GET
CHANGED

Kat Farmer, creator of the *Does My Bum Look 40 In This?* blog and Instagram account, is a fashion stylist and digital-first talent, known for her role in the BBC1 styling show *You Are What You Wear* and the fashion segment on ITV's *This Morning*. Kat is celebrated for inspiring people to dress for themselves and to innovate, using both old and new pieces from their wardrobe. With a following of more than 335,000 across her digital platforms, Kat documents her journey as a UK-based fashion stylist, offering an honest, no-holds-barred opinion on fashion trends, interiors and beauty products.

As an authoritative voice in the fashion industry, Kat's advice has featured in the *Guardian* and the *Telegraph*, culminating in a stunning Christmas cover shoot for *Stella* magazine. Described as 'a hugely successful one-woman brand' by *The Times*, Kat is proud to have worked with a variety of prestigious brands, including Marks & Spencer, The White Company, Whistles and John Lewis.

@doesmybumlook40

GET CHANGED

Finding the New You through Fashion

KAT FARMER

Mitchell Beazley

First published in Great Britain in 2022 by Mitchell Beazley, an imprint of
Octopus Publishing Group Ltd
Carmelite House
50 Victoria Embankment
London EC4Y 0DZ
www.octopusbooks.co.uk

An Hachette UK Company
www.hachette.co.uk

ISBN 978-1-78472-778-9

A CIP catalogue record for this book is available from the British Library.

Printed and bound in China

10 9 8 7 6 5 4 3 2 1

Publisher: Alison Starling
Editors: Ella Parsons & Sarah Kyle
Art Director: Yasia Williams
Designer: Lizzie Ballantyne
Illustrator: Janelle Burger
Production Controller: Serena Savini

Cover
Design © Octopus Publishing Group 2022
Artwork © Hanna Buck 2022
Illustrator: Claire Huntley
A note from Kat: this drawing was inspired by Alexis Amor glasses, one of my favourite
fashion brands that I have been wearing for many years.

Contents

Introduction

How to change your life – one outfit at a time

Fashion Saved My Life. Not last night, it wasn't a DJ and I'm not being overly dramatic when I say fashion saved my life. If you're my husband, right now your eyes may well be rolling so far back in your head that you could be auditioning for *The Exorcist*, but actually, I'm only being 'slightly' dramatic. I will explain more later, but suffice to say I have learned that a good outfit truly can change your life.

So imagine what you could do if you had a whole wardrobe of them!

This is a book about how I realized the true power of fashion. It's about how I was able to completely reinvent myself, thanks to fashion. And how you, too, can not only reclaim but also rewrite your identity, wear it proudly and be the person you've always wanted to be.

How is this book any different from all the other fashion books you've read? I'll be honest, they can be daunting. You sort of know what you should be doing, but it's the equivalent of trying to do your kid's maths homework…WHEN did they make long division so complicated? So, first of all I wanted to make sure this book would be as simple as possible and super digestible for EVERYONE. I decided to break down the process into its fundamental parts and make it really practical and user-friendly.

Putting together an outfit doesn't have to be any more difficult than following a recipe. In fact, I've borrowed from a simple recipe structure to provide a recipe framework for this book. I'll guide you through the Preparation, the Ingredients and the Method for cooking up your new style.

More than anything, this is a true and honest, tried-and-tested guide to how you can not only rediscover yourself but also reinvent yourself using fashion, especially if you feel you've lost your way in life and your sense of self. It's a guide that works. It isn't difficult to do, but sometimes it's so much easier to see the wood for the trees if you have someone pointing it out – and decoding the fashion myths, expelling out-of-date, suffocating 'rules' and taking you on a journey, step by step, to discover the you who you've always wanted to be.

It's not about spending loads of money; it's not about losing loads of weight; it's not about simply putting a belt with everything; and it's NOT about following 'rules'. One size does not fit all. It's about starting your own journey and having the tools to find your own personal fashion path (I really feel like I should be bursting into 'Follow the Yellow Brick Road' right now…just call me Dorothy – and, yes, I do like red shoes, but I'm not implying that you're either a scarecrow, a lion or a tin man!).

This book is for anyone in need of a transformation, and I'll be holding your hand the entire way. Take it from me, as someone who's been in this position, I know a way out.

Who is Kat Farmer?

So how am I vaguely qualified to write this book?
And who even am I? (Not Dorothy.)

My name is Kat, and I was that person who had lost their way. To backtrack, I was in my mid- to late 20s, living in London, the proud owner of a high-flying career in the City, who knew exactly what she was doing and what she should be wearing (although I did have a Burberry checked mac with the check on the OUTSIDE – I swear that at one time, before it all went a little bit Pete Tong, it was the epitome of elegance. TRUST ME. I used to wear it with ankle-length cropped trousers, loafers, a thin knit and a huge scarf. It worked...).

I got married at 30, had a baby at 31, went back to work and managed to keep all the plates spinning. Had another baby at 33 and moved out of London to the country (OK, it was the country to me, having always lived in a city). Truth be told, it was a commuter market town just outside the M25, but it may as well have been another planet. There were lots of trees and I had really bad hayfever, and you couldn't get any form of food delivery AT ALL, or a taxi after 11pm. Essentially the boondocks.

I still freelanced for my old job as a City headhunter. I had pulled on my big girl pants; I could do this. I was used to dealing with CEOs and board directors. Looking after a two-year-old and a newborn on my own (my husband was a City lawyer working 12-hour days; I don't think he did bath time in four years) – how hard could it be? In fact, it was obviously 'such a doddle' (not so rose-tinted glasses as fluorescent pink here) that I went on to have another baby and ended up with a three-year-old, a one-year-old and a newborn.

And then I basically rocked in a corner for a couple of years. I had completely lost myself. I felt I had been put out to pasture at the grand old age of 35. I was utterly woman without portfolio, and I was CERTAINLY woman without a clue what to wear. When I had

been living in central London, working in a corporate/smart-casual world (anyone remember Dress Down Fridays?), I knew exactly what worked: well-cut suits with silk blouses and heels if you were going out in the evening; cropped trouser suits with neat-fitting tops, ballet flats and a trench to ring the changes. I had the perfect mix-and-match wardrobe that worked for every occasion, from city meetings to cocktails in the evening. And not a hint of concern about getting a mushed-up banana on anything (no one warns you about the stain disaster that is The Banana...or a half-sucked Pom-Bear).

But I digress – and that's exactly what used to happen. My brain was all over the shop: distraction and the inability to focus on the task in hand was the norm. There was no time to think of anything else as I already had a billion other things on my mind. And when it came to fashion? Where did you get any inspiration? There was no Pinterest, no Instagram, none of my friends had a clue either – we were all in the same boat, wondering if a huge alarm was going to go off were we to venture into certain high street shops that were clearly aimed at a much younger market. Yet we didn't want to shop in those stores that stocked a lot of tweed and everything had a matching blazer that you wore with sensible shoes – especially when you lived in the country.

Was I allowed to still wear heels? (The answer is, one looks rather foolish tottering along pushing a double buggy complete with buggy board and three screaming toddlers while sporting heels. Been there, done that, looked a right tit and nearly broke an ankle at the same time.) WHAT was I supposed to wear and, more importantly, WHO was going to tell me? Who was there to talk to about it? Magazines either spoke to those in their 20s, most definitely without children, or to the older generation of women who sported a gilet and wore a raincoat with a 'fun lining'.

In an effort to make a change and reclaim the Chic Me I knew I had once been, I had the worst haircut known to man – seriously, they don't sell wigs that bad – think the love child of Jon Bon Jovi and Jane McDonald from that cruise programme. I had a FRINGE cut in. I have hair like wire wool – a fringe is never a good idea – I looked like I'd stapled a vole to my forehead. I admit, I was attempting Anna

Wintour, but neglected to mention 'bob' so ended up with 'mullet'. I was trying to find my style. I KNEW it was in there somewhere among the baby brain, weird post-pregnancy hair, stretch marks and saggy boobs. I thought I was the epitome of cool; in hindsight I was possibly better dressed in my school sixth form, but I just put my newly found eclectic look down to hormones (I'm still lamenting a bottle-green, puff-sleeve very fitted blouse I had, which I specifically remember buying from a shop in Amsterdam with my mum when I was going into the lower sixth).

It wasn't only the not-knowing-what-to-wear, the not-knowing-where-to-shop – it was more than that. Underlying everything was the fact that I had lost my direction in life completely. I thought that all I had ever wanted was to be a mum and stay at home with my babies. Turns out, it wasn't enough for me. And it's taken me the best part of too many years to be able to say that THAT'S OK!

As prophetic as it sounds, I could see that once they were gone (I'm a planner, so it was obvious to worry about what I was going to be doing in 18 years. Totally obvious…), there was still a long time ahead of me and I couldn't spend the rest of my life living vicariously through them. But I didn't know how to change, I didn't know what to do – I just knew that something had to give. So, my amazing husband persuaded me to go and see a psychiatrist, who (after I had sobbed on him for two hours – proper, full-on snotty sobs) declared that I was suffering from 'Loss of Identity'. Who knew that was even a thing? It is, and it's a lot more common than many of us realize.

I recognized that it wasn't just not knowing what I wanted to do; it was not knowing who I wanted to be. And a very, very large part of that came down to getting up every day and getting dressed. I had lost every element of my sense of identity.

There are generations of women like you and like me, who were told that we could have it all, that we should want to have it all, that we could study, get good grades, get great jobs and the world would be our oyster.

They told us that we could. But they didn't tell us how. What they also didn't tell us is that we don't have to stay doing what we started doing in our 20s. They didn't tell us that we are allowed to change, that we are allowed to start over, that we can have more than one career in our life. They didn't tell us about life stages and about how we don't have to stay being the same person. AND no one ever told us that the way we dress and the way we look TO OURSELVES can be the most important element in how we feel and an integral part of our confidence. No one ever told us that an outfit could be the first place to start rebuilding ourselves. We are allowed to change.

The realization was life changing – this was after a lot of therapy, by the way. I was hugely lucky and privileged to be able to talk to a therapist. They showed me how this loss of identity had burrowed its way into my psyche and how I might confront it. And now I'd like to tell you. I sat down and thought about what I loved and what I did, deep down, know about: it was fashion. As my friends said, even with the dodgy haircut and slightly random 'out-there-trying-to-find-myself-post-baby-number-three' look, I still had a style radar – the signal had just gone a bit skew-whiff. Nevertheless, I knew there was a style goal I was trying to achieve and was determined to work towards. I just had to rewire and find the confidence to trust in my radar again.

I wanted to open a clothes shop. I wanted to open the perfect boutique. I did a business plan, I found premises, I spoke to suppliers. I was ON THIS and I was going to make it work. And then a friend came back from Canada and said that her mother-in-law paid someone to come to her home and do exactly what I did for all of my friends for free! In Canada, it was called a Personal Shopper and they got paid. I had always taken friends shopping for clothes. I'd rifled through their wardrobes, finding them gems they'd banished to the depths of Narnia; I'd find them a dress to wear for that occasion, which would work with accessories and shoes they already had and would be able to wear again; I'd advise on the perfect jeans and the right blazer for their shape.

Ten years ago, personal shoppers for 'normal' people were really thin on the ground. It certainly wasn't a run-of-the-mill thing that everybody paid for, hell no. A personal shopper or stylist was something that only the super wealthy or celebrities could afford.

But on thinking about it, I realized it needn't actually be expensive – it could also be seen as an investment. In the long run, it could save money and time: by paying someone to work out exactly what it is that you are missing from your wardrobe, by sorting the wheat from the chaff among those clothes that you've had for years, by taking you shopping and making sure you don't make any expensive mistakes, and by ensuring that you have a wardrobe of clothes that you love, full of outfits that you can actually wear – surely that is an investment worth considering? Especially for those who are either time-poor or who simply hate shopping. Or for those who just can't see the wood for the trees.

I would also leave them armed with guidance about how to shop in the future and ensure that they wore nothing but outfits of perfection for years to come. So, I did it (this was also after the husband pointed out that one venture required a billionty pounds of investment, plus was a seven-days-a-week commitment, while the other was free and I could fit it around the children).

At the same time as setting up my personal shopping and wardrobe detox business, I started a blog. This was on the advice of another friend who had come back from the US and declared that no one was writing for the over-40 market and I should do it. I'll be honest, I had to rewind a couple of steps first and ask her to explain what a blog was…

The opportunity to write (which was something else I'd always loved doing) was just BLISS and genuinely as good a therapy for me as shopping and living and breathing fashion. It was also the perfect marketing tool for the business: a place to advertise how I could help; the level of detail I would go to just to find the perfect black jumper; how to wear new styles and trends and which ones were possibly worth swerving; what were the perfect shoes for a pair of jeans; and what jeans we should all be wearing.

I knew that I couldn't be the only person on the approach to a big number, who had essentially had a mid-life crisis and who was stumped at how to navigate new trends and had no idea how to straddle that hideous line between mutton and frump (and did that line even exist?) And so, *Does My Bum Look 40 In This?* was born.

I hadn't realized how many people the personal shopping service and the blog would appeal to. I knew that I had found it difficult losing my way in my late 30s but I never imagined how many women all over the world lose their way and do not feel able to find it again. I had first-hand experience – both personally and from my hundreds of clients – of how finding your style again and having a wardrobe of clothes from which you can make outfits you love can really make a difference to your confidence. If you feel great, you will look great: it's as simple as that. It's not shallow, it's not fickle. It can be the difference between feeling horrendous about yourself and hating the way you look, and holding your head high and exuding confidence and sass.

It wasn't just me who was recognizing this either. Just after starting the blog, in pretty short order, along came Instagram. I admit I was quite sceptical, as my photography skills were (and still are), quite frankly, non-existent. But it so happened that people liked the authenticity (code for amateurishness) of them. They weren't polished (some of them weren't even in focus), they weren't on a model: they were me in real life as a real person, heading into my 40s like a steamroller. I had found a whole generation of women who didn't want to dress like their mum, who found themselves at a crossroads (or so they thought) of going to the 'cool kids' shops or those shops that were either full of tweed and twinsets or outfits for the Mother of the Bride. No one else was talking to those women at that time, and the retailers hadn't considered them in any of their marketing plans.

And then that changed. The Sunday newspaper supplements suddenly caught on that THESE were the women who had influence, experience and disposable income, and started a conversation with them. The retailers realized the same thing and wanted to pitch to the discerning shopper. Again, the conversation changed. Over the past decade, fashion has no longer been seen as the stomping ground of the whippersnappers. There is no such thing as a trend that can't be worn at any age (I reserve the right to include the odd exception, but it's usually on the grounds of taste).

And so, my new career took off in a totally different direction from my old life. From a love of fashion and a renewed confidence,

I had found a voice and a platform. I had a blog channel, a rapidly growing Instagram page and a flourishing Facebook community. I partnered with retailers to try to change the way we dressed, to support our high street while at the same time preaching that it wasn't about buying more; rather, it was about buying better and wearing it more. I wrote for magazines on how to wear trends and how to cherry-pick the best items for sale that could add versatility and longevity to your wardrobe without having to sell a kidney. I spoke to an entire generation of women who had never been spoken to before. I was picked as a stylist for the first fashion show that the BBC had produced in almost 15 years: *You Are What You Wear*, which essentially was a living and breathing documentary of what I had been saying for the past decade: an outfit CAN change your life. We met real people who had totally lost their way AND their style. While they may have come through the trauma that threw their life upside down, they still weren't themselves as their confidence was gone. And they hid – behind clothes that didn't reflect the new them.

But I did that – all of it – from a love of fashion and a passion and a desire to change.

There has never been a better time to take hold of your own destiny, to change the way you feel, and the first step on that ladder is to GET CHANGED. As utterly trite as it sounds, the way you look can completely change the way you feel. And YOU can do that, one outfit at a time. It helps, of course, if you have a whole wardrobe of them and I'm here to show you how it can be done.

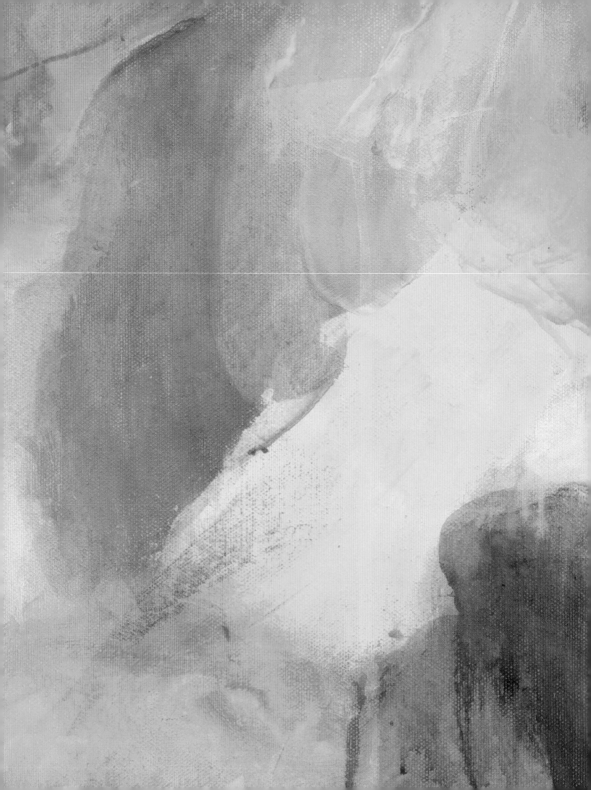

1

Preparation

Reviewing the situation

It's literally impossible to read that title without singing it in a Fagin-style manner, so apologies for leaving that earworm with you for potentially the rest of the day.

But the fact is, we do need to review the situation. Once we understand why so many of us are feeling so… discombobulated (is the word I'd use – bet Dickens wished he'd used that one), we can start making changes and, most importantly, make sure that we don't end up in the same position again.

Before we even start thinking about clothes and about what we wear, if we want to make a change that will last (and not just solve your dilemma of what to wear out on Friday night), we need to go back to the beginning. Preparation is key.

It's exactly the same as with cooking. You don't just swan into the kitchen to prepare a dinner party, and the recipes for the three courses magically appear in your head – and work for the vegan, the coeliac and the dairy-free guests you've got coming…Oh, and the fridge

is miraculously full of all the ingredients that you need. You need to plan. And it's the exact same process when it comes to our wardrobes.

So what's stopping you from having the perfect wardrobe from which to select a sublime set of outfits every day? The obvious answer is that you just don't have the right clothes in there, but to take it back a step further: why don't you? Whether it's because you can't decide what to wear, you don't know what to wear together, you don't like anything you own, nothing fits you properly or you simply can't be bothered or don't care any more, it all leads back to one major thing.

Confidence. Or more significantly, the lack of it. And the simple question of where did it go? Or maybe you never had it in the first place.

There's an assumption that confidence is something you're born with, or that it's a result of your upbringing. Yes, I would absolutely say that's true: an element of nature and a lot of nurture. But that doesn't mean that if you don't have it, you never will; or that if you'd had it and lost it, you'll never get it back.

Loss of identity and loss of confidence is something that is, as I mentioned in my introduction, so prevalent in our society that it's heartbreaking. What's even more heartbreaking is that it's hardly ever addressed. It's almost as if we're supposed to adopt the stiff upper lip and accept our fate, because to be seen to rail against it comes across as moaning and whining.

But to not do anything about it doesn't improve the situation. This isn't something that time can necessarily fix. Time can, in fact, be the worst enemy of change, because the longer you live with something and in a certain situation, the more that becomes the norm and the more you accept it as the status quo, forgetting who you once were or who you once wanted to be. Sound familiar?

And surely we owe it to, if not ourselves, then our families and friends to be – as trite and as clichéd as it sounds – the best version of ourselves. Yes, there is a little bit of sick in my mouth as I type that, but the irritating fact is that it's true. The old sayings, 'you can't run a car on empty', or 'fix your own oxygen mask first' – and a whole slew of other hackneyed self-help phrases – really are true.

While I didn't want this to be a self-help book in the inspirational sense of the words, I do want it be a practical manual. Think Haynes but with prettier things than carburettors and exhausts. I genuinely believe, and know from experience, that the key to being happy with your style and how you look is down to confidence.

Confidence breeds confidence. Let's break the chain and prove to the next generation, and the next, that growing old doesn't mean you have to be put out to pasture.

But how are we in this mess now?

Simply put, women for years have tried to do too much. We were told we could have it all. And I'm sure some are able to juggle the balls and spin the plates of home, kids, family, husband, career, social life and themselves with utter aplomb.

Good for them. Hats off to them. I will go so far as to say that's not the norm. I'm going to throw it out there that most of us are not superwomen (well, OF COURSE we're all superwomen deep down, but some have a cape).

What happens so often with women is that we give ourselves to everyone else first. We put ourselves at the bottom of the list of priorities until we're so low on the list that we're not even on it. We focus on others and give our time to putting other people first, leaving nothing for us.

And that's not even the tip of the iceberg when it comes to the checklist of shite that can happen in our lives to undermine our confidence. Separation, redundancy, abuse – the list of other things that can throw us off kilter long enough to lose direction and reduce us to a shadow of our former selves is long. It's very, very, long.

Not to mention the whole shape thing. Yes, just for shits and giggles, the older you get, the more importance gravity and metabolism have in our lives and, suddenly, not only do you not feel like yourself, you also don't physically look like yourself either. Congratulations if you're one of those people who bounced back after having a baby, or have maintained your weight from your early 20s, or haven't yet entered the dreaded menopausal mausoleum of weight gain. For many, a significant change in shape, or not being the shape that you want to be, can be the hugest dent in your confidence.

When you think about it in that much detail and break it down into what women these days have to deal with (some a LOT more than others), it's no surprise that so many of us feel that life has given up on us. I truly believe it's not a case of us having given up on life; it's that life has thrown us so many curveballs, it's easier simply not to play ball any more.

It's no thunderbolt, then, that we get to a point where we look in the mirror and don't recognize the person looking back. And until we learn to love ourselves again (we should possibly play glib self-help-phrase bingo, shouldn't we?), it's virtually impossible for others to see us as we would like them to.

The very first step on the road to rediscovering ourselves, then, is to acknowledge that there is an issue.

To some, it may be seen as a sign of weakness to admit that you've lost your direction, you've no idea where your sense of style has gone or whether you even had one in the first place. There's also the thorny issue of if you admit it, then it means you might have to do something about it and, frankly, you may have neither the brain space, the wherewithal, nor the inclination to tackle it. As it's hard. And where do you start?

Here.

Here is where you start. Baby steps. And if you start at the very beginning (OK, I'm going for musicals bingo as well as pithy self-help bingo – so far we've done *Oliver!* and *The Sound of Music*) and take it step by step, with proper preparation, taking time to cherry-pick your ingredients, then understanding and executing the method, you'll be set for life.

It's not difficult, but it is time-consuming, as most things worthwhile doing are. But you're allowed to spend time on yourself. It's not seen as being fickle or shallow to spend time preparing fabulous and healthy food for yourself, but to spend time on making yourself look and feel great on the outside has a whiff of self-indulgence about it.

Wrong. Wrong, wrong, wrong. There have been countless studies into how appearance can affect mental health. It's no secret that the outfits we choose give an indication of how we want to be perceived, be that intentional or not. It can influence how we are treated by other people, which can have a direct impact on our mental health – again, this could be positive or negative.

And so it makes sense to put forward the argument that we should be allowed to have control over those perceptions. We have the right to take time to make sure we look our very best – that the signals we give as a result of how we look are positive ones.

It's also of vital importance that the outfits we pick and the styles we choose to re-create are ones that are true to us and represent how we actually want to look, as opposed to just copying someone's style or a new trend, thinking that it will work on us as it works on them, but then realizing it doesn't and you actually just look and feel like a potato (believe me, we have ALL been there). This leads to thinking that the whole effort you went to is a complete waste of time, so you don't bother and, hey ho, guess what? Your confidence is swimming around in the gutter with the potato outfit you threw there in disgust.

Once you've got your head around it being mentally beneficial for you to ensure that you look and feel your best, it's time to think about the practical preparation steps. It may sound ridiculous to say that we 'allow' ourselves to want to look good, but I honestly feel that any physical self-improvement has, for so long, been seen as vain and indulgent that we have to get over that hurdle of guilt. There's no guilt or shame in wanting to improve our diets and expand our cooking repertoire to impress; why should we harbour these feelings of remorse towards wanting to rediscover ourselves and feel great again? The knock-on effect can be so powerful that, frankly, it seems insulting to suggest it's something we should have to justify.

So we're starting with baby steps. Nothing painful, nothing tricky, and the best thing is, you can sit at home in a onesie for the rest of the prep. Chocolate/coffee/wine optional (but recommended).

Defining your style

OK, hands up (baby, hands up...see what I did there?), this does sound like a particularly I've-disappeared-up-my-own-behind fashiony saying.

Well, it's not. We all really need to get over this feeling that to discuss fashion using certain semantics is pretentious and 'not for us'. Style is a GOOD thing, and it's something that everyone has. It's simply the way of defining a look: a certain style. To be fair, while I say it's 'a good thing', there is no doubt that some will think that certain 'styles' are very bad, I'd go so far as to say downright hideous – and therein lies the reason why it's a good thing, even if it's a bad thing. It's a personal statement. It's subjective. Clear as mud?

Style is what defines the way we, as individuals, dress. To each of us, there will be bad style and good style, depending on our personal tastes. The only thing that we need to actually worry about is: are we happy with our own style?

If, currently, you look in the mirror and are not enamoured with the image that is staring back at you, then, no, you are not happy with your style.

And the first step in your preparation is coming to terms with the fact that, nope, your style ain't rocking your world.

Style lingo

The very, very first step is to think about vocab. The words that describe the way you would like to look and how you want to feel while wearing something.

If you're not sure what I actually mean by this, again, let's take the food analogy. How often do you think about what sort of thing you'd like to make for dinner? What do you fancy? Something light, something spicy, fishy, warming, creamy, tomatoey, meaty, cheesy? Do you like a certain type of cuisine? Indian, Mexican, Italian, French, British – flavours from all over the world are at your fingertips (providing you do the right preparation and have the right ingredients...see where I'm going with this?).

And the same principles can be applied to style. How do you want to look? Think of the word or phrase that describes your style – and it doesn't have to be just one. Hell to the no. You are more than welcome to be a fashion magpie, but try to be a couple as opposed to a whole flock.

I don't expect you to come up with a slew of fashiony words. That isn't what we're after here. Rather, it is anything that describes the sort of style you would like to emulate. Yes, there are more fashion-focused terms but, genuinely, any description of how you want your outfit to make you feel will work.

Sunny, jolly, happy, calm, young, quirky, elegant, fun, mature, individual, different, beautiful, pretty, eclectic: the list of words is endless and totally up to you.

Style focus

Right now, I appreciate you may be thinking, well that's all well and good, but why is she doing this and how on earth does it translate into me looking elegant/French/like the rock chick that I would love to be? Oh, and WHY can't I be a whole flock of fashion magpies? The main reason is to give you FOCUS (and unless you have the shoe collection of Imelda Marcos with the closet space and budget to go with it, there is no way that you can be every style).

How many of you have a wardrobe full of wearable clothes but you don't actually 'like' any of them? You put them on and they merely fulfil the functional job of ensuring you're not walking around in just your pants and bra. You don't love them (although if you think about it, they probably do deserve some credit for saving you from regular nakedness…), and they don't make you feel special. And WHY shouldn't you feel special and great every day? You should. You've just not got the right clothes to match how you want to feel…and that comes down to knowing your style. It's no more difficult to put on an outfit that makes you feel amazing than to put on one that is just 'meh' to you, but you need to have those clothes in your wardrobe in the first place (and you WILL get there!).

Having a honed style description gives you a starting point on which to build, a focus point from which to start. And if you don't have a starting point, you can't go forward. The end goal will be worth it, but you need to start somewhere. With just ONE word at least. One word that sums up how you would like to look and/or how you would like to feel. It can be vague…it doesn't have to be worthy of a write-up in *Vogue*. And fear not, if you want to think in terms of people (I see you at the back, one step ahead, yes, you've got it) – but hold your horses (or your Audrey Hepburns, Kate Mosses or Michelle Obamas), the next chapter is for you.

Dressing for your lifestyle

Before we go all style icon and let our imaginations run wild, there is one other 'admin bit'. The boring but very, very necessary part of the process and one that can lead to major wardrobe malfunction if you don't get it right. It sounds so simple but, from years of styling, I've learned that it's one of the major things that prevents people from having something to wear every day. Dress for the lifestyle that you have, not the one that you want.

That's it. A tiny phrase that has huge ramifications if you don't remember it. And it's so easy to forget (or ignore). We unravel the repercussions and view the evidence later on when we detox your wardrobe (see page 196) – no sins to be hidden; but for now, I want you to think about those things that you bought because you loved them. The reality is that you simply have no occasion to wear them, however great they look on you OR however much they are 'your style'.

And that's why you need to focus, or else you risk ending up with a wardrobe full of unworn clothes and nothing that you can 'actually' wear on a daily basis. Confidence back in the gutter (together with the potato), and we're right back where we started.

For some, it may be a question of 'refocus', of recognizing that you want to look a certain way but your lifestyle doesn't entirely suit that style. It's a question of acknowledging and adapting; again, all things that, step by step, you will hopefully be aware of on your journey to discovering the new you. Once you know what the problem is, it becomes so much easier to fix.

For some, it will be that they simply don't have the right clothes for their every day. Which, let's face it, is the majority of the time.

You will also find that if you start buying for the lifestyle you have, not the one you want or only have for three per cent of the time, you actually spend less on clothes as you're wearing the ones you already have more. You'll be acing the chapter on sustainability without having even read it. Saving money and the environment while looking great every day? That is why we focus and we find our style that works for our everyday lives.

Dressing for your shape

This sounds so easy and so obvious, doesn't it? Well, duh...of course everyone should be dressing for their shape. But the reality is that it is trickier than you think. We're not going to go into detail here on how to dress for your shape (fear not, that is coming up, see page 56), as the first thing we need to do is to get to grips with the shape we are.

Just like dressing for the lifestyle we have and not the one we want, so we should be dressing for the shape we are and not the one we once were. Or the one we want to be...It's a cruel turn of events but our figures change over the years, especially as we get older. Life events mean that curves are in different places from where they once were and may have multiplied with the decades.

That's not to say AT ALL that there are things you can't wear; rather, that there are other styles that are potentially more flattering. It just takes a tweak here and a tweak there to make all the difference. But if you're trying to shove a square peg into a round hole (not implying that any part of you is a square peg...), you're probably finding that it's not working for you. Which is why you may well have a wardrobe of clothes that you don't like and that don't look great any more.

I appreciate that I'm just writing this down in an offhand manner, when the truth of the matter is that these are not entirely pleasant facts to have to face. But trust me: the acknowledgment is the worst part. Once you've done that, you will be able to see the wood for the trees and, by the end of the book, you will realize that it wasn't that hard at all. And the results are so incredibly worth it.

Just remember, it's baby steps.

Nutritional information

> First, know that you are in good company. There are millions of us who get to a certain age and realize we have lost confidence and lost our style direction, often without even noticing.

> Get ready to acknowledge that you want to change, you can change and you can do it in baby steps.

> Appreciate that it's OK to want to look great so that you feel great. It's a myth that taking pride in your appearance is fickle and vain.

> Psychologically you owe it to yourself and to those around you to make sure you love the way you look.

> Start to think about identifying your style.

> Think of words that describe how you want to look and how you want to feel.

> Understand the need to FOCUS! It will be worth it in the end and it will work wonders for your confidence.

> Dress for the lifestyle that you have and not the one you want.

> Dress for the shape that you are, not the shape you once were.

Identifying your style

This chapter is where it gets exciting. Well, it's where I think it gets exciting. It's where we get to be Mr Benn. Think Fashion Mr Benn. It's where we will work out the style that you aspire to and learn how to make it suit you. We're still very much in prep mode and this is a key step on our GET CHANGED journey.

Without understanding how you want to look, it's almost impossible to build the wardrobe of your dreams that will enable you to get dressed every day and love the way you look. We need to set ourselves goals of how we want to be, and the best way to do that is to find inspiration, otherwise we don't know what we're trying to achieve in our fashion choices.

There is simply too much choice out there. Where do you start? The method that I follow should help you to streamline the process of identifying your style and, at the same time, live out your childhood Mr Benn fantasies. OK, I can appreciate that the latter might not rock everyone's world. But imagine if I said you don't have to move from the comfort of your sofa and could just let your imagination go wild…

It's once again about focus. To revisit the food analogy I mentioned earlier, it's like when you're wondering what to cook for dinner. If you set parameters and break down the thinking process into bite-size chunks, it becomes much easier to decide and seems far less daunting and insurmountable. So, thinking about whether you fancy Chinese, Indian, Thai, French, Italian or Spanish food (feel free to swap out the cuisines for ones you prefer) channels your thought process into something far easier to digest (literally). And you can then take it a step further: veggie, vegan, chicken, fish or pork (again, feel free to choose a protein of your liking)? You've narrowed down the choices and eliminated the options that won't work. In my experience, once you have less to choose from, it makes the actual selection process a lot simpler.

And the same principles can be applied to finding your style.

First off, we should address the smirky faces I can see at the back, at my liberal bandying about of the phrase 'identify your style'. Yes, I understand that this comes across, yet again, as me sounding all fashiony and at the risk of disappearing up my own arse any second.

It's not fashiony at all. Well, to be fair, it is a bit, in that we're talking about fashion and we're talking about style, but that's something we all need to accept as NORMAL. You get dressed every day in clothes that you have made a conscious decision to wear – you have made a FASHION CHOICE. You might not think you have, but you have. As we discussed in the previous chapter, regardless of whether or not you think you are making a statement in what you've put on, to other people you are. Their reaction could be a conscious or subliminal one, but your outfit still reflects you. And once you've got this process and your wardrobe nailed, it's JUST as easy to wear an outfit that you love as it is to wear things you've grabbed from your wardrobe (or floordrobe in my case; maybe you have a chairdrobe...) that you're not fully on board with and that don't make you feel fab.

So now I can hear the panic starting to creep in...let's nip that in the bud. It's not judgment. I'm not saying that we should dress for other people, I'm saying that we should see this as an opportunity to own the narrative. To know that we can look exactly how we want to look. To LOVE the way we look every day. To look in the mirror and feel confident and, well, the best way I can describe it is to look in the mirror and to see YOU looking back. You can be the person you want to be, and one of the easiest ways to start doing that is to look at what's on the outside: know your style.

But hang on...'it's about what's on the inside that's important'...Isn't that what we've been told for years? And here we come full circle. THAT is why, when we talk about finding our style, it's seen as being 'fashiony', slightly (possibly very) pretentious, shallow and vain. The confusion comes when people assume we're doing it purely for others, whereas it's actually the first step to taking control. We can start writing our own story and being the person we want to be, and that begins with identifying our style.

How? I appreciate it's somewhat ironic, when I've been banging on about finding the person who YOU want to be, yet my very first piece of advice is to think about the person whose style you would most love to channel. Bear with me caller, there is method in my somewhat hypocritical madness.

When I say someone whose style you would love to channel, it's not about becoming that person. It's a visual aid. It's a starting point from where you can jumpstart your creative vision and translate a specific style, which you admire and would love to emulate, into a wardrobe that works for you. It's a visual way to focus and narrow down your choices by thinking 'what would *insert Style Icon* wear?'.

And to make it even easier, rather than just asking 'what do you fancy cooking?', I've broken it down into a broad range of cuisines. For the purposes of fashion, these are essentially styles. And then within the style sections, there are your icons, who are great representatives of the style.

Like with cooking (bear in mind we're not baking here, we're cooking), this isn't an exact science. Your style icons won't embody their main style all of the time and you may have a different style in mind to the ones I've outlined here. And that is the joy of fashion. There are no rules. Feel free to make different decisions – so long as you love them, that's the main thing.

For those who are looking for a starting point, who would like some guidance, I have always found this a fabulously easy way to channel my thinking when it comes to putting outfits together and making sure that my wardrobe works and I look my best every day.

The other thing to remember is that you don't have to be just one style. BUT, if you do happen to be the owner of a roving fashion eye like I have, it's almost more important to have that focus and really think about channelling a few styles, rather than loads.

That's not to say it can't work if you don't follow this line of thinking; some people are able to put clothes together effortlessly, without channelling someone else's style. I will hold my hands up and say that isn't me. I like the focus and I think of it as a two-step guarantee. So while I might love an item, think it would work with myriad outfits, trust my gut and be ready to buy, I will always at the last minute do a style safety check: 'would *insert style icon* wear it?' (depending on the style I have in my head).

I will also add the caveat that this method doesn't always work; sometimes I get said item home and try it on with all the outfits that I had put together in my head and, hey ho, I actually look like a potato. BUT because I know my style, I know my lifestyle and I know my shape, I know that it doesn't work and so back it goes. We will all still make mistakes but the more knowledge we are armed with, the better we get at recognizing them.

I did just throw in there about dressing for the lifestyle that you have... and it is an interesting factor to take into consideration when you're honing down the style you love. But I do believe that most styles can be adapted to suit most lifestyles. I should probably point out, though, that if you have a uniform to wear to work, I'm all out of help as that just is what it is! But when you shed the uniform and can be YOU, the style you choose can be adapted to most lifestyles.

Remember, it's YOUR life you're dressing for. You're not choosing the lifestyle of the icon, you're just taking inspiration from their style.

Minimalist elegance

When thinking about elegance, you could really just ask how long is a piece of string? And you'd be right. For one person's elegance may very much not be another's. Same goes for classy (I actually dislike the word intensely, which is why I haven't used it) – but surely it means something different for everyone – classy is in the eye of the beholder perchance?

For some context, when I describe an elegant style – for the purposes of this style it's definitely Minimalist Elegance – yes, I do mean something that can stand the test of time. But rather than being reminiscent of another time, a minimalist elegant style is one that stands on its own, year in, year out, season in, season out. With Minimalist Elegance, you can't pinpoint the era in which it was worn; the outfits are ones that you can re-create from current clothing stock. Your style is timeless.

The ethos of Minimalist Elegance is the element of simplicity. You nearly always keep colours neutral, prints are pared back and subtle, and your silhouette is clean. Tailoring is a key feature, along with a neat finish, while accessories are kept to a minimum.

You favour well-cut trousers and skirts. They may be flamboyant in their shape and sometimes volume, but added details are kept to a minimum – you're not a fan of frills and fripperies. Knits in classic styles are your favourite additions, along with luxurious fabrics for blouses, shirts and tees. Dresses may be glamorous in their silhouette and material but are never ostentatious in extra detail. Outerwear is timeless and well cut.

The joy of Minimalist Elegance is that it very much suits a capsule wardrobe – there are very few dress codes for which the minimalist elegant style doesn't fit perfectly (you lucky duck!). And it's a style that is easily obtainable year after year. As reticent as I am about describing a style being 'in fashion', it's safe to say that if you do want to attach that moniker to a style, this one wears it with pride.

For some, it may be seen as the safe option. You're certainly not going to raise any eyebrows with regards to controversy if this is your personal style, but you will definitely raise eyebrows for wearing a style that exudes sophistication and timelessness.

Style icons: Grace Kelly, Audrey Hepburn, Victoria Beckham, Coco Chanel

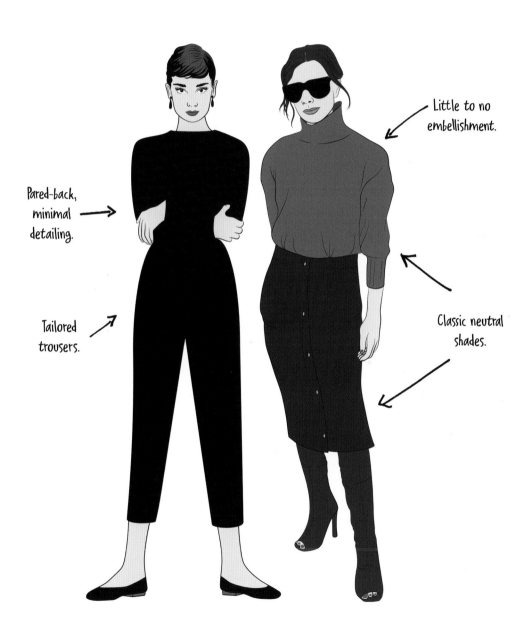

Little to no embellishment.

Pared-back, minimal detailing.

Tailored trousers.

Classic neutral shades.

Classic chic (sometimes corporate, always composed)

As much as you may assume this style starts in the boardroom (the clue is in my throwing the corporate bit in), this is a style that transcends a formal setting. It is the perfect style for those of you who need to follow a more corporate dress code in the work setting but also want to like what you wear when you leave the office.

Not that you're besuited the whole time, but the classic, feminine look is one that you're most comfortable in. The key is feeling composed and radiating a confidence that stems from looking and being entirely comfortable in your own skin while not rocking any fashion boats. Even when Classic Chic is dressed down, there is still an element of 'smart' about it.

Like your Minimalist Elegance cohorts, you prefer a classic look. It's not about wearing the latest trends, it's about having a wardrobe that always makes you feel put together with an element of comfort. Unlike Minimalist Elegance, though, there is more print involved, and the biggest difference is colour. As a Classic Chic, you embrace colour and choose either block colours or florals and most definitely stripes – there will no doubt be more than one coloured Breton top in your wardrobe.

Accessories also play a larger part in your Classic Chic wardrobe. Scarves are key, again in both colour and print. While statement dressing isn't your bag, there may well be a pair of shoes or two (or trainers or boots) that do the talking.

If you do have a more corporate style to your life, you will have a host of well-cut, timeless suits that you mix and match at the weekend with a plethora of jeans, tees, shirts and blouses. You may love a pencil skirt for work or an evening out, or a more soft-flowing maxi or midi for off-duty moments (basically, I mean when we're not at work, although you may have a job where you can wear them to work, in which case they are no doubt a wardrobe staple for you). Dress-wise, the world is your oyster, as long as they are not too 'out there'. You love to dress them up and down, and may go for a more fitted, glamorous style or prefer a lighter, prettier number.

Classic Chic styles are the personality behind the clothes. The statement your outfits make is that you are confident and comfortable with who you are: you wear the clothes, the clothes don't wear you.

Style icons: Michelle Obama, Holly Willoughby, Naga Munchetty, Catherine, Duchess of Cambridge

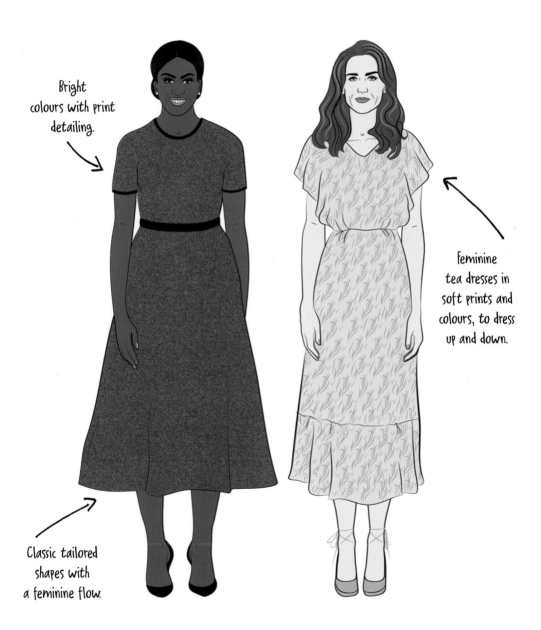

Bright colours with print detailing.

Feminine tea dresses in soft prints and colours, to dress up and down.

Classic tailored shapes with a feminine flow.

Boho

From one extreme to another. The Boho style isn't necessarily fully flamboyant but there is nothing pared back about it. To some, it can be an assault on the senses, as the key to this style is an utter mishmash of glorious fabric, colour and texture. And there are no rules. Not that there are fashion rules anyway, but within outfits (as we'll see) there are guidelines that lend your look a better aesthetic. Bin that concept for Boho. If you like it, throw it on. OK, so that's easy to say, but for many (dare I say, me included) the thought of doing this will leave you with a feeling of abject horror.

But not if you're a Boho at heart. It's about mixing vintage with new fashion, breaking proportion rules that somehow don't matter because you've created your own rules that work for your shape, creating outfits with a riot of texture that are rich, vivid, eccentric and dynamic. There is a vintage vibe that transcends a specific time in fashion. The look is simply Boho. It can be light and airy; it can be brilliantly rich and dynamic.

Fabrics are decadent and flow. The Boho style has a length to it – which, as I type, doesn't appear to make much sense, but that's exactly what it is. It's an elongated style, it flows and drifts and sways. It has a movement that conveys length. It's also not for everyone! Those with a Boho style seem to have an innate ability to mix fashions from different eras so that they look like they belong together, while creating a unique and distinctive style.

It may seem that it has a 1970s vibe to it (and it can indeed), but, as a true Boho, you're able to mix different styles that have the same feel, leaving the rest of us wondering what the era is – it looks like the styles belong together but we know they don't. You weave different elements from different tribes together but the ultimate look is one of pure ease.

As a Boho-style aficionado, you love different textures, fabrics and finishes. Attention to detail is what counts – be it a fringe, a section of embroidery, a clever collection of accessories that just finish your look perfectly. You can appear, to the rest of us, effortlessly stylized while looking completely natural.

Style icons: Lisa Bonet, Sienna Miller, Florence Welch, Zoë Kravitz, Erykah Badu, Dame Judi Dench

Accessories make all the difference.

Rich, decadent, flowing fabrics.

Invest in accessories and wear them your own way.

Boho can work at any age.

Seventies magic

There is, it has to be said, a fine line between Boho, Eclectic Vintage and Seventies Magic. You can easily be a bit of all three. But there is something about the 1970s specifically, something about the styles that has really bled into the fashion of today, and the decade holds a very special place in many people's hearts.

Maybe it's a generational thing; I was brought up in the 1970s and, to me, so many of the extravagant styles, prints and colours are still so evocative of the ultimate in elegance and, well, pure FASHION! They're origins of my sartorial goals.

Having said that, I also spent a great deal of my childhood in the 1980s and, funnily enough, the hankering for a shell suit or a corkscrew perm didn't make it past 1989. Maybe the next generation will be agog for Heather Shimmer lipstick, pedal pushers, ra-ra skirts and fishnet tights fashioned into fingerless gloves.

The 1970s, though – the huge floral pints, the maxi dresses, the platform shoes, the knee-high boots, the flares, the suede jackets, the leather trench coats, the rise of the band tee (although originally seen as early as the 1950s) – I am actually salivating writing this list. And we haven't even discussed Disco yet. Sequins, sequins everywhere. Huge collars, ruffles – if I had to wear nothing again but 1970s clothing, I easily could.

However, when it comes to adopting Seventies Magic, most people don't tend to go the whole hog. If you're looking for a head-to-toe 1970s ensemble, then you really belong in the Eclectic Vintage or Boho tribe (depending on which style of the 1970s takes your fancy). The thing about 1970s fashion is that most people aren't aware that it's become embedded in our more mainstream fashion, these days. So it is seen as being a lot more acceptable and less eclectic than it was in years gone by.

But true mavens of the 1970s will know that the jewels in your wardrobe are large-print florals, maxi dresses, flares, band tees and a great tailored blazer all woven neatly into other styles to give a hint of Seventies Magic without the full quirk of an Eclectic Vintage.

Style icons: Donna Summer, Bianca Jagger, Farrah Fawcett, Pam Grier, Margo from the BBC sitcom *The Good Life*

Tailored blazers and jackets balance the wider trousers perfectly.

Sequins are for life, not just for Christmas.

Classic flares always work.

Androgynous flair

As we move through the styles, you'll notice that there's an element of overlap between them. And it helps to have a broad concept of what 'style' is in your mind. Because at the end of the day, fashion is purely subjective. It's about the style you're looking to find. Not anyone else's, as theirs may well be different. Just yours.

One woman's Eclectic Vintage may be another woman's Androgynous Flair. Some may think that Androgynous Flair is very similar to Classic Chic with a less feminine touch. And they would be right. However, it's important to remember that the key point of the prep stage is to get your creative juices flowing and think about the concept of your style, rather than just throwing on the first two things you grab out of your wardrobe. Although, by the end of the book, you WILL be grabbing the first two things out of your wardrobe as you will know they're there for a reason, they will go together and you WILL look amazing.

But before we get there…Androgynous Flair. How I adore this style category! It's one that is best described as a preference for masculine-looking clothes but with a feminine twist. So it's not about actually wearing men's clothes (not to say it can't be, though); it's about taking their styles and shapes and adapting them to create an individual look that is both masculine and feminine. Oh hello, that will be Androgynous Flair.

You should be thinking wide-leg trouser suits, men's-style button-down shirts, waistcoats, brogues, loafers, chunky work boots or tuxedo jackets or trousers, possibly worn together as a suit. Accessories are kept to a minimum and are often male-inspired in their aesthetic – a tie, cufflinks, a masculine-style hat – and generally colours are neutral.

The joy of this style is that it's easily adapted to give your look a more feminine edge. Lots of you will have an Androgynous Flair vibe in the base elements of your outfit: say, a classic tailored suit to which you add a girly twist with a ruffle shirt or a print blouse. A silk pussy-bow blouse is the perfect antithesis to a sharper-cut suit. A wide leather belt over your suit can, again, soften the look, or it could be as simple as wearing a tailored jacket over a full skirt with chunky work boots to top and tail the outfit with Androgynous Flair.

Style icons: Diane Keaton, Marlene Dietrich, Katharine Hepburn, Janelle Monáe, Grace Jones

Go bold with the accessories.

Think variations on classics, such as the pinstripe suit.

Men's tailoring, but in a fitted style, adds femininity.

Add a belt for a more form-fitting, feminine edge.

Parisian chic

It's not all about the Breton. Don't get me wrong, the Breton is a worthy flag bearer of all things Francophile and, for many, is the ultimate Wardrobe Gem, but there can be more to Parisian Chic than a stripy top.

There are layers of similarity that run across many of these styles. The key thing about Parisian Chic is the level of effortless elegance that it portrays. Many of the items that Parisian Chics put together in outfits are ones that we all wear, but just not necessarily (or never) at the same time.

It's a pair of skinny jeans, a tailored white shirt, a sharp blazer and heels. It's a casual tee, leather trousers, slouchy blazer and heels. It's a leather pencil skirt, sheer blouse and trench coat. And heels. It may be jeans, a slouchy jumper, a vintage (classic, not really Eclectic) coat, sublime handbag and ankle boots... which have a heel. As much as the ballet flat is seen to be the epitome of French style, for our style icon purposes I have positioned it as the footwear fetish of Minimalist Elegance, while for all things Parisian, we're craving a heel.

It doesn't have to be vertiginous. In fact, French designer Vanessa Seward once told me that she had designed her boots with the perfect heel height for walking around Paris ALL DAY, and that was 7cm (2¾in). For the record, I obviously did then buy the boots and I can confirm that you are able to walk around in them all day. I may have three pairs, and do you know why? Yes, I love the boots and, yes, they are really comfortable, timeless, versatile and go with lots that I own. But I'd be lying if I didn't say it was because SHE told me that and because I am a SUCKER for wanting to think of myself as walking around Paris all day, embodying Parisian Chic. There may even be a Breton thrown in for extra Gallic points.

But until I get to Paris, these boots are the basis for many of my outfits because, frankly, they make me feel like I am living my best Parisian Chic life, and that gives me confidence. And makes me happy. Do I care if other people think that's crazy? No, because I would love them to get to a place where something they wear has the ability to make them as happy as some of my clothes make me.

Style icons: Emmanuelle Alt, Vanessa Paradis, Carine Roitfeld, Ines de la Fressange

Statement jackets complete any outfit.

Think detail - a pussy bow or a belt to transform an otherwise plain outfit.

Jeans can be the most glamorous clothing.

Classic neutral prints in texture are key.

Think boots for all occasions, ideally with a heel.

London cool

For the purposes of my London Cool style category, I am talking 'cool' (much to the eye rolling of my teens – I can hear it now. And, yes teens, if you're reading this, I CAN hear an eye roll...).

The epitome of hip, a little bit grungey, a lot of rock chick and an element of Eclectic Vintage that all work together to become a style that we recognize. Yes, it's rock chick, but it's more than that. There's a softness to it, an elegant aesthetic that comes from an innate inner confidence in being able to put together an outfit that simply says 'I know exactly who I am'. There can be colour, but cut open the beating fashion heart of the London Cool style and the blood runs black.

There's leather and there's leopard. There's a hint of Androgynous Flair to it, there's a whiff of Eclectic Vintage, there's a scent of Boho, but actually it very much stands up as its own style. Am I being fair by calling it London? Not at all. Apologies to any other metropolitan British city, and please don't take it personally but because it's where I grew up, London is where this style is most definitely cemented for me.

It's the style that really has stood the test of time in its essence. Each new generation and each new season, there are tweaks to the ethos of the look but at its roots there is always an inner rock chick fighting to get out. A little more leopard, a couple more studs, a change to the shape of the leather jacket or the leather skirt, maybe some more colour, maybe a sequin blouse or maybe a logo knit or a graphic tee. Boots are high on the leg or high on the heel. Shoes can be anything so long as they're fierce. What remains constant is the attitude. It's undeniably British in style, if not birthright, and it's worn with a confidence that can't be denied.

Denim has a key part to play. It can be classic blue, true black or a faded charcoal. It can be a skinny, a boyfriend or a wide-leg jean (and any other jean style you can think of, to be fair). We'll even throw in jacket form. The key thing is – it's lived in. Chunky knits and cashmere in the autumn/winter, a tee or silky blouse in the spring/summer, but there's always an element of fabulous black.

Style icons: Kate Moss, Debbie Harry, Chrissie Hynde, Claudia Winkleman, Mary Portas, Amy Winehouse

Leopard and black are the perfect combo.

A mix of grunge and femininity is the name of the game.

Perfect black skinny jeans, in denim or leather.

Boots are either high on the leg or high on the heel (or both!).

Eclectic vintage

Not to be confused with Boho – although, to be fair, if neither of these are up your strada, both will seem equally intimidating.

The main difference between the two is that there are even fewer rules when it comes to Eclectic Vintage. I say fewer, I mean none. Absolutely anything goes. If you thought that Boho was an idiosyncratic statement, let me introduce Eclectic Vintage, which takes it to another level.

This is an unashamedly unique and in-your-face representation of personal style of any description. It most definitely isn't going to be a style that appeals to everyone. And you may well look at people who are avid adopters of Eclectic Vintage and not really appreciate the vibe, but you have to acknowledge that they wear it with panache. They own their aesthetic and don't care what anyone else thinks. We may not wish to emulate them but we can absolutely admire the conviction those who pull off Eclectic Vintage have in their style. Which is, when it comes to confidence goals, right up there at the top of the tree.

The key to successful Eclectic Vintage is simply wearing what you love. At the end of the day, that's it. It's not about carefully matching pattern or print or colour or texture, or thinking about a specific style that you'd like to adhere to; it's the fashion equivalent of wearing everything but the kitchen sink. It's definitely, DEFINITELY, the more the merrier. True Eclectic Vintages have absolutely no need for this book as they are simply the masters of their own daily outfit destiny.

What many of us may want to emulate is a hint of their rebellion. We love the idea of adding a slightly quirky element to our wardrobes – a small hint of individualism that can really personalize your look – but if you're not an inherently Eclectic Vintage individual, there is the genuine fear of looking like you got dressed in the dark. It's very easy to have the best intentions but fall slightly (very) wide of the mark.

True Eclectic Vintages wear many styles at the same time, but unlike their Boho counterparts they won't be making any concession to ensuring these have a similar look and theme. Their outfits are a smorgasbord of styles rather than a representation of one. If we're looking to borrow a bit of their vibe, the key step is to try for the 'more is more' look by actually only wearing a little bit more.

Texture on a plain colour takes it to a new level.

A true Eclectic Vintage still understands proportion and shape.

Absolutely anything goes – if you love it, wear it.

The brighter the colour and the more eccentric the mix, the better.

As an Eclectic Vintage, you think nothing of wearing a tulle skirt, a Breton and a leather jacket with heels, trainers or Dr. Martens. Kaftans with 35 necklaces in every colour of the rainbow. For you, it's often not about mixing diverse items of clothing to create an outfit that is cohesive, rather it's the pieces themselves that you fall in love with and want to wear. A floral vintage maxi dress with a suede blazer and cowboy boots. It could be that you're channelling your inner Laura Ingalls Wilder and love a more theatrical look – not going to lie to you, I could have worn every single outfit from any episode of *Little House on the Prairie*. And I'm frequently asked by my teenager if I'm worried that my outfit is a bit too *Handmaid's Tale*. There is something about taking a theatrical piece and teaming it with more modern wardrobe elements that creates a really unique, albeit eclectic style. It sounds like it shouldn't work, but on the right person it does. And as an Eclectic Vintage, this will be your comfort zone in its entirety.

Alternatively, it could be what looks like a whole level of crazy. Most definitely good crazy. Think outfits that we simply can't imagine working on anyone but you; they somehow do. Literally anything goes, so long as you wear it with cojones of style (not an actual thing but they so should be, and if you embrace Eclectic Vintage full on, you are no doubt a proud

owner of a virtual pair). Bright orange faux-fur coat, head to foot in a tartan suit, bright pink full-length velvet frock coat, yellow knee-high boots: you can somehow pull these off and make them look conventional.

It's often the juxtaposition of wardrobe pieces from different styles that you put together in an outfit that makes this look work. And that's the info we need to nab to add a hint of eclectic to our style. We can borrow some ideas from our Eclectic Vintage cousins (without nicking the kitchen sink that they're possibly wearing). Think what shouldn't work, think what wouldn't normally work, then do it. But with only one or two items. Start small, maybe with accessories. Perhaps a pair of vintage sunglasses. And you can go as far as you like. OR, OR, OR – and here is the beauty of finding your style – you don't have to! But if you do have a penchant for being a bit of a fashion magpie every now and then, taking it one item at a time is the best way to start.

Laid-back LA

This is probably one of the easiest styles to emulate – even if you have to add a coat or jacket of some description, depending on the climate in which you live. However, the essence of the style is one that will appeal to many: laid-back, casual, but still with an elegant edge. More laid-back, effortless sass than laid-back, 'I'm still in pyjamas and you can sort of tell as I'm wearing half my breakfast as well'...

Mastered by the crème de la crème of Hollywood glamour on their off days, it's a style that we aspire to and can, with a little bit of creative curating, actually achieve. The key to their seemingly nonchalant style is actually a wardrobe of carefully coordinated essentials that are easy to dress up or down. Colour is kept to a neutral, or at the very least pale shades, but there are nods to trends and new fashions – worn in a wearably realistic way by keeping the rest of the outfit classic. It is casual sartorial elegance at its finest.

Jeans can be baggy or skinny, ripped or spanking new and in any colour – although extra Laid-Back LA style points if they're off-white or ecru (and clean, obvs). And therein lies one of the reasons this isn't a style that I gravitate towards. I might be one of those people – the only person perhaps – who wishes it was

the done thing to still wear a bib to eat at the age of 48 (at the time of writing). As well as having the ability to wear clothes, I also have the unenviable skill of frequently wearing my dinner.

Other trousers that grace the Laid-Back LA wardrobe are likely to be a selection of cargo-style ones – either baggy, tapered or skinny – as well as long skirts that are loose and flowing. However, the legs do get a voice, and there's a very high chance that you have a pair of shorts or a skirt of the shorter variety, most likely in denim or a cotton chino fabric.

You have an enviable collection of tees – neckline and shape to suit – ditto an array of casual shirts. There may be – what am I talking about, there absolutely is – a crisp white shirt in your collection, which you wear dressed down with your jeans, cargo pants, shorts or skirts.

But you may also have a selection of softer shirts, perhaps in worn linen, chambray or silk.

Jacket-wise, well, you're in LA so you don't need a jacket, but if you happen to NOT be in LA (*everyone raises their hands*) a jacket and a coat are what you need. Not to mention knits to layer. The palette of your coats and knits are muted; there may be soft tailoring but it's unlikely to be overly structured.

Shoes are again casual, but you may favour a heel or two in the stylishly comfortable and not the glamorous stakes. Heels are chunky or a wedge, as opposed to a vertiginous stiletto.

Laid-Back LA types add interest to their look in the form of accessories: huge scarves, hats (to keep the paparazzi away in LA; to keep the rain off or to hide your roots in the UK – needs must) and bags can definitely do the talking.

Style icons: Sarah Jessica Parker, Jennifer Aniston, Gwyneth Paltrow, Kate Beckinsale, Nicole Kidman, Halle Berry

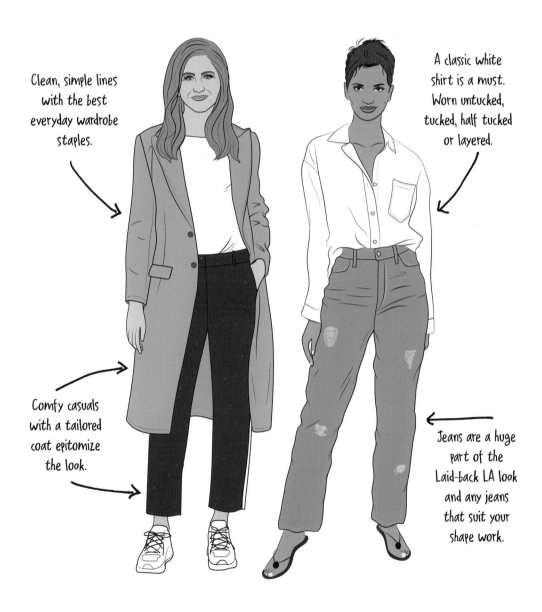

Clean, simple lines with the best everyday wardrobe staples.

A classic white shirt is a must. Worn untucked, tucked, half tucked or layered.

Comfy casuals with a tailored coat epitomize the look.

Jeans are a huge part of the Laid-back LA look and any jeans that suit your shape work.

Nutritional information

> To help define YOUR style and to jumpstart your creative vision for your wardrobe, start by selecting which style category you most identify with.

> There's no need to stick with just one style; a combo of a couple absolutely works, and you can be a different style on different occasions. But, in order to focus, it's probably best not have too many (or all of them!).

> The best way to find your own style icon is to get your thinking cap on and get googling. As much as I have made suggestions, there may be someone whose style you love that you want to channel. Have a look at what they wear and see if you can dissect their style and categorize it – it will make it a lot easier for you. Think 'What would *insert style icon* wear?'

My style category suggestions

Minimalist Elegance
Neutral colours, pared-back simplicity, tailoring and structured shapes with fabric and cut being at the forefront of your style.

Classic Chic (sometimes corporate, always composed)
Timeless, classic looks, well-cut and elegant clothes, embracing both neutrals and colour, with a plethora of accessories adding the personal stamp.

Boho
Mixing vintage prints and fabrics from similar eras with modern-day touches to complete the look.

Seventies Magic
All about the full-on disco, glitter, sequins, huge prints and bright colours (there may be similarities between Boho and Eclectic Vintage). More is more is more.

Androgynous Flair
Adopting the shape and style of typically masculine clothes but with an added feminine edge.

Parisian Chic
Taking wardrobe classics but putting outfits together using pieces that traditionally wouldn't be worn together. And nearly always with heels (even a little heel).

London Cool
Essentially the ultimate rock chick – think leather, leopard and also denim – but mostly black.

Eclectic Vintage
A smorgasbord of styles from any decade, worn with panache and confidence (not to be confused with Boho).

Laid-Back LA
Dressed down but with a nonchalance that is casually elegant and simply chic, with classic fabrics and informal styles.

Dressing for your shape

The first thing to point out about body shape is that we are ALL perfect. The media's portrayal of the 'perfect body' for many years has done nothing to improve our self-confidence, when basically we're not all models. It IS great to see that in recent years there has been a broadening of body shapes and types depicted in magazines, and certainly the rise of social media sites such as Instagram and TikTok (I think that's how you spell it...suffice to say that, at 48, the dancing thing has not entered my world) have worked wonders in dispelling the myth that all women's bodies are a size 8 with perky boobs.

But old habits do die hard, especially when we may, at a certain time in life, not be the same shape that we once were. We need to stop punishing ourselves for not having the same body we had 20 years ago, and we need to stop making apologies for our prosecco protrusion and trying to hide away behind mountains of fabric.

It's about understanding the shape that we are; it's about buying clothes that fit well; and it's about buying clothes that flatter. At this stage in the book, we hopefully have an idea of the style that we would like to be and have taken into consideration the lifestyle that we have and that we need to dress for every day (not the lifestyle that we would, perhaps, like to kit ourselves out for!).

I'm pretty sure that I've said numerous times already (and if I haven't, trust me, I will): 'The most popular question I am asked is...'. Well, this one is. Or, at the very least, it's definitely one of the most frequent questions: 'How do I dress for *insert petite/curves/small boobs/big boobs/tall/big tummy/big bum/no bum/ad infinitum* shape?'

I get asked it so often, I wonder if anyone is what society considers 'normal'? And while we're here, what on earth is 'normal' anyway? What is the shape that we all 'should' be? The simple answer is: ANY SHAPE. But the answer that people are mostly looking for is: in proportion. And the obvious follow-up question to that is, what is 'in proportion'?

And down a rabbit hole of what is perceived to be anatomical perfection I went. As fascinating as it is (ish...OK that's a lie – if it's your thing you will no doubt find it fascinating, but I'd much rather talk about what shoes are going to make your outfit sing and ultimately make you happy), it's a whole other debate for another day and, frankly, since at least as early as 300BC people have been wrangling about what is and isn't the set of perfect proportions.

Suffice to say, within Western culture there is a broad idea of what we perceive to be in proportion, and it's essentially the silhouette that we strive to emulate when we talk about fashion and making sure that our proportions are balanced. Whether we agree with it or not, we are conditioned to think that there should be a balance to an outfit and that it looks 'better' when that balance is achieved.

It has NOTHING to do with size. And in case my attempt to use capitals didn't quite convey how strongly I feel about this, let me repeat it in capitals and bold: it has **NOTHING** to do with size.

People may say that the 'ideal' is an hourglass shape, which is all very well and good if you have a fabulous waist, but many don't. So beating ourselves up about not having a waist, if anatomically we're never going to be able to achieve one, is all sorts of daft. If you have one, wonderful. If you don't, it doesn't mean that you can never be in proportion.

For me, the key element to focus on, which is much easier than trying to take away flesh, is where you can ADD balance. And the two main areas that are really the only ones you have to make sure are balanced are your shoulders and hips. That's it. You can obviously make it more complicated if you would like to, but so long as your hips are balancing your shoulders and neither one is overly wider (or narrower, depending on which way you look at it), that's as 'in proportion' as we need to worry about.

The other thing you could consider further down the line after you master the basics is body-to-leg ratio. Seeing as I've just mentioned something that sounds a bit 'mathsy' and I am horrendous with numbers, the golden rule is that you're looking for your legs to be longer than your body. If you think of your legs as being roughly half your

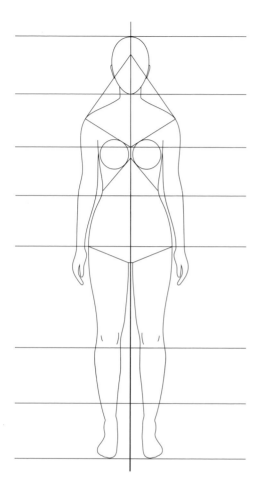

It doesn't matter if you're not the 'perfect proportion'. It's understanding how to achieve the balance through clothes.

height, that should give you an idea of what sort of balance to aim for. The thing is – as with the waist – legs either are half your height or they aren't. So worrying about the minutiae of the ratio seems like a big old waste of time to me, with most of us having a lot more to address! And, of course, there are always tips and tricks that you can employ to give the illusion of perfect ratios and even a waist. But this is very much the icing on the cake. First and foremost, the main balance that you want to achieve, so as to hit the golden proportion ideal, is between your shoulders and your hips.

Which is why it's important to understand your body shape and know the best way to dress for it.

Seeing as we are all individuals and literally no two people are exactly the same, for me to cover every single body shape in one chapter frankly isn't possible. BUT while we may all be different shapes, many of us have the same NORMAL attributes that aren't seen by those who make clothing as being NORMAL, meaning we struggle to buy clothes that fit.

And so we have to be creative, which I've always found really interesting, by which I obviously mean *insert swear word* irritating, as I'm pretty sure you

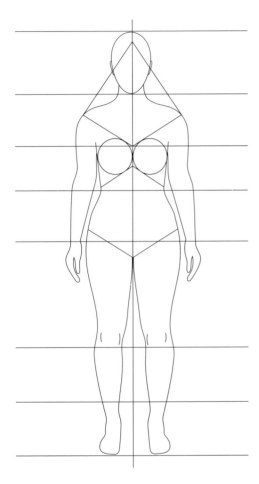

Proportion isn't about 'size'. It's about looking to achieve a balance and is the same for petites, plus size, tall and short.

can count actual 'normal' body shapes on one hand versus the rest of the female population. But we are where we are, so rather than moaning about it, there ARE ways to dress cleverly and find the perfect wardrobes for our body shapes AND match the style that we want to be.

We have boobs, we are petite, we have TUMMIES, we have love handles, we are tall, we have wide hips, we have small shoulders. We most definitely don't have all of those at the same time but we probably do have at least one, plus some other random attribute that makes it tricky to find clothes that we love.

There are very few 'media perfect' bodies out there, but every single body IS perfect. And there are solutions and options for every shape and for every height. There is an element of acceptance that we all need to face. In an ideal world there would be a huge selection of clothes for every single size and shape, but that's not commercially feasible for retailers – especially with us knowing just how many different variations there would be to cater for, and with us hopefully moving towards a more sustainable retail model.

Partly it's about finding retailers that specialize in your shape, partly it's being cleverer about how you shop, but mostly it's about knowing what works for you and focusing on the options that suit your shape and your style (not the ones that you'd like to wear but can't). There ARE options out there. You're special, you're really special, and you deserve to spend time on yourself making sure you can look and feel truly spectacular.

Hopefully this advice will go some way to help you cheat the fashion system and find a set of clothes that genuinely works for you.

There are many, many ways that I could divide up the different body shapes and you could still guarantee that I wouldn't have everyone covered. Instead, I'm trying to keep it simple by looking at heights and then shapes.

Think of it as a pick 'n' mix or a smorgasbord of shape advice. You pick the height that you are and then the shape that best describes you. Fingers crossed there will be something in there that sings to you.

Height

Petite

I'm not going to tell you that good things come in small packages (although they most definitely do) as you've no doubt been told that all your life (and if you haven't, you should have been). And, frankly, while it's nice to know, it's about as much use as a chocolate teapot if everything you wear simply drowns you; literally zero use to you when nothing you want to wear fits. There are a few key general pointers to take on board before we get to the tips and tricks.

● **Hunt out retailers that specialize in petite ranges.** Practically every high street store now has a petite range. You may not be able to get what you want from one store, you may have to shop around to find the clothes that work for your style, but there is definitely more choice now than there ever has been. It may be that a shop doesn't have a specific petite section, but often online each item has different leg lengths and sizing options.

● **Make friends with a seamstress** (assuming you're not handy with a sewing machine). OK, they don't actually have to be your friend, but finding a good one who can make adjustments

Keeping an outfit tonal
- in the same shade -
gives the illusion of height.

Long flowing trousers
add length to your look.

to garments so that they fit means you have a wider pool to shop from. The more you have altered, the more you will understand what can or can't be made smaller or shorter – that in itself is a really handy piece of knowledge when you're trying something on and know that with a nip and a tuck here and there it will be perfect, as opposed to having to take a garment apart to make it fit! Some things are much easier to alter than others and the more you know, the more choice you will have.

● **Don't dismiss children's ranges.**
I fully appreciate that this may well be up there in the patronizing stakes and for that I apologize profusely (I feel like I'm playing Petite Bingo – how many offensive things can I say? Small packages, kids clothes…), but look on it as an advantage. For a start, they're a lot cheaper (no VAT) and teen ranges these days aren't like they were when we were growing up. Don't get me wrong, they may have evolved the other way and I am absolutely not advocating a wardrobe of cropped tops, pelmet skirts or dressing like your daughter (although if that floats your boat, knock yourself out). There are great wardrobe staples that can be found among the younger ranges: classic denim jackets, jeans, cargo trousers, plain tees,

fab sweatshirts and hoodies. Yes, you will probably find that you're looking at a more casual style and chances are you'll not find a whole wardrobe, but there are gems to be found. Especially when it comes to footwear. Trainers, boots, ballet flats, sandals: I often look at the range with envy and wonder in reality how many toes I actually need…

● **Print.** You absolutely can wear print but, to make it flattering for your height, keep the print small. The issue with a large print is simply that it will overpower you: there won't be enough of the print and you'll just see the odd huge flower. A repeat of lots of tiny flowers or paisley is a lot more flattering. But vertical stripes are your friend. If vertical stripes are your thing…although I can't remember the last time I saw anything in a vertical stripe, BUT if you have a gem that you love, whip it out and get it on. They draw the eye upwards in a vertical manner, automatically making you seem taller. That's not to say you can't wear horizontal stripes as well, you absolutely can. What size stripe may depend more on your shape than your height, although the general rule of thumb is the more petite you are, the smaller the print and so a smaller stripe would be preferable.

● **Find what works for you.** As frustrating as it is not to be able to find the perfect petite sizing in everything that you would like, there are tips and tricks that you can use with regards to individual clothing pieces. Embrace fashion where it works for you in adding height, and see if you can benefit from these tips in your chosen style:

> **High waists.** High-waisted everything are your friends. They give the illusion of a longer leg, making you seem taller.

> **Wide-leg trousers.** Don't let anyone tell you that you can't wear these. High-waisted wide-leg trousers are a game changer for the petite and there's a pair out there for pretty much every style. Add height with shoes, not necessarily heels, although they are ideal under long wide-leg trousers, ditto wedges. Flatform trainers, pumps, espadrilles and loafers are also genius for adding height.

> **Maxi and midi skirts and dresses.** First up, you can absolutely wear these if you're petite. The key is to find one that fits your petite proportions, but there's nothing to stop you buying a 'regular' midi skirt and wearing it as a maxi. The main thing to focus on here is the fabric. You don't want swathes of material and lots of layers and frills. In an ideal world, you're looking for fabric that skims and flows and isn't excessive. The more voluminous the material is, the more it will look like the dress is wearing you rather than the other way around.

> **Necklines.** I'm slightly reluctant to mention necklines as I genuinely think you should wear what you feel comfortable in and it also depends on your bust size. But, as a rule, the lower the neckline, the more flattering it is. Why? Because the larger the space you create between your neck and clothing, the more your neck is elongated, yet again, giving that wonderful illusion of length and height.

> **Footwear.** So the ludicrously obvious statement here is to say 'wear heels'. And, yes, it is ludicrous as who on earth wants to wear heels all the time? If you do – absolutely go for it, and I genuinely have footwear envy as I am too clumsy and too lazy to live a life in heels (in the next life, I will simply rock a heel every day). But you can still get height from flats: oh hello the flatform. Which is essentially a fancy fashion word for a shoe that has some height in the whole sole as opposed to the heel alone. These are now very much everyday accepted

footwear – not a high fashion item – and are available everywhere. Platform heels are also great as they give you the height in the heel while the platform aspect means that you're not really walking on a heel that's impossible to balance in. Chunky boots with a cleated sole are a given and can add inches but also chunkier trainers, pumps, brogues, loafers and sandals. A couple of extra inches on the sole is the ideal way to add valuable height.

> Colour. I truly believe that you should wear whatever colours you love, but if you are looking for a trick to add the illusion of height, stick to wearing one colour palette. Which is pretty difficult (and perhaps dull), but you can cheat by wearing a longer coat or cardigan in a single colour over your outfit, which again means the line isn't broken and you look taller.

> Hair. Make your hair bigger. This sounds like the most bonkers thing EVER but it's a genuine thing if you'd like it to be. A high ponytail, a huge head of curls, a top bun – all will add a good couple of extra inches.

Tall

I will confess to having a certain vested interest in this element of the book as I fall into this category being 5ft 10in (178cm). I feel your pain and have lived and breathed your misery in trying to find anything to fit for 48 years (give or take a few at the beginning where it was my mum's issue and not mine. Am still scarred by my First Holy Communion dress, though, as I wasn't allowed a pretty, full tulle one like all my friends had. Oh no, apparently tall girls couldn't pull off 'pretty' so I had a broderie anglaise one that would have been ideal if I was heading for the nunnery, but the frothy princess dress that I really wanted and all my friends had? Not so much – scarred I tell you!).

If you're tall, you will no doubt have spent a good proportion of your life being told how lucky you are. Well yes. Any luckier than being average height? Many tall people would tell you probably not. Especially if you've ever tried to buy things to fit you properly in the leg, in the torso, in the arms – actually pretty much anywhere.

Are there shortcuts (excuse the pun) to make finding your perfect wardrobe easier? Here are some that I have relied on over the years.

● **Hunt out retailers who specialize in extra length.** 'Tall' it's usually called (no flies on them). You will be aware that

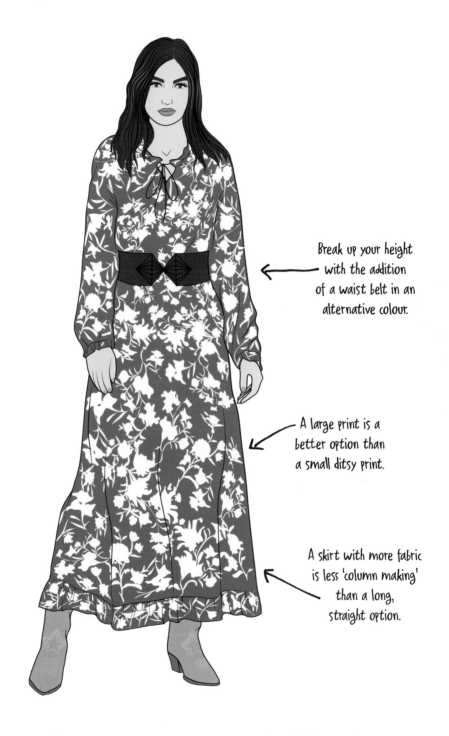

Break up your height with the addition of a waist belt in an alternative colour.

A large print is a better option than a small ditsy print.

A skirt with more fabric is less 'column making' than a long, straight option.

there are far fewer of these than there are for petite people (I'm assuming there are more of us at the diminutive end of the scale than there are at the 'can you see snow up there' scale – don't you LOVE that comment?). As is the case for the petites, rather than having specific categories, some retailers will just have extra length options on the product pages, and it's always worth noting and bookmarking those sites.

● **Befriend a seamstress.** Like our petite allies also in clothing hell, yes, we should all be friends with a seamstress, but it's not quite as simple. It's a lot trickier to add fabric (especially when you don't have the fabric...). You can't simply make something bigger. ARRRGGGHH!

But...you can buy things in a bigger size for the length and have it adjusted. You do need to think creatively but you can always buy two of the same item and 'add' length from one to the other, essentially using one as extra fabric. Add a tier or a ruffle to a skirt, have longer sleeves made – no, it's not the cheapest way to buy a piece of clothing but you are getting something unique and you will get something that fits. The other obvious option is to simply have things made for you. I say 'obvious' and 'simply' implying that this is the easiest thing to do when we all know it's not. It's time consuming, it can be expensive, and there's always the danger that you won't like it once it's been made (I may or may not be speaking from experience with regards to the latter...). But if there's a shape of dress or trousers or skirt or whatever it may be that you love, to have one or two items that you adore and will wear again and again is a lot more beneficial than having a whole wardrobe of clothes that you never wear because they don't fit properly!

● **Find the retailers that cut things more generously.** They are out there. Often, now, lots of online retailers give the height of the model wearing the outfit. Ridiculously useful, because they don't always use the traditionally lofty lady. A maxi skirt may look maxi but if the model is 5ft 6in (168cm) and you're 6ft (183cm), maxi it ain't gonna be on you (weeps; again, I may or may not be speaking as someone who's been there, done that, bought the skirt/trousers/dress that was way too short). Some are on the high street, for others you may have to look at more expensive brands. Some retailers make a 'true' maxi that's actually long, others call it a maxi but we all know that it's only going to be mid-calf (and a midi is knee length). Ditto sleeve length. Some retailers always make lovely long arms, others always skimp on arm length. Once you've found them and they suit your style and you know that the clothes fit you well, have them on your sales list. Make a note of what it is you have your eye on and as soon as the sale hits GO, GO, GO.

● **Be open-minded to shopping in men's departments.** Now bear with me caller on this one…to some, it may sound as patronizing as suggesting that the small but perfectly formed shop in kids' shops BUT it can work. I'm not suggesting we all embrace Androgynous Flair as there are absolute classic wardrobe staples that we can find. Think extra-fine merino knits, cashmere polo necks, denim jackets and shirts. The latter is trickier if you are blessed with breasts but you could easily still adopt a man's shirt as an overshirt, wearing it undone. And it would fit in the arms and it would be long enough. NOVELTY! Knitwear is a real find though. I would suggest just taking a size down (in S, M, L and so on) from your usual size.

● **Embrace what you can.** In an ideal world, yes, our sleeves would always be long enough as would our trousers. But they're not. Rather than being constantly hung up on finding trousers that are the right length, think creatively about what you've got to work with.

> **Skinnies and leggings** can always be a little cropped, especially when you wear a pair of boots over them. Or bridge the gap with a pair of hightop trainers.

> **The 7/8ths style** can be your friend. Of course, ideally we would have a FULL full-length pair of trousers but 7/8ths length can work for pretty much any style.

> **Skirts** that you'd love to have an inch or two longer: try wearing them slightly lower on your hips. Again, this is where I tend to size up so they sit lower on the upper hip, rather than right on my waist. A larger size also means it's not cutting into you. OR buy maxi skirts and wear them as midi skirts.

> **Footwear.** Try wearing dresses and skirts that could be longer in length with knee-high boots to lessen the amount of leg on show. Shoes with ankle straps and hightop trainers will also make your legs look less lanky.

> **Sleeves.** Always an issue. Never long enough. Not sure I can remember what long-enough sleeves are like, other than in a man's knit or shirt, but it's no longer an issue for me as there is a cunning plan you can employ. Arm candy. Be it a chunky watch, a cuff, a selection of finer layering bangles. Even a skinny silk scarf tied around your wrist. Ideal for bridging the gap between cuff and hand. Adornment on your wrist takes away the excess flesh that would usually be on show and, hey presto, no one notices that your sleeves are too short. It looks intentional.

Shape

Curve

So I've actually divided this up into where you've been blessed with extra loving, as it does make a difference to how you dress. And if you have a lot of love to go around, there will be tips that you can cherry-pick from each section BUT hopefully most people will be able to recognize themselves in at least one part. The most important thing to remember is: we're trying to balance our proportions. It really is as simple as that. It's about finding those clothes that work for our shape at the same time as meeting our style requirements.

There are tips for dressing a curvier shape that go across the board. One trick that everyone would do well to remember is: accentuate the positive. I think it goes without saying, but I am going to reiterate it, every single body is perfect, regardless of shape or size. However, having been styling for more than a decade now, I know that everyone has something about their body they don't like. And that's what they tend to focus on. They want to hide it, and I get that.

But how about you flip this on its head and LOOK for the positives (rather than focus on the negatives). There will be something about your body that you love. It may be something that you think

is seemingly insignificant – your hands, your ankles, your hair – but these are things that you should be celebrating and highlighting. You may not feel like accentuating the rest, but the attributes that you love are the ones you can draw attention to.

> **Hands.** Lots of bracelets and big, gorgeous rings.

> **Ankles.** Make sure that your trousers or skirts are the right length to flash a bit of ankle.

> **Hair.** Pretty self-explanatory...make sure your hair is great at all times. Another way to accentuate the barnet is to have great earrings as well as hair accessories. Scarves, bobbles (showing my age there; my 16-year-old still rolls her eyes when I call them that), hair clips, headbands.

> **Feet.** I will throw it out there that my feet are not the most attractive part of my body – think Skeletor on a skinny day, bony with toes like fingers. BUT there are people with gorgeous feet out there. Trickier to show off in winter (flipflops in the snow are not a good look), but in the summer let your feet be the hero of your outfit. The brightest nail polish, the sparkliest of shoes; your feet should be the crowning glory of your look (at the other end!).

Curve with a bust

For those blessed with breasts. To be honest, this could also be for those who are not necessarily large but still have a gorgeous rack. First up, I have had so many requests from people over the years for advice on how to hide them. Now I'm not advocating whipping them out and having them on show as if you're working for Hooters, but frankly you can't strap them down and you're never going to be able to hide them. So there's a middle ground that we need to try and hit.

Your very first port of call should be the perfect bra. Your boobs deserve it. YOU deserve it. For the perfectly logical reason that without a really good bra, your breasts won't even be in the right place. And if they're not, no clothes are going to sit well as they're cut for boobs to be in a certain position. If yours are swinging low, clothes are just going to look wrong. Lots of people assume that it's the clothes that aren't working for them, when the reality is they're not wearing the right bra. Before you go through all your clothes that you assume don't fit properly on the bust, it's definitely worth investing in a new bra and trying them on again.

The perfect bra also changes the way you stand. I know this sounds all sorts of bonkers but it's true. With good scaffolding doing the job it should, you will stand up straighter and look more confident. Trust me.

Once you've got your bra in place and your assets are looking the best they can, here are some other suggestions to make sure that you're showcasing what God gave you (without having someone's eye out…).

● **Necklines.** The easiest way to show off your assets in their best light. It's not all about the cleavage (although if you want to flaunt it DO!). It's about making sure your shape looks the best that it can in the most flattering neckline. Generally for the larger of bust, that is a V-neck, a low square neck or a low scoop neck. A higher neckline can work if it's a boat neck: straight across with a hint of collarbone on show.

● **Style of top.** The most important things are to make sure that they're long enough AND that they fit properly. Anything with a high neckline is going to be trickier to wear and anything that's very loose, well, you run the risk of looking like the bow of a ship. As much as it may seem that a more fitted shape accentuates the bust, it actually flatters rather than draws unwanted attention to it – so long as you stick to the neckline rules and the top doesn't pull over your bust. Those are your key considerations with a top. But there are two specific styles that can work really well.

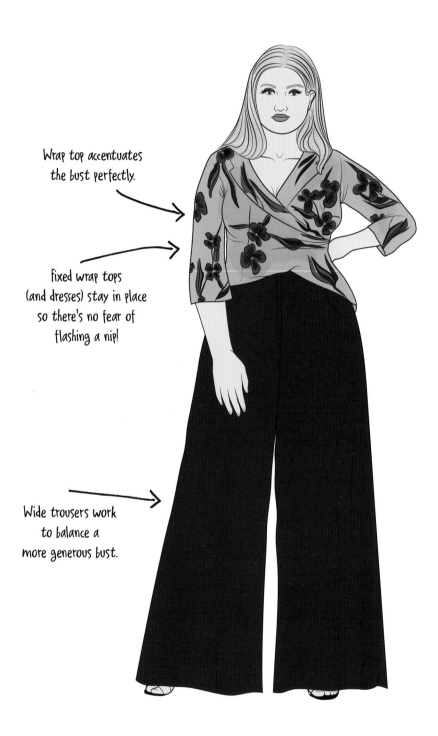

Wrap top accentuates
the bust perfectly.

Fixed wrap tops
(and dresses) stay in place
so there's no fear of
flashing a nip!

Wide trousers work
to balance a
more generous bust.

A V-neck is another neckline that works perfectly if you're more blessed with breast.

A wide-fitted waistband under the bust accentuates your curves rather than hiding them.

> **Wrap tops.** Ideal, so long as there is enough wrap in them...anyone with a larger bust will have tried and wept at a wrap top that doesn't actually wrap anything (see above point about making sure tops fit properly). You might prefer to find a fixed wrap top as opposed to one that has a manual wrap, as in my experience, even with pancake boobs, these have a tendency to unwrap themselves. And it doesn't matter how flattering a top is when it's done up, if it's prone to flashing what God gave you to the masses, it's a no-no. A fixed wrap top is one that has the appearance of a wrap top but is actually sewn at the sides.

> **A good, fitted, collared shirt** can be superb for drawing the eye away from your cleavage and up to the décolletage and neck, BUT the key is to make sure the shirt fits properly with no gaping. There are specialist suppliers that make superb shirts and, if this is your style, it may well be worth investing in one or two that fit you perfectly as they can solve many style problems. Easy to dress up with extra jewellery for a special occasion, ideal for work and also superb for weekends with jeans or over casual skirts. Fitted is also the key here: trying to tuck in a shirt creates a whole wealth of other issues, so one that skims over your tummy and hips is ideal.

> **Peplum tops** are also great for balancing out your proportions. A peplum top that fits you under the bust and then flares out over the hips is perfect for creating a flattering look.

● **Sleeves.** This depends on whether or not you love showing your arms. If you do, just go for it. If you prefer a sleeve, then keeping it simple with no frills or ruffles is a more flattering style – you're not looking to draw extra attention to the part of your body that is your largest.

● **Dresses.** Again, the fit is key. Shirt dresses are fab as they generally offer a great neckline that can be undone as far down as you see fit, meaning you can create the perfect neckline for you BUT they must not gape. It's always very tricky when you are well endowed, which is often why specialist retailers cut more generously to accommodate your best assets – same applies to shirts. Back to the wrap shape à la top (and the wrap rules...no unwrapping on my watch, please) and any dresses that are nipped in at the waist with a fuller skirt (thinking back to the peplum top) add balance to your proportions and give you a gorgeous shape.

● **Jackets.** Single-breasted. End of conversation. Longer line are generally better as they draw the eye downwards. More fluid fabrics are also more flattering as they skim over your bust, rather than hitting your breasts to create a shelf. No one wants to look like a fridge. Drapey, soft fabrics give you a much better shape.

● **Jewellery.** It can really be your friend and offer the most aesthetically wonderful distraction. Go for gold (or silver, rose gold, beaded, pearl or jewelled – whatever takes your fancy) with the earrings. If you're not looking to draw attention to your boobage, create a party elsewhere. Necklaces are also amazing, not ones that fall exactly between your boobs – they sort of defeat the object – but ones that fall higher on your chest. Statement necklaces or a set of layered finer ones – anything that you love and that works with your style and personality.

● **Stripes.** You CAN wear stripes. AND horizontal stripes. So long as they are wide stripes. If a narrow-striped top is fitted, as it extends and stretches over your assets, the stripe becomes distorted and, as you can imagine, it just looks weird. And that is where the eye is drawn immediately, as it's something that doesn't gel. A wider stripe distorts less, if at all. The exception to the rule is if something is in a narrow stripe and a looser fit that glides rather than clings so that the stripe isn't distorted.

Curve with history around the middle – also known as an 'apple shape'

Or, as many know, the Menopause Middle. Yes folks, it is a cruel fact of life that you can be one shape all your life and – suddenly – the big M hits and you're faced with a body you don't recognize. Or you may have been simply prone to this shape as you've got older and have never quite mastered the most flattering styles of clothes. I call it 'history' as this is the shape that often people who were slimmer when they were younger morph into. After having babies, C-sections or just being a lover of all things wine related (substitute wine for chocolate or Jaffa Cakes – my personal jam – if you like, although it's not called a booze belly for nothing). And they were GREAT things that happened in our life. They are our history, which some may slave away in the gym to unburden themselves of, but for lots of us, yes, it's on list of things to do but we're busy, life takes over and before we know it we have a shape that we're not used to dressing – thanks to our 'history'.

When it comes to proportion, I actually think that having no waist and being rounder in the middle is potentially the most difficult shape to master (especially if you have boobs as well). BUT do not fear, there definitely are styles that work better and certain tips and tricks you can use to make yourself feel great. One of my best friends is this shape and she always says 'I just want to look less like a Weeble'. And if this is your shape, I'm sure you know exactly what she means.

First off, let's just face facts: it's very difficult to hide your midsection. There are no Spanx on the planet that can contain that bad boy without giving you a stomach cramp that, when you get to a certain age, you simply don't care enough to suffer. Don't get me wrong, shapewear is one incredible tool that can give you a much smoother torso to dress, but it's not going to give you the flat stomach you had when you were 12. So again we need to think of the art of distraction. Highlight your best features – often arms, legs, bust or even collarbone. But there are certain clothing choices you can make that help minimize the middle.

● **Tops.** You're looking for tops that don't cling to the area you're trying not to highlight. Basically, a tight, stretch top on a larger tummy is slightly more reminiscent of a sausage trying to break free from its skin than we would like. We've all been there. Instead, look for tees that are looser without being oversized. They should skim your middle without clinging. Tees that have a split hem (where they have a little notch cut into either side of the seam on each side) are a great idea. Tucking in can be both a blessing and a curse. You can tuck in and bag the top ever so slightly over your waistband (great for hiding a muffin top) BUT the risk is that you have extra bunched fabric where no extra padding is required. So the other option is the good old half-tuck. Sometimes called a 'messy tuck', recently known as a 'French tuck' (nothing French about it – coined after Tan France from the series *Queer Eye*, who favoured it). Whatever the semantics, the key is to not tuck in all of your top. It could be just the front half, leaving the back swinging free, or it could be half of one side, so you have half in and half out (hence the name…!). You therefore get the best of all worlds: the muffin-hider tucked bit, only a little bit of extra fabric to deal with and a hint of shape from accentuating your middle. Still better, work with more fluid fabrics so that the bunching is less obvious.

> **Fitted shirts.** Great as well, so long as there is no pulling on the buttons. Other shirts can work – see the half-tuck trick above!

> **Tunics or blouses.** Neither of which sound like the most appealing garments on the planet, but they are probably what most of you have in your wardrobe that isn't a tee or a shirt. Loose, swing shapes are perfect BUT make sure they hit below the waistband while remaining above the bottom of your bum cheeks (technical term there folks). So hiding the tummy and hips but not too long, otherwise you

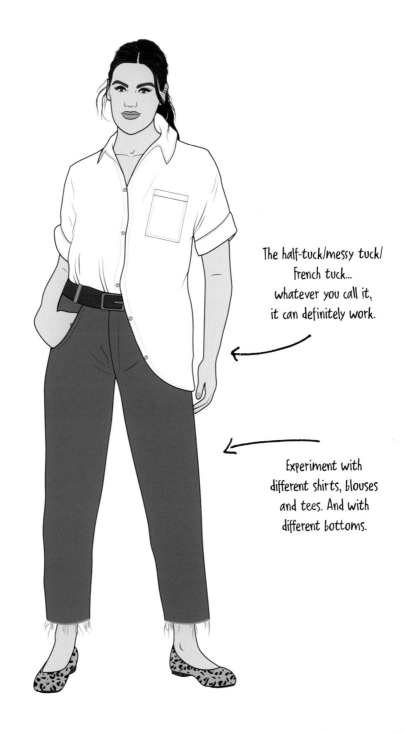

The half-tuck/messy tuck/ French tuck... whatever you call it, it can definitely work.

Experiment with different shirts, blouses and tees. And with different bottoms.

Floaty, loose tunic tops (they don't have to be Boho) that hide the history around the middle but aren't so long that they look like a shroud.

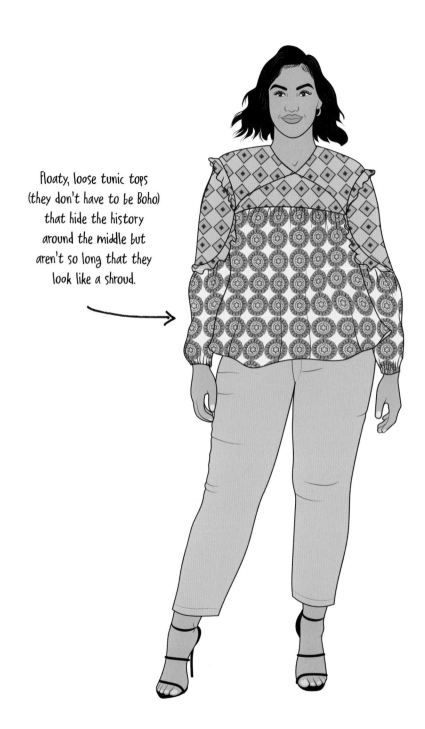

veer into maternity wear. They can be any fluid fabric that doesn't cling, but not so voluminous that you look like you're wearing a tent.

● **Jumpers and sweatshirts.** People don't necessarily agree on this BUT I've always found it a great tip for the apple-shaped and those with a tummy: jumpers and sweatshirts that have a waistband. Bear with me caller, that sounds weird, I know. They can still be quite loose and slightly baggy in the body of the top but they finish in an 'elasticated' band. It's not a stretchy, gathered elasticated band; it's often a ribbed edge to the bottom of the top. These are genius. There's no tucking in to faff about with. The fact they are slightly baggier above and then go IN at the waistband gives the illusion of shape. They hide a multitude of sins under the baggy bit (what's not to love about that) and work over trousers, skirts and even dresses. Most people of this shape really struggle with a muffin top and tucking things (although do try a half-tuck and do practise – it can take a couple of goes to get it right. I still often tuck and untuck, as sometimes it just looks plain wrong diddly). So a top that you can just put on and go, and does the work for you, is a find.

● **Shoulder pads.** Not a piece of clothing in their own right. Please do not take this as licence to go out in just shoulder pads. I mean as part of a top. These really can be the magic ingredient in your wardrobe. You can buy ones to sew in tops, or go old school and just tuck them under your bra strap à la 1980s (admittedly a risky strategy – how many times did you end up with an extra boob and realize that it was your shoulder pad migrating down your body?!). These will give you back proportion and balance your rounder middle, taking the eye up to the shoulders and minimizing your largest area. If, of course, you already have really broad shoulders, there's no need to accentuate them further (no one wants to look like that massive blue Eagle from *The Muppets*).

● **Dresses.** Actually the easiest thing for an apple shape to wear.

> **A dress with a fitted waist.** Not a self-wrap, not a loose dress with a fabric belt (the worst – think tying a ribbon around a balloon – does literally nothing bar draw attention to the fact you have absolutely no waist!). A fitted waist does the work of creating a seamless waist for you. Generally with a looser dress that has a fitted waistband, there is excess fabric above and excess fabric below. The fixed waist nips you in exactly where normally there would be no nipping in and, hey

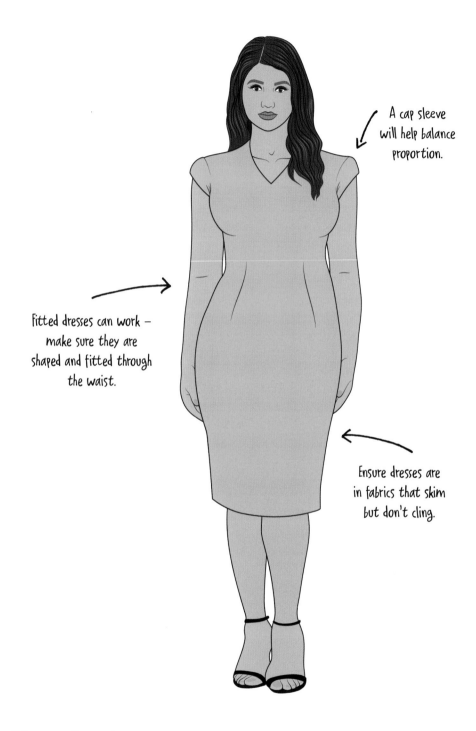

A cap sleeve will help balance proportion.

Fitted dresses can work – make sure they are shaped and fitted through the waist.

Ensure dresses are in fabrics that skim but don't cling.

presto, you have a waist! It's the perfect illusion. Drawstring waists are also an option. They work really well as the cut is designed to taper in at the waist, unlike their thin-belting counterparts where you are doing the belting for them.

> **Loose and floating.** With no accentuation on the waist, this style can be worn as is. Or, think about creating the same shape as a dress with a fitted waist by adding a stretchy belt. Not a super-narrow one, but neither does it have to be hugely wide. Elasticated is great as it forces a waist – unlike a flimsier belt. Think back to our balloon, but this time putting an elastic band around the middle of it (I appreciate it's slightly tricky to pull off BUT you get the idea...). It creates shape that holds. You may think it's pulling and you've got stuff coming out above and stuff squeezing out below (OK, too much stuff means that the belt is too tight). But in a loose, light-fabric dress, I promise this is OK! It's hidden under the fabric and all of a sudden you have a waist.

> **Fitted.** Again fitted dresses are great as the shape is created for you by the cut of the dress. If you are narrower on the shoulders, it might be that you want to think about adding shoulder pads to give you some proportion. The dress can either be straight fitted, if that's your style, or a looser shirt dress.

● **Skirts.** Similar rules to dresses. Skinny, paltry elasticated waistbands are going to do you no favours. If the skirt has an elasticated waistband, it needs to mean business and hold that waist in shape. So a wide, sturdy band, please. Or a fixed waistband – again, the wider the better as it holds your history in. Pleated skirts are not going to be your best bet unless they are flat fronted and the pleats start from hip height. Or the pleats are fixed (as in sewn down so they can't move, stretch and distort over your history) until hip level where it works if they're then properly pleaty (not a word, but hopefully you know what I mean). Full skirts are great: you can wear tier skirts but you do need to be mindful about where the tiers start – if the first tier is very fitted, it can draw attention where you don't want attention being drawn. A wide, loose A-line is definitely the best shape: clean, simple, works perfectly in balancing your proportions while sitting beautifully flat over the stomach and hip area. Length-wise, it really depends on your height and your style.

● **Jumpsuits.** These, like dresses, are the best friends of an apple shape. Loose above the waist, loose below, but either a fixed waist or a drawstring waist gives you the most amazing shape. TRUST me, you will look like a different person in one. Of course, if they're not your style, you might look like a person you

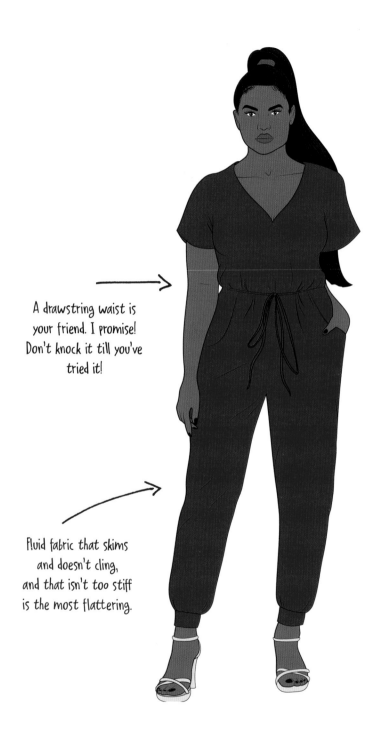

A drawstring waist is your friend. I promise! Don't knock it till you've tried it!

Fluid fabric that skims and doesn't cling, and that isn't too stiff is the most flattering.

don't actually want to look like, but think about how perhaps the fabric of the jumpsuit, the colour or the rest of your outfit could work for the style you would like to be. Or think about accessorizing with shoes, outerwear, scarves and jewellery that make it more your style if the basic shape of the jumpsuit works.

● **Trousers and jeans.** The key to perfect trousers and jeans is to find ones that fit around your middle. They must fit. No one likes a muffin top.

> **Skinnies.** So you may well have been told that high-waisted skinnies are not for you. I remember years ago, someone whom I was styling said she had been told not to wear them as they would make her look like Humpty from *Play School*. RUDE! Well yes, if that's all you wear. But skinnies are the most comfortable and versatile trousers, and if you think of them as a staple and a base layer of your outfit, there is absolutely no reason why you can't wear them. You need to be mindful about proportions. If you hold all your shape in your middle, you need to think about balancing the top and the bottom. So with your skinnies, think about your footwear. A chunky boot or shoe will help to balance you out at the bottom. With your top half, you're wanting to draw attention up and away from your middle and have some balance in the shoulders.

So a chunky knit, perhaps a polo neck, a shirt with a wide lapel, a jacket with wide shoulders, a trench with epaulettes. Just make sure you don't tuck anything in to your high-waisted skinnies. Not the best look (to be honest, unless you're Elle Macpherson or 14 years old, it's a tricky look for anyone to pull off, regardless of shape).

> **Wide-leg trousers.** The trousers of dreams for those with history around the middle. Flat-fronted trousers work better than pleat-fronted ones, which just serve to accentuate the stomach area. The joy of this style is that the wide leg works wonders in lengthening you and taking attention away from your midsection – balancing the bottom half of your body with the larger middle area.

● **Jackets and coats.** Like with those blessed with breasts, it's better to avoid double-breasted jackets and coats as, again, you're looking to minimize excess bulk around the area you're not looking to add bulk to. Single-breasted is better. Fitted is ideal: a fitted blazer that is cut to nip in at the waist is a winner. Cropped can also work, or a longer-line coat or jacket. A straight jacket that cuts you off just at the hip is really the shape to avoid here. Anything that has epaulettes on the shoulders is great as they take your eye up and away from your middle area.

Curve with extra loving around the booty and thighs – also known as a 'pear shape'

Like the others above, it's a tricky shape to dress, but if you focus on balancing out your silhouette and drawing the attention from below the waist, up towards your shoulders, you're there.

Like with all shapes, it's about accentuating the areas that will balance your proportions and those areas that you love. To be fair, that may well be your more generous derrière, in which case, get those buttocks on show (preferably with some sort of clothing over them, unless you're a Kardashian...). But if you are more conscious of your shape, there are ways in which you can minimize and dress to make the best of the assets you've been given.

Distraction, again, can be the easiest weapon in your arsenal. The most simple and effective way to do this is to make sure you have a party on your top half (taking into consideration the size of your boobage – rules above do still apply if it's generous). All the colour, the print, the ruffles, the sleeve detail can be as outrageous as you like. Off-the-shoulder is a fabulous shape for widening your top half. Or think about drawing the eye away, like a magpie, towards earrings, large necklaces or hair accessories, as bold as you want to go for your style and your lifestyle.

Other clothing ideas...

● **Skirts.** The easiest bottoms to wear for those prone to the shape of pear. Ideally ones with more rather than less fabric, as the fabric does the job of hiding what you don't want to show so well. Even though I have mentioned thinking about less fabric if you're petite, you can still have a certain volume, just not swathes of the stuff. A lighter, more fluid fabric, such as silk, recycled polyester, light velvet, thin cotton, is better if you're petite, whereas if you're taller, you can get away with a sturdier fabric, such as a heavy velvet, thick, crisp cotton or cord. A-line or full skirts are ideal; pleats can work, so long as you take into consideration the shape of your tummy (see apple shape, page 73), as can tiers. Length-wise, it depends on your height and style. Straight skirts are possible if you're wanting to let your booty do the talking, but be mindful that it may be trickier to find one that's a good fit as they'll always be loose on the waist. Saying that, you may find it an issue with all skirts that have a fitted waistband so do bear it in mind or keep an eye out for elasticated ones. Lots have an elasticated back and a flat front, which is the best option. But once again, you should be making friends with that seamstress.

● **Dresses.** Like skirts, these can be the saviours in your wardrobe. The issue that you will have is finding ones that fit. I can hear you at the back...they fit on

Bardot tops work perfectly and balance wider hips.

A full skirt works wonders for hiding more ample loving on the thighs.

the top but then don't on the hips, or they're fine on the hips but you can fit two versions of you in the rest of the dress. Look for dresses that are fuller through the skirt part. Flared skirts are the dream that you're on the hunt for. Full shirt dresses are perfect. Most pear shapes have the most incredible waist, so take advantage of that by building a collection of belts that you can add to anything or everything (admittedly only where a belt is required – that's just me being very envious of anyone who has a waist, and I encourage them to show it off at any and every juncture). Style and length again depends on your height and, funnily enough, your personal style.

● **Tops.** So when it comes to style of tops, so long as you're not larger in the bosom (if you are, see curve with a bust, page 69), you can pretty much have free rein. Well, I say that. The one thing you need to do is make your shoulders seem broader. First up, making sure you have a great bra, so that your boobs are being lifted properly and are in the right place, has a huge effect. It also immediately makes you stand up straighter with your shoulders back, so a lot of the job has already been done for you. But there is another trick that I have mentioned already and, as randomly easy and stupid as it seems, it's the good old shoulder pads again. 'WHAT?' I hear you cry.

I promise you, these can work in most tops. We're not talking Krystle Carrington numbers here (although I do have a personal penchant for these); we're talking a more subtle squaring-off of your shape to balance out the width of your hips. Pear shapes are literally a shoulder pad away from being Marilyn Monroe.

● **Trousers.** I have had, over the years, so many pear shapes tell me they can't wear trousers. And I sympathize. But it's not that you can't wear them, it's that it's very tricky to find ones that fit properly. The gaping on the waist…I've got you. So, first off, think about the waistband. The obvious choice is an elasticated waistband, which doesn't need to be as retirement home as it sounds. Or a drawstring. Like with skirts, more trousers these days have an elasticated back waist with a flat front, which is the best of both worlds. Your two other options are belts or a seamstress on speed dial. OR, thanks to Kim, Khloe and Kourtney (no idea if that's how you spell them, but we do owe them a favour), there are more options now that cater for the more generous of booty among us. Shape-wise, if you're not looking to show the roundness of your bum, trousers and jeans that are looser through the legs are a better idea.

> **Wide-leg trousers.** The obvious choice and they are superb.

Epaulettes and cape detailing on coats are an excellent way to draw the eye away from your hips and balance proportions.

Barrel-leg jeans are great for pear shapes as they're more generous on the thigh, but don't be afraid to size up.

> **Culottes.** Worth thinking about as the perfect hybrid between a skirt and a pair of trews. Basically a cropped wide leg although culottes are often shorter.

> **Boyfriend jeans.** Barrel-leg trousers are also great options, so long as they are loose enough. I am huge fan of sizing up (it's only a number on the label), as they will be looser – a trick I always employ, being tall, as there's simply more fabric and they're not 'too big', you're just deploying the fabric in a different way.

● **Jackets and coats.** This again comes down to thinking about proportion. No swing coat that means the bottom half of your body is even wider than the top; no jacket or coat that finishes on your hips at the widest point; and no dropped-shoulder coats (unless they're very oversized everywhere and hide a multitude of sins). The easiest way is to think about adding breadth to your top half.

> **Cropped jackets.** Fab.
> **Double-breasted.** Great, being mindful of where it finishes (which should be either above or below your widest area).
> **Shoulder pads or epaulettes.** Ding, ding, ding.
> **Trenches.** With a cape-style top they are perfection, and you lucky sods can even wear them belted.

Skinny

Please don't read this and think WHAT?? How hard is it for a skinny person to get dressed? For many, no, it won't pose a problem, but there are those out there who, not for want of trying, are very slight. And if that's your struggle, that's as big an issue as any issue is to anyone.

First up, you don't have the problems that others have in that you're trying to disguise parts of your body or draw attention away from them – it's more the look as a whole. There is also the issue of not being able to find clothes small enough (like petites) and, yes, all too often the tiny sizes are the ones that sell out first (as do larger sizes), and the simple reason for that is supply and demand. As a 'general rule' there are more people who make up the middle section of the size range and so they're the clothes that they make more of. But the issue comes when they don't know how many of the sizes they could have sold, were they in stock. This isn't really a short-term problem-solver BUT, on websites, if your size is out of stock and there is an 'email me when back in stock' option, always click on it. Even if you don't want the item when it is back in stock, it will give the retailer an idea of how many they could have sold and therefore a better indication of demand. This also works at the other end of the scale – actually it works for any size, to be honest! It's the closest things retailers

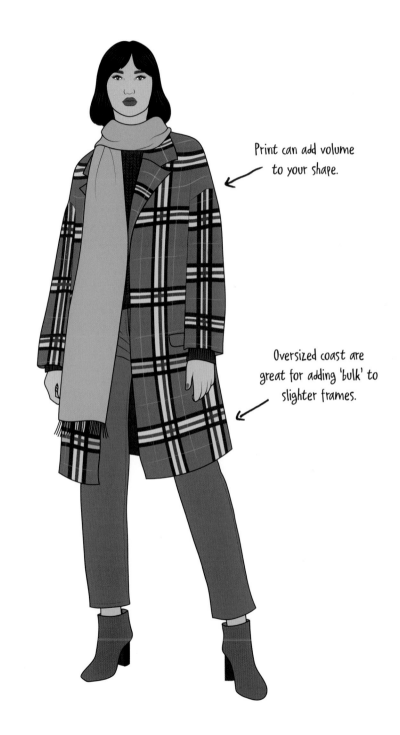

Print can add volume to your shape.

Oversized coast are great for adding 'bulk' to slighter frames.

have to people saying, 'I would have bought that but it sold out in my size, please make more next time.'

Even if you are able to get things in your size that fit and suit your style, there are some basic tricks to have up your sleeve to look less, well, skinny and beanpoley (says she who was this for her formative years and hated it!).

● **Layering.** Imagine you're going on a budget airline and your hand luggage is too big or too heavy (isn't it always?). So, rather than selling a kidney to check it in, you decide to wear a whole load of your clothes, piling them all on. OK, not exactly that – there are more stylish ways to layer, but your ultimate goal is, basically, to add bulk. If you're tall and lean, you can break up your height by making natural breaks in your outfit with layers.

● **Accessories.** Along the same lines as adding bulk with layers, the curves that you don't have naturally you can create with accessories. Large scarves add volume and texture. We're back to distraction: big, bulky jewellery, or think of wearing layers of finer, more delicate necklaces, earrings and bracelets. Think about the shape of clothes. It's not about simply adding bulk with lots of oversized, baggy clothing. Think about creating shapes and the illusion of curves that you might not have. So while barrel-leg trousers (which are

perfect for pear shapes to hide their extra loving underneath) will have no padding on you, the cut of the trews gives the impression of a curvier figure. Same with balloon-sleeve tops. Puffed shoulders are ideal, and baggier shirts and blouses tucked in to the waist give you a shape you may not naturally own.

● **Colour.** We all know that all black can be slimming, so it's not beyond the realms of logic to think about avoiding wearing all black if you're very thin. But sod that, some people really want to wear black. Employ the layering concept, think about the shapes of dark colours and potentially breaking up the look with print. One head-to-toe look in any colour can work, so long as your outfit is made up of different pieces that interrupt the line of vision.

● **Fabrics.** Like with layering, a variety of different fabrics and textures adds dimension to your outfit and makes it – and you – look less 'flat'. Be mindful of your height: the texture of fabrics that you layer will differ depending on how tall you are. If you're taller, it's easier to add volume with more weighty fabrics – a stiffer, heavy cotton or a rich, luxurious velvet or a thick cord. The more petite among us should think about lighter, more fluid fabrics such as a whimsical fine silk, airy cotton, polyester, needlecord or delicate velvet.

Nutritional information

> First step is acknowledging the shape that you are. Whichever shape you are, you are perfect and you CAN dress to suit the style that you love, and ultimately look in the mirror and love the person looking back.

> Always remember proportion. It doesn't matter what your size, it's thinking about maximizing your proportions that counts.

> Cherry-pick from the categories below to find tips and tricks on how to dress for your shape.

Height

Petite

> Find your favourite retailers that specialize in petite.
> Have a seamstress on speed dial.
> Remember there are bargains to be found in the children's section.
> Keep print small -- head to toe is a GOOD thing.
> Keep stripes narrow – vertical stripes are also good.
> Styles that you should look out for and tips on how to wear them:
> - High-waisted trousers elongate your legs.
> - Wide-leg, high-waisted trousers with heels add length and height.
> - Maxi/midi skirts and dresses, but make sure they're the right length and there's not too much fabric (ensure the fabric is as fluid and unstructured as possible).
> - Necklines – depends on your bust, but ideally lower to create more space between your neckline and your neck, which has an elongating effect.
> - Footwear – chunky soles, wedges and heels all add height.
> - Colour – wear WHAT you love, but if you keep the colour tonal in an outfit, it will again add height by not breaking up your silhouette.
> - Cheat with big hair!

Tall

> Hunt out retailers that specialize in tall.
> Find a competent seamstress and think laterally and creatively.
> Search for generic retailers that are simply more generous in their cuts.
> Don't dismiss men's clothing.
> Styles and tricks that you would do well to bear in mind:
>   – Don't mind skinnies and leggings that are cropped – think boots/hightops to cover them.
>   – Become more comfortable with 7/8ths-style trousers and try to work them into your style if you love wearing trousers.
>   – Size up so you can wear skirts lower on your hips.
>   – Dresses – think about investing in knee-high boots to make them look longer.
>   – Sleeves too short? Disguise the gap between fabric and hand with arm candy – the more the merrier – watch/bracelets/cuffs/scarves.

Shape

Curve with a bust

> Necklines: V-neck, low square or low scoop.
> Style of tops:
>   – Wrap top.
>   – Fitted shirt.
>   – Peplum top.
> Sleeves – avoid a ruffle or frill sleeve.
> Dresses – the most important point is that they fit and that the neckline works.
> Jackets:
>   – Single-breasted.
>   – Longer line is also a good shout.
> Jewellery – distraction is key. Big earrings, layered necklaces.
> Stripes:
>   – Keep stripes wide in more fitted clothing.
>   – Narrow stripes can work but only in looser items.

Curve with history around the middle – also known as an 'apple shape'

> Style of tops:
>   – No tees that cling to your middle – ones with side vents are a great option.
>   – Remember that the half-tuck can also be your friend.
>   – Fitted shirts that fit.
>   – Tunics or blouses, swing versions are ideal, not too loose and not too long.
> Jumpers and sweatshirts – ideally ones that have a gathered/elasticated waistband OR oversized are your

friends (depending on the rest of your outfit).

> **Shoulder pads** – get with the shoulder-pad programme.
> **Dresses:**
>   – With a natural fixed waist.
>   – Loose and floaty – worn loose or with a belt. NOT a fabric belt. Thicker and elastic or a fixed-waist belt are preferable.
>   – Fitted.
> **Skirts:**
>   – Sturdy waistbands, not thin elastic. Fixed is best.
>   – No pleats from the waistband.
>   – A-line skirts.
> **Jumpsuits** – with elasticated or drawstring waists.
> **Trousers:**
>   – You can wear skinnies but try balancing at the bottom with a chunky boot or shoe.
>   – Wide-leg trousers but always FLAT-FRONTED ones.
> **Jackets and coats:**
>   – Avoid double-breasted.
>   – Fitted coats, jackets and blazers.
>   – Long and fluid.
>   – Epaulettes.

Curve with extra loving around the booty and thighs – also known as a 'pear shape'

> **Skirts** – full skirts.
> **Dresses:**
>   – With fuller skirts.
>   – Shirt dresses.

> **Tops:**
>   – Think about making your shoulders look broader.
>   – Embrace the shoulder pads.
> **Trousers:**
>   – Wide-leg trousers and culottes.
>   – Boyfriend jeans.
>   – Barrel-leg jeans.
> **Jackets and coats:**
>   – Cropped.
>   – Double-breasted.
>   – Trench with cape top and/or epaulettes.
>   – Belted coats.

Skinny

> **Layering** – think about adding extra dimension to your shape by layering clothes. Not always bulky layers – long, fluid lines will be just as effective.
> **Accessories** – the more the merrier. Add large statement accessories or layer finer jewellery to 'bulk up' your look.
> **Adding shape** – Think about adding shape through your clothes – fuller skirts, shoulder pads, oversized coats all give the illusion of shape.
> **Colours:**
>   – If you want to wear one colour, think about shape and texture to add 'bulk'
>   – Mixing colours is ideal.
> **Fabric** – mix fabrics and textures. You can of course mix colours to add bulk to your look, but tonal colours can work just as well, so long as you add a selection of fabrics to create depth.

2
Ingredients

Colours
(and a bit of print)

First up, thank you for your patience in reaching this chapter as I know some of you will be chomping at the bit to know what to buy (or what to keep in your wardrobe). Well, we're very nearly there but, before we move on to the actual items themselves, we've done body shapes but we haven't done colours.

Colours, colours, colours. Sounds so easy, doesn't it? But this is where the whole lot can go totally Pete Tong in an instant. Yes, the shape and style of what you buy is utterly crucial, but if it's in the wrong colour, well, your whole outfit can go to hell in a handcart in a second.

But what do I mean when I say 'the wrong colour'...is there such a thing as the wrong colour? Oh, I can hear you: 'But she said so long as I love it, it's OK to wear it.' THIS IS TRUE. There ARE no rules. I fully stand by my conviction, but that's not to say there aren't guidelines that, if you're not sure and need some advice, you can look over and may find super useful to check in with now and again.

You probably think I'm going to wax lyrical about getting your 'colours done'. Knowing which colours work for your skin tone and your hair colour; whether you're a winter, spring or some other season...not yet...but I will get there. V soon.

First up: find your neutral.

Neutrals

These are basic colours which, if you have them as the building blocks of your wardrobe, make it so much easier to mix and match outfits, therefore creating more looks from what you own and wearing more of your clothes more of the time, WHICH is the ultimate goal here.

Now, I do not want you all to think: oh, so that's black.

No. Well yes. It could be. And I will fess up right now and say this is the colour that I live and breathe for (even though one of my smart-arse children will no doubt tell me that it's not a colour; it's a lack of colour, or something equally pithy, which I will assume they've learned at school but they'll then inform me: oh no, from YouTube).

Whatevs Trevs, I LOVE black. But I fully appreciate that it's not for everyone. If you've ever had your 'colours done' (I did say I would get to this…), chances are you have been told that you shouldn't wear black. And actually this is probably a subject that I should put out there now, as it can absolutely be a good idea. Those ladies with their colour wheels, telling you from your skin tone, hair and eye colour whether you're a spring, summer, warm, cold, tepid…and what colours and shades you should be wearing, do absolutely have their merit.

For a start, most (whom I've ever heard of or spoken to anyway, which IS a sweeping generalization so a huge, huge apology to you if this isn't you) recommend that you avoid black, because as our skin gets older, it can be a draining, unflattering colour. It sucks the light from your face (not literally – I don't want anyone to be picturing my beloved black as a vampire) and drains away any hint of vitality and youth (you can see why people want to avoid it when you put it like that…). Navy is the alternative that (in my experience again) is always offered. It's a warmer tone, it's more flattering, it's reflective and is more suited to skin as it ages. I wholeheartedly agree.

However.

Not everyone wants to get rid of the black – for many, that would mean binning the vast majority of their wardrobe, which probably isn't financially viable and certainly doesn't tick any sustainable box.

And as much as I love navy, can it ever replace black? For some, it absolutely can. For me? I'm going with…maybe one day but not just yet. For me, it epitomizes the ultimate in glamour, it's grown-up (slightly ironic when said by a woman in her late 40s, but true, I think we'll find), it's sophisticated, it makes me feel simply better by just wearing it, it has absolutely magic qualities and I could never not wear it. OK, so slightly swept away by theatrical over-exaggeration with those last two points but, the fact is, whenever I need to be completely on top of my game and I need to Boss It (admittedly those moments are few and far between these days), I always look to a black outfit. I will also say that it comes into its own when I'm heading off to an occasion and I don't know what others will be wearing. It's a loose dress code; if I want to make sure I will fit in, then I turn to black. For me, at the end of the day, it's the ultimate confidence builder.

And therein lies the trick in finding your neutral (yes, that is what we are discussing!). Finding that perfect foundation on which your ideal outfits can all be built.

It definitely doesn't have to be black. As we've said, there is always the (more flattering, for most, for sure) navy. And while we're here: let's remember that there is navy and there is navy. There are bluer navys and there are the delicious darker, midnight versions (which, if you are prepared to eschew the black but it's with a heavy heart and a reluctant hand, you will want to check out). There is a navy for everyone.

But it doesn't stop there. Oh hell no, we have neutrals aplenty.

We have camel. There's also grey. And let's not forget about khaki. Essentially what makes a neutral colour is a shade that pretty much all colours work with and that acts as the perfect backdrop against which you can then layer other colours and prints.

Let's start with some of the paler colours. Take some lighter shades, for example. Camel, beige, taupe, oatmeal, fudge, caramel: all shades of…camely, beigey, taupey, fudgey colours. Again, there will be a shade out there that works for you. 'Aha!' I hear you cry, 'but how do I find the shade that works for me? I can't wear any of those shades, they wash me out.'

Well. Here's the thing. You could go along to one of those colour people who hold up a trillion (sorry, a few) swatches of different camel/taupe/even dark peach/sand shades against your skin to show you that there WILL be a shade that you can wear. As there will be. And you will be sorted.

Until it's time for you to go and actually find a garment in that exact shade. Good luck with that. I have styled people over the years who would love to wear a larger selection of shades but they've never

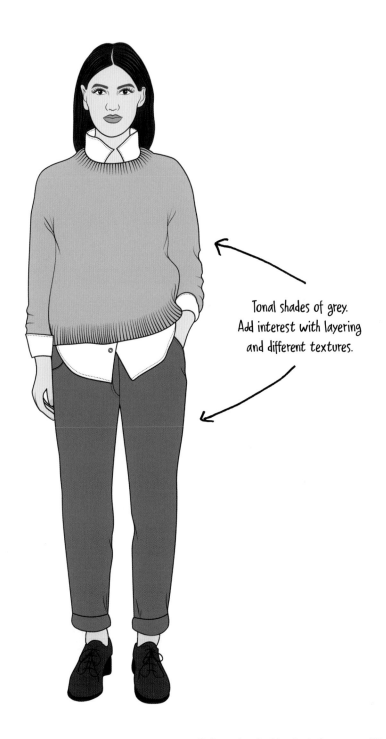

Tonal shades of grey.
Add interest with layering
and different textures.

been able to pinpoint the exact tone that they've been advised suits them, so they just stick to what they know.

There is a different way to do this and, yes, it might be a tad trickier in the short term, but in the long run, once you've built up your confidence, I promise that it works. AND it doesn't just work for camel shades. I TOTALLY accept that not everyone is going to even vaguely want a camel/tan/taupe shade as their neutral. No, this is a trick that I want you to take to heart, to learn and to use, as it works for every colour. It also works for print and, dare I say, it works for styles of clothing too. But, right now, we're focusing on it from a colour aspect.

I'd love to say that it's a newfangled trick that I've pulled out of a hat with a flourish. Embarrassingly it's not. BUT it's something that is often overlooked and something that the whole crux of this book is about.

The trick is to look in the mirror and to trust your instincts. Your gut feel. Right now, that might not seem like it's possible – you may not know how – but trust me. YOU DO! You've just either forgotten or you've never given yourself a chance to find out. Those instincts are there, even though they may be buried under 25 tons of work issues, lack of sleep for a billion reasons (the heady memories of thinking that once they were toddlers we'd get our sleep routine back – oh, how we laugh, as we gaze at our teens and then grandchildren), homeschooling, which has darn near killed many of us, and just life in general. Which, as we've covered, has taken over and you've lost you.

Well here is another chance to reclaim a bit of yourself. It's super simple. You hold a colour up to your face and look in a mirror. Or, if it's a jumper, blouse or top, just slip it on. I should add, at this point in the proceedings, please do make sure that you are wearing a modicum of make-up. I'm not talking club-level, full-on slap, but the make-up you would wear on a normal day. I don't know about you, but the older I get, the absolutely no make-up thing doesn't do me many favours, whereas in years gone by (a LOT of years gone by), the no make-up look had a fresh, girl-next-door, natural vibe going on. Now, a 'few' years on, we're talking more exhumed corpse – think dug-up chic. Which isn't how I would normally go out and about. As we're looking to perfect a wardrobe that we can go out and about in, may I suggest you put on a bit of make-up (NOT that I'm assuming you all could be joining me as dancers in the 'Thriller' vid sans slap, but it's *just* a suggestion).

And look in that mirror. You will know instantly whether you think 'bleurgh' or 'hmmm, actually I like that, it doesn't look too bad'.

So…I hear you at the back…'I can't do that'. You can. You just think you can't. And there are a couple of tricks (maybe I do have something else up my sleeve, just not in my hat…) that might give you a helping hand.

If you look in the mirror and really have no idea whether or not it suits you, go and find your favourite top. The one you love, the one that your husband loves, the one that your kids say looks great (OK, thinking out loud, I'm not sure any of my kids have ever said that so maybe swap out 'kids' for 'friends'). Look in the mirror, making sure the mirror is in a good light (as in there actually is light), and – as it's your favourite top – hopefully you will be happy with the reflection looking back at you. You should be able to recognize that you like the image you see.

Now, put the other item on. The one in the colour you're not sure about – or simply hold it up to your face. Right now, the only question you have to ask yourself is: do I like it as much as I like the other top? If so, then it's a hit.

Do I like it almost as much as I like the other top? If the answer is yes, then you're still onto a winner.

Am I indifferent to it? In that case, it's still not a no, but you could possibly do better.

Do I hate it? And you will know if you hate it as it will just be – like I said earlier, for want of a better, more professional expression – bleugh. If it's BLEUGH, then it's a big fat no. Don't wear this colour next to your face. It's as simple as that.

However, it's not entirely as simple as that. If you've learned anything this far in the book, I am not one for being told what to do. I really don't like being told 'no', or 'you can't do that', and don't even get me started on 'you shouldn't wear that'. As I've said before and I will say countless times again, this isn't a book that gives you rules. It gives you advice on areas that you might want a little bit of advice on.

SO, if a colour is bleugh, does that mean you can't wear it? NO! It just means that you shouldn't wear it next to your face. But can you wear it as a pair of trousers or a skirt? Absolutely you can. You can also wear it as a coat or as a cardigan. This is where it does get slightly trickier, as that means, in an ideal world and to eliminate the bleugh factor, you probably want to wear another colour that loves you back between your skin and the 'bleugh' shade. Which does mean

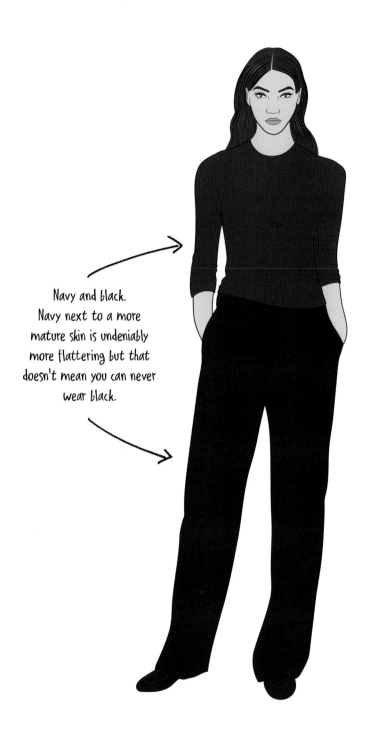

Navy and black.
Navy next to a more mature skin is undeniably more flattering but that doesn't mean you can never wear black.

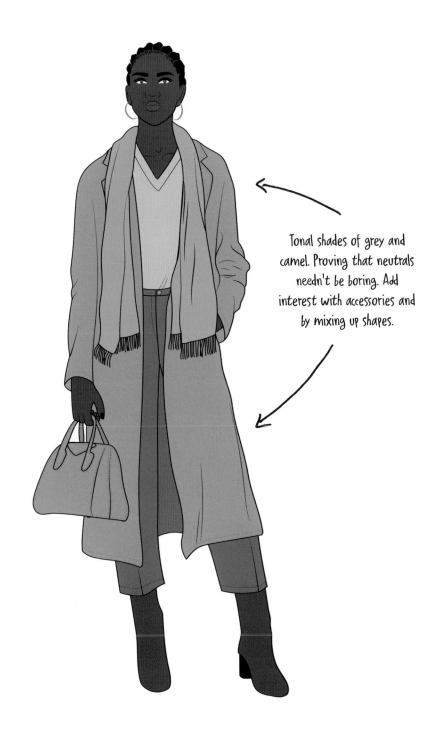

Tonal shades of grey and camel. Proving that neutrals needn't be boring. Add interest with accessories and by mixing up shapes.

it requires a bit more thought, which means that you might just want to wear something else. Which, let's be honest, is what usually happens.

It DOES sound very confusing, but actually once you start doing it, it becomes second nature. As Rod Stewart says: the first cut is the deepest... I promise you, once you've got it sussed, it will be the most natural thing in the world to trust your gut again.

And this rule of thumb doesn't apply purely to camely/taupey/fudgey colours. It works with ANY colours. But we're talking about neutrals right now, and for all neutrals it works. With khakis: does a khaki with a browner hue suit you or are you more of an olive shade (with more green tones)? And with greys: are you drawn to the darker shades of charcoal grey or the paler silvery tones of a dove grey? And whites: can you do a bright white or is ivory more your tone (this will be very familiar to anyone who's bought a wedding dress and heard themselves uttering – or thinking as it sounds so stupid to say – 'I don't like this shade of white on me'...YOU SEE? It's a thing!).

But hang fire there with the decision making...there's one more very important piece of advice that I need to impart. You don't have to decide on just one! 'WHAT?' I hear you cry.

The joy of a neutral palette is that the colours all work together. So grey and tan, olive and camel, black and navy (yes, you read that right), navy and brown. Any shade can be layered, and I really don't see why there should be any limit to the number of different neutrals you have in your wardrobe.

I do genuinely think people are drawn to certain shades, though. Have a look in your wardrobe (a sneaky peak, as we're coming to the wardrobe bit later!), and you are likely to have a definite preference for a specific neutral. BUT it's OK if you're partial to a few as they will all work together.

You can even go tonal with your neutrals. It's OK to be 50 shades of grey. Again, just be mindful about which ones you're wearing next to your face.

ONE last thing to point out here and it's something that I'm asked all the time, plus it's something that I'm all too aware of personally. What happens if I change the tone of my hair, the colour of my hair, when I go grey? The colours I loved, don't seem to suit me any more.

And...alas that's probably true. BUT there's no need to throw the baby out with the bathwater. There will just be some tweaking here and there. And – here's the very good news – it needn't necessarily be with your clothes. Have you made any changes to your make-up? So often, the reason people don't recognize themselves in the mirror after a new hair colour (slight exaggeration there unless you've been on *Extreme Makeover*, but hopefully you get the gist) is because they've not made any changes to their make-up. As simple and obvious as that sounds, it is amazing how a simple fine tuning of your blusher, a bit of bronzer, definitely a slick of lipstick and even eyeshadow can suddenly realign your view on what works when you look at yourself.

Actually, lipstick can be the key weapon in your arsenal if there's a colour (in clothes) that you love but that doesn't love you back. A different lipstick can completely change the compatibility. Again, we've got back to the gut instinct and trusting in yourself to see if it works, but a variety of lippie shades can make the hugest impact on what you can and can't wear.

If that doesn't work, it may be that you need to change the tone of the colour that you used to love. Or...it may be that you need to pair it with something different in your outfit. A perfect example of this is someone who once said to me that after going grey they couldn't wear lilac any more as it made them feel like a pantomime dame. Now I'm sure they didn't LOOK like a pantomime dame (I should perhaps have asked what exactly the lilac item of clothing was). There's more on combining colours later in this chapter (see page 110), but by teaming lilac with, say, navy or...wait for it and brace yourself...leopard print (just hold that thought peeps), you're taking away any hint of Widow Twankey and are making it YOU again.

Back to black

Before we do move on to COLOUR (we will get there), I do want
to have another little word about black. Because I've spoken about
finding your neutral in the shade that works for you, and some
may be thinking, but what about black? There aren't tones of black.
(I can literally hear my kids jabbering something about, 'yes, that'll
be grey, Mum' – I SO didn't let them proofread this book...)

If you feel that black no longer does you
any favours yet you're still drawn to it like
a 1980s *Corrie* barmaid to leopard print,
I have a few tricks that you might like to
give some airtime.

Instead of thinking about shades of
black, think about texture. We're talking
different fabrics. If we tackle the issue of
why black appears to be less flattering
to more mature skin and come up with
a solution, it means...drum roll...that
black is back.

A flat black, non-reflective cotton
is probably going to be draining unless
you're sub 25 (doesn't stop me wearing
it – wait until we get to the bit on
accessories). It's not the most flattering
way to wear black. But if we think about
fabrics that create a reflection, ones that
don't drain the luminosity from your
face, they do the job of reflecting light
back onto it. So think satin or silk. One
of the easiest 'cheats' to achieve this is
a tuxedo blazer. No, not just for black

tie, and don't go nicking your husband's.
There are lots around in a huge variety of
shapes – loose, double-breasted or fitted
– to suit your style, but the KEY thing
is the satin lapel. That's all you need as
it's the nearest part of the jacket to your
face, and that's where you want the light
reflected back.

The other major win in a reflective
'shiny' fabric is that it does make black
tonal. So it's not black black (which to
many, as we've already said, is a no-no).
Depending on what you wear it with
and the light you're standing in, the very
nature of the fabric means it actually
does not look black. It can look a dark
shade of grey, an inky-dark midnight
blue or even have a slight silvery tone to
it. All and any of which are GOOD and
circumvent neatly the theory that black
isn't for everyone.

And then there's the neat little texture
trick. As we've mentioned, a flat black is
cold and not entirely forgiving. But when

you warm it up and give it some texture – suddenly it's a lot friendlier colour to embrace. A bouclé jacket (if it's good enough for Chanel…just saying…), a linen shirt or tee, a sheepskin coat, a textured knit jumper (something chunkier and 'bobblier' – not old and bobblier, the good bobblier type) works. The texture, even though it may only be a slight texture, creates shadows and suddenly your flat black has different tones to it. It's almost like creating a pattern of black and shades of grey/midnight – again, depending on what light you're standing in.

But now, it's on to what many of you probably assumed this chapter would mostly be about.

There are always ways of wearing black. Think texture, think fabric, think tone. Trust me, they'll be burying me in black.

Actual colour

Right. This isn't going to be nearly as detailed as I think some people might have suspected it would be.

Because, as I've said earlier on, I truly believe that when it comes to colour, you should wear what you love. This could be full-on bright colour; it could be a mix of colours; it could be clashing; it could be tonal. BUT the key thing is that you must love it.

Over the years, I've learned that there are three groups of people when it comes to colour:

1. Those who love it.
2. Those who hate it.
3. Those who are pretty much terrified of it.

Let's tackle the first group, although 'tackle' isn't really the right verb to use as I am preaching to the converted. What can I say? Nothing bar, I APPLAUD YOU. You know the sorts of people I mean: those who embrace all shades of colour or are head to toe in one bold tone – those who really own the courage of their colourful convictions. They are a pure joy to behold and their confidence means that even if the outfit, in theory, shouldn't work, it always does. You are not needing of anything but my utmost admiration.

So it's on to the second group. Those who hate it. People who live in neutrals. Those who eschew bold colour, probably print as well. Maybe you live top to toe in black. This is always, in every area of styling I've been asked to consult on, seen as a no-no.

Well. I don't necessarily agree (I so wish I could chuck in an emoji here… the shocked one à la Edvard Munch). I know…it's not the done thing to say that I don't think there's anything really wrong with an all-black outfit IF… it makes you happy (me). IF…you're purposefully harnessing your inner mysterious, elegant self (me in my dreams) and IF…you are wearing it for carefully chosen sartorial reasons (me).

If, however, you choose to wear black because you think it makes you look smaller, or you're using it to hide behind, or you really don't know how to pick something else and you're not channelling your inner Morticia, then it really is worth considering some other colours.

And how to do that? Well, again, there is the option of visiting a colour consultant. As I've said, some people do find them very useful, but personally I feel there's a much greater sense of satisfaction and ultimately a much more personal style if you're able to do it by yourself. And 'hopefully' by the end of this book, you WILL be able to.

It's like anything: once you've made that first step, it doesn't seem nearly quite as intimidating or difficult. And you might even start to enjoy it!

Interestingly, I don't think the first step to finding the colours that work for you is down to the colour itself. As random as that may seem, there is (as always, albeit sometimes vague) method in my madness.

And...here's the GREAT thing: you have already done the hardest part. That is, identifying your style. This has everything to do with colour. Finding your inner style icon, your inner muse, the person whose style you love and would love to emulate – which hopefully you have already done or have already started thinking about – gives a real insight into the sorts of colours that you're drawn to.

First teensy-tiny hurdle complete. Which has hopefully helped you climb one rung on your confidence ladder. Once you start envisaging who it is you want to be, the actual process of getting there becomes a lot less daunting.

This is a mighty good thing, as next up it's time for that old looking in the mirror and trusting yourself gig again.

INSTINCTS. You have them for a reason and while yours may be slightly rusty – or you may never have used them for this before – I want you to have faith in them.

Look at the colour wheel overleaf and pick the colours you would love to wear in a jumper. I've given you the task of a jumper as it's something to focus on as opposed to just looking at the colours. Otherwise it's very easy to get sidetracked into thinking: would love that colour in a sofa but I wouldn't want to wear it. And, right now, that's about as much use as a chocolate teapot. If you'd rather not do a jumper, you could do a tee...or a blouse...Just pick an item of clothing of your choice.

That's it.

It's not a trick question and it's not the caveat for the only colours you should ever wear. BUT, and here's the thing, I bet if you go and take a look in your wardrobe – should you own anything of colour, that is – you will find something in there of a similar hue. If your wardrobe is more the funereal vibe, then I wager you'll be able to think of something that you may have once worn in that colour. I still remember the party dress I had when I was about 8: it was the most incredible print of pinks, and to this day, whenever I see anything in a similar set of shades, it makes me smile and feel happy.

And THAT is what colour should do. It should make you feel better about yourself. I want you to be able to look in the mirror and smile and feel good. Because if you're smiling and feeling great, you are climbing up that confidence ladder like a seasoned firefighter (sans hose).

Colour Wheel

So as suggested, you can use the Colour Wheel to just practise getting used to understanding which colours you actually like. As trite as that sounds, while we all probably know what colours we favour, it helps to focus on which ones you'd actually like to wear.

And you can also use it to start on the journey of mixing and clashing colour. Keeping it very simple, there are three different options that you have, building up in ambition from 1 to 3.

1 Choose tonal colours that are within the same colour segment.

2 Choose colours that are in adjacent segments – up to two or even three (or team two with a neutral).

3 Choose colours that are opposite each other.

If you want to experiment, it's always good to start with the second colour as an accessory – be it a scarf, a belt, a handbag, shoes, or even just a piece of jewellery (earrings, necklace or bracelets) in a statement colour.

BUT, as I've said, if that all sounds a tad too experimental for you, just start by focusing on the colours that you're drawn to and would love to wear in a knit and build up your colour confidence. And if a jumper is too ambitious, how about a scarf? The world will not fall off its axis if you wear an orange scarf with a navy suit... or even denim. Go on...give it a try!

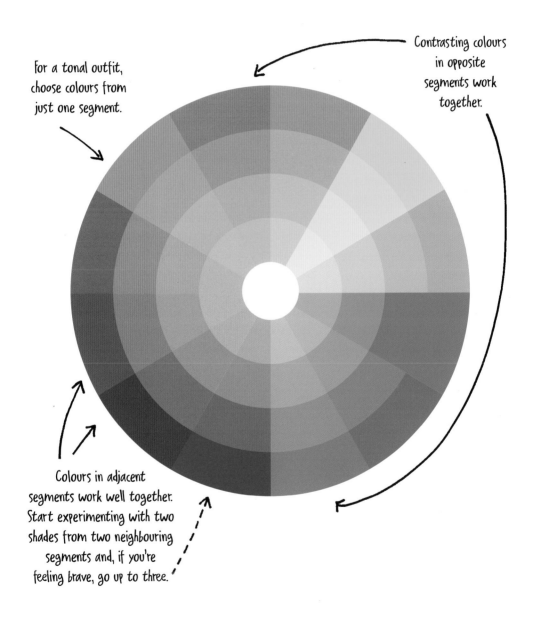

For a tonal outfit, choose colours from just one segment.

Contrasting colours in opposite segments work together.

Colours in adjacent segments work well together. Start experimenting with two shades from two neighbouring segments and, if you're feeling brave, go up to three.

Combining colours

Perhaps for many of you, wearing colour is not a new concept at all, but I do know that for some, where it gets trickier is putting colours together. Hands up whose mum told them 'blue and green should never be seen?' (Although my mum also used to say 'red coat, no pants' so, to be fair, I did take most things she said fashion-wise with a pinch of salt. For the record, whenever I have worn a red coat, I have ALWAYS worn pants and have never thought that anyone I saw wearing one may well have been commando. Just to clear that up.)

Going back to the specialists who recommend what colours you should wear together. Yes, it's all well and good, but what if you don't like those colours? What if you DO want to wear lilac and green. Or red and orange. Or green and blue. Or pink and camel.

So I did say that I took most things my mum said about fashion not entirely seriously, but there is one fabulous thing she said that I've never heard anyone else say but it SO works.

Just look at nature. Do you ever look at a garden and think, that flower really doesn't work; that green stem with the pale pink outer petal and the coral inner bit with the red bit elsewhere? No. It looks gorgeous. The different shades of green on a leaf; a leaf that starts to turn and is a coppery colour with a brown, camel edge and a redder hue on its underside. All these colours together are beautiful. Now I'm not saying that we should channel our inner Monty Don and become floral enthusiasts, but just bear in mind that colours you may not have thought work together really CAN.

The most important thing to remember is that you must love them. You must put them together and...as I've said before and as I will say again... they must bring you joy. An uplifting effect is what you're looking for. Not least, because you're on your way to creating your very own style, and having confidence in your own style means having confidence in yourself.

And speaking of nature...and flowers...that brings me neatly on to the second part of this chapter, which is as, if not more, important than colour, and that's print.

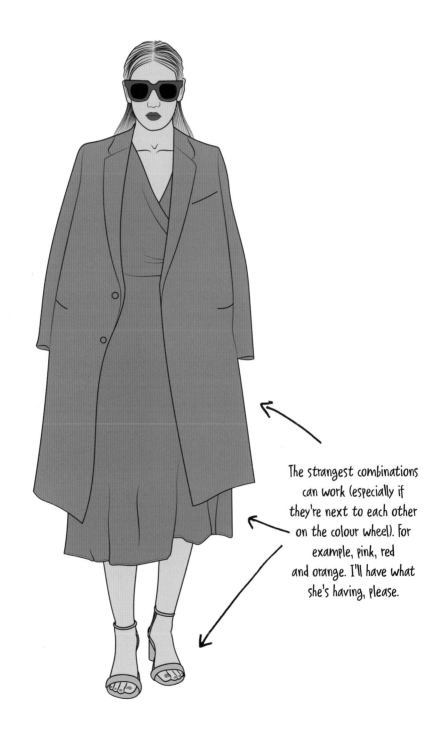

The strangest combinations can work (especially if they're next to each other on the colour wheel). For example, pink, red and orange. I'll have what she's having, please.

Print

There is the potential of a print for everyone (although some I may never convince and THAT'S OK TOO!). As it's not just a floral print. We have big floral, little floral, paisley, tartan, check, geometric, stripes, polka dot and every animal print you can think of: leopard, cheetah, zebra, snake, tiger, snow leopard. An exhaustive list that we will probably never get to the end of. Ultimately, I want to make you see that it's highly likely there is an option for you.

If that all sounds a tad overwhelming, please don't panic – you have already DONE the hardest bit of thinking about print: deciding on which colours to wear. You've also worked out what shape you are and you've sussed what size of print is going to work best for you. All you need to work out now is how to find a print that you love.

I know I'm perhaps making it sound easy, but trust me, it really doesn't have to be hard. And if you're able to trust me, then I want you to be able to trust yourself. Yes, that's right, we're about to get on that confidence horse again.

I want you to be able to trust in your instincts and feel confident doing so. I know I'm starting to sound like a stuck record, but if it's something you really think you can't do, believe me, by the end of this book you will be able to. You will get that gut feel back.

How do you find a print that you like? You look at a print and you work out whether you like it or whether you love it or whether you think bleugh. Yes, it does sound familiar as it's exactly the same as the colour test. Which is sort of embarrassing as it does seem like the most obvious thing on the planet but, if you're not used to doing it, it can take some getting used to.

And so, I am setting some homework: print practice. I actually do this on a regular basis, not to keep me on my toes but because I'm a print junkie and the joy of finding one you love, is just the best feeling (on typing this, I appreciate I could possibly do with getting out more).

I find the best place to wallow in print paradise is the Liberty fabric website or Instagram page. A smorgasbord of visual delight where there is definitely something for everyone.

Full print head to toe needn't be scary. It's often easier to wear than trying to match your print with another item of clothing.

It also doesn't have to be bright and in your face - print can be subtle and pared back.

Although while I say everyone – hold your horses there – you don't necessarily have to love print. If you hate it and prefer clean, smooth block colours (or lack of colour, oh black fans), that is absolutely fine. At the end of this chapter I have some hints and tricks as to how you can inject a bit more personality and interest into your outfits that aren't colourful and without a print in sight (see page 120).

But back in the room for the pattern lovers. Go through the prints and simply click on ones that make you feel lighter, on ones that give you an INSTANT reaction of 'I like that'. I find the best way to collate them is on the saved board of Instagram or Pinterest, but you can always bookmark them on a computer or phone.

Again, it's definitely helpful if you have in mind that it's a print to wear, not a print that you'd like to have as wallpaper in the downstairs loo (although if you happen upon one of them in your search, then happy days – multitasking at its finest).

The more you practise and familiarize yourself with the prints you love, the easier it will be to identify a print piece you love when we start shopping.

But then, how does it go in your wardrobe? Right, here's the clever thing. I am willing to bet my mortgage (hefty), on the fact that the print you've picked already goes with something in your wardrobe. And the easiest way to pair them is to pick a colour in the print that marries with clothing you already have.

Most prints have many more shades in them than you think at first glance. There will be a colour in there that you have to search for, but when you find it, then a top (if it's a skirt, for example) of the same colour will be a perfect match. I promise you, it can be as tiny a detail as the edge of a petal, but if it's the same shade as your jumper, the job's a good 'un.

The alternative is to pick out a neutral. Very, very rarely will there not be a neutral in a print, be it navy, black, khaki (often with a floral) or even white. And often more than one of them, which gives a great choice with the neutral basics that hopefully you should have squirrelled away somewhere.

How to wear print

This is again one of those things that very much comes down to personal preference, as well as taking into consideration what works for your shape.

We've already covered this in how to dress for your shape (see pages 56–91), but the very basic rule of thumb is: the smaller you are, the smaller your print should be. Those who are tall or curvy are able to embrace a larger print. And the same theory applies to stripes.

It's true that you can also create illusions (as in tricking the eye, not as in full-on David Blaine numbers) with print. So a head-to-toe print in a dress or jumpsuit (or a matching top and trews or skirt) makes you look longer and leaner, rather than breaking the print up with a plain top (or trousers).

And now we've mentioned them: print pants (trousers not knickers – to this day when I think of print knickers I remember my then four-year-old's look of disappointment when she realized that women, generally, didn't have pics on their pants: 'But, Mummy, do they not even make them for grown-ups with Hello Kitty on?'). A quick note on them. Some people love them – a wide palazzo pant in a print can indeed be a striking affair. But as a rule, I do think they are slightly trickier to wear without having a whiff of the jim-jams about them. That's not to say they don't ever work, but in my experience, it's easier to stick to a skirt on the bottom, a dress or a full-on print jumpsuit – although, I will be honest, if you're not used to wearing print, you might want to work up to the latter. That's like starting with a phaal when you've never been for a curry before. There's something trickier to wear about a jumpsuit because you're breaking up the print in the legs, in contrast to a swathe of the print in a skirt. It's more for the eye to focus on and can be more confusing, which is why you may look in the mirror and think, 'what the actual chuff?' – as opposed to being a lot more comfortable in a full-on print dress.

Now, you would think that the easiest way to break yourself in with a print would be to go for a simple top. In theory, that sounds about right. However, as bizarre as this sounds, I would start with a dress. Yes, there is more print but it's just one thing you have to think about as you don't need to wear anything else with it. In true caveman stylee: wear dress. Go.

We have proven that it's not as tricky as you may think to match your print clothes to things you have in your wardrobe – yes, but that's colour-wise. Once you're familiar with print as an integral part of your outfits, this will come naturally to you. But, at the beginning, even a plain tee and a print skirt can create difficulties. Do you tuck it in, do you half tuck, do you untuck? When you sit down, does it come

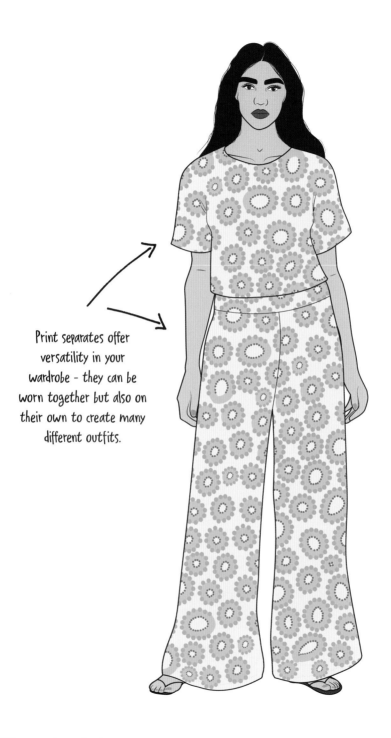

Print separates offer versatility in your wardrobe - they can be worn together but also on their own to create many different outfits.

untucked from whichever tucking option you went for? Discombobulation is what you may well have going on.

If you're stepping outside your comfort zone with your print escapade, anything else that is a mild inconvenience and wouldn't normally bother you, will suddenly become as irritating as not being able to find the end of the Sellotape at 2am on Christmas Day when you're still wrapping presents (just me?). Until you get used to it. And you will get used to it, and it will become second nature. But if you're at the start of your print journey, I would invest some time in finding the perfect print dress in a style and pattern that works for your shape and makes you smile. As bizarre as it sounds, a full-on print dress IS often easier than a top or a skirt.

Neutral prints

No, that's not a contradiction in terms: there is such a thing as a neutral print. Now you may well think that this would therefore be the easiest place to start, but I don't think it's any more simple to get your head around than a floral. It's just personal preference and what pleases you. Which makes you smile?

A neutral print is one that is essentially made up of neutral shades and usually only two of them. Yes, it's that simple. Except not all prints made up of neutral shades are neutral prints. Clear as mud? The following prints are what I would count as neutral (although this isn't an exhaustive list):

1. A two-tone stripe
2. A polka dot
3. Any animal print (which may have three or four different colours in it but they're variations on the same shades so they sneak in under the radar)

As neutral prints, they therefore work with other prints. I know that doesn't sound like it should work but it actually does. I am not saying that you must combine them with other prints – hell to the no, not at all. You are more than welcome to wear these neutral prints on their own with your usual favourite colour combos. Or they work perfectly and breathe new life into an outfit of your tried-and-tested neutrals.

Two 'neutral' prints are the easiest way to print clash. Leopard and stripes - yes, they do work!

Neutral prints are also the perfect place to start if you've never embraced anything print before. As much I would love to say, go large or go home when it comes to print, I have met more than my fair share of print-phobic people over the years who love a pattern on others people but never feel they can quite pull it off themselves. Well you can. You so, so can. At any age, in any outfit, regardless of what shape or size you are, there is a neutral print out there with your name on it.

You may have twigged that I've just thrown in 'animal print' there. As if you might not notice. But I'm sure you have, so let's just put one of the thorniest topics in fashion out there: Is it acceptable to wear animal print? Yes.

That's it really. Well, it should be. But just to be a bit clearer for all those naysayers who say it shouldn't be worn by women over a certain age (don't even get me started; I've got a whole chapter to bang on about my feelings on that later in the book); it's cheap and should only be worn by soap-opera barmaids. If that's your opinion, good for you. But keep it to yourself.

I'm not here to convince anyone who has strong feelings that they should do it differently. If you're happy to stand up to the courage of your convictions when it comes to a certain style, then that's GREAT. But I am here to say to those who WANT to embrace their inner leopard-loving self that you absolutely can and you absolutely should.

Both we (the royal we) and it have come a long way in the past couple of years. More of which I wax lyrical about later in the book when I talk about the elephant in the room: AGE. Although in this case, let's swap elephant for leopard. The print that, for too many, has a really bad rep. But the joy of animal print is that it really does go with everything – pretty much anything – especially florals. Think back to what I said earlier about nature. Anything that you can see in nature will work in an outfit. Leopard and floral print – what's not to love about that? Which brings us VERY neatly on to how to mix your prints.

If you are feeling more adventurous, there's always the option to step up your print game and GO for the clash.

You may well look at these combos and think 'that is not working for me, no siree, I would simply look like I had got dressed in the dark', AND, yet again, that's OK. It would be a very dull world if we all liked the same thing, but I want you to be aware that if you do want to clash your prints, this is the safest way to do it. Of course, if you are feeling a little bit brave but not quite sure about going the whole hog, there is always the option to layer with a print: over a stripe top, you could always wear a knitted tank or throw over a plain-coloured cardie to break up the mass of pattern.

Texture

I'm ending this chapter by peeling those who are scarred by the very mention of mixing print off the ceiling. For some, it is too much, but there are other options to add that little bit of extra into your outfits.

I have mentioned it previously when extolling the virtues of black, but it also works as a great option in other colours. It adds, well, I'm not going to say 'personality' as that makes it sound as though if you don't do it you're on the bland side, which is frankly rude and not what I mean at all. It's more something that gives you an option to elevate your wardrobe if you're looking to add to a classic look.

Texture.

It doesn't sound like much but texture can give a plain colour a totally different look. This is partly, as I've already mentioned, due to the texture creating shadows that can give the illusion of different shades as opposed to a single flat one, or even create its own 'pattern'.

Textured fabrics to consider are: sequins, velvets, linen, silks with a sheen, satin, tweed, bouclé or a chunky knit. You can either add one item in a texture, for example, a bouclé blazer over jeans and a plain cotton tee, or mix up your textures, perhaps a chunky knit over a satin skirt.

If you are thinking of mixing them up, I would suggest going for different textures from each end of the touchy-feely scale, instead of two that are quite similar. So rather than a satin and a silk together, go for a silk blouse with a sequin skirt.

At the end of the day, the most important thing, when it comes to colour, print or texture, is to have fun and take it one step at a time. If in doubt, take baby steps and experiment with one new element rather than throwing it all on together.

This chapter has verged on *War and Peace*, but there's a lot of info to get through. Hopefully, the nutritional information (see opposite) will be useful for you to refer back to.

Nutritional information

Learn to be confident in your colour and print choices (brights or neutrals, prints or no print) and make sure they work for your style and for your wardrobe.

Neutrals

> Make friends with neutrals – all shades of navy, camel, khaki, cream, grey – these will form the backbone of your wardrobe.
> Identify the shades and colours you love.
> Try combining your neutrals. All neutrals will work together – they can either be building blocks for adding colour or print, or work together to create an outfit in a purely neutral palette.
> Get to grips with looking at yourself in the mirror (see homework, page 122).
> Bear in mind that changing your make-up can really alter the way a colour looks on you.

Black

> Remember that it is OK to love black.
> But black should never be worn to hide behind...
> Think about different textures of black fabrics that will reflect the light back onto your face.

Actual colour

> It's OK to love it, hate it or be terrified by it.
> You don't have to love colour – it's OK to live in neutrals.
> BUT there are ways to find colour that works for you (see homework, page 122).
> Trust your gut and if you can't yet, practise until you can.

Combining colours

> Remember what works with nature.
> Practise with colour combinations that you may already have.
> Make sure you love the colours you're combining, because confidence is half the battle.

Print

> Again, you don't have to love print. That's OK!
> The rule of thumb for finding a print that works for your shape: the smaller you are, the smaller the print.
> If you're curvy or tall, embrace the larger print.
> Do your print practice (see homework, page 122).

Neutral prints

> Pick a print containing one colour that matches an item already in your wardrobe.
> Start to introduce print into your wardrobe with a print dress.
> Polka dots, two-tone stripes and animal print.
> You may not love leopard print but there is NO reason not to wear it (if you can't say anything nice, don't say anything at all).
> A neutral print is the easiest way to clash your prints. Team a neutral print with a print print.
> Practice makes perfect; practise the clash.
> Again, it is OK not to love even a neutral print.

Texture

> The final option for those who don't love print or colour.
> Look for bouclé, satin, silk with a sheen, velvet, sequin, tweed or a chunky knit.
> Try mixing your textures, but ideally mix textures that aren't similar. Think about both ends of the touchy-feely scale.

Homework

The 'bleugh' test

> Look at yourself in the mirror wearing a range of different colours.
> Learn to really appreciate which ones you love and which ones are bleugh. Try changing your make-up to see if that makes a difference.
> Then...when next shopping, try on a range of different coloured jumpers, starting with neutrals and moving on to colours.
> Make a note of the ones that you love and the BLEUGH ones – both are equally important.
> If you only buy things in colours that you LOVE, you will actually wear them.

Print practice

> Find an online site or an in-store fabric department with a host of different prints on offer. Simply go through them and, on immediate GUT instinct, pull out the ones you LOVE. Make a note (I have a file of photos on my phone).
> The more you practise, the more you will instantly be able to recognize a print that you love AND you'll have the confidence that it's right for you.

Don't be bullied by other people into wearing things they think suit you. Learn to trust YOUR gut. If you love the tones and patterns of your clothes, you're far more likely to actually wear them.

Pantry staples

Some call this a capsule wardrobe, to others it may be your wardrobe essentials. I like to think of them as pantry staples. Which sort of gives you an idea of how important it is to get them right. You know, those things that you simply can't cook a meal without, those ingredients that form the base layers of most of the meals you cook. And if you have a selection of these in your cupboards, you know that your meal (up to a certain point and until you start adding in unknown things) is bound to be a success.

Think of these staples as building blocks. The foundation of your wardrobe on which all outfits can be built. They're timeless, they're often able to be worn all year round and, from a sustainability point, they're ideal as you'll wear them again and again and again.

I'm making it sound simple and, ultimately, it is – once you've worked out what pantry staples work for you. I've seen lots of lists over the years, which are amazing but also don't give options. And let's face it, one of the things we've worked out so far is that everyone is different and one size does not fit all. Therefore why would one set of building blocks work for everyone? Taking it back

to the ingredients analogy: yes, there are a couple of basics that everyone has, but after that one man's meat may well be another man's (or woman's) poison. I am a sucker for a jar of passata, frozen garlic and onions, but I have a friend who is allergic to garlic and everyone in her family hates tomatoes. Won't be finding those ingredients behind the Frosties (which aren't an essential of mine, by the way, and other breakfast cereals are available).

So, how on earth do you write a chapter about a set of pantry staples that will be different for everyone? Good point. Not going to lie, this has taken me more time than it should have to work out. It's very easy to advise on a one-to-one basis, but how to be all things to all (wo)men without it ending up an encyclopaedia?

Back to basics. Essentially there ARE a set of basics that everyone has. It's just deciding on what that basic is for you. For your style, for your shape, for your lifestyle and for your budget.

For example, you need to be clothed from the waist down. End of story. You need to wear something on your feet, assuming you're not Sandie Shaw (spot the child of the 1970s whose mum was obsessed with *Eurovision*). And unless you're planning on having your bazookas swinging free, something to cover the top half of your body is also an idea.

Essentially clothes. We all need clothes. And once you have a selection that works together, that you can mix and match, it's genuinely easy to look totally composed and put together AND...of course...you will automatically feel and therefore look more confident. As I always say, once you have the right wardrobe staples, it's as easy to put together a great outfit as it is to put on a crap one.

I also advise against looking at a very separate set of winter and summer clothes. Seeing as the seasons in the UK are more, let's say, fluid than that (in other words, temperatures pay scant regard to when it should be hot and cold or wet and dry), there are obviously going to be crossovers in what clothes you can wear throughout the year.

For some, a capsule wardrobe is their only wardrobe and, yes, it can work. Even without anything else, you will have timeless outfits that suit your style and your shape. Personally, I am a complete fashion magpie and love to have other options that I can layer on top of my pantry staples. And that's OK. Once you've got the basics covered you always have a great outfit at your fingertips, and you can then go wild in the aisles when it comes to adding in the colour and the print to the style you've identified with (see pages 30–55).

The harder part is narrowing down the style and neutral colour that you want. 'Neutral?!', I hear you cry, 'How dull!' No, not dull. Practical. And useful. Which means that you will actually wear them, which is very much the whole point. Having a wardrobe of fabulously brightly coloured impulse purchases is all well and good, but having clothes that offer versatility and from which you can actually create a whole host of useful outfits – that's the point. Hold that thought on adding the extras, we've got to get the basics right first.

It's the pick 'n' mix option. Because fashion, like food, is completely subjective. Are you a fizzy cola bottle or a jazzie sort of girl. For the record, I am 100 per cent jazzie (those discs of fake chocolate covered in hundreds and thousands), white mice and chocolate-covered raisins. You can keep all the gummy, fizzy sweets. Fake chocolate is my friend. And you can either pick a whole variety of different sweets to have in your bag, or keep it simple with a pared-back selection.

Without further ado, let's get menu planning with our pantry staples.

Please do remember, though, you don't have to have one from each category. So long as you have a selection from the bottoms and the tops – and all-in-ones (dresses/jumpsuits) if you like, but not actually necessary – you're good to go.

As always, there is a handy menu in the nutritional information section at the end of the chapter for ease of reference (see page 173).

Bottoms

Trousers

First up, trousers. If you have a good-fitting pair of trousers in your wardrobe, you will always have something to wear. That's the easy part (so long as you have a top to go with them – I'm assuming you're not Mr Tumnus). The thing about trousers is that they're more versatile than people think.

There is no reason to think that a pair of 'smart' trousers can't be worn in a more casual way – it's all about what else you wear with the trews. A good pair of trousers can be worn to work; they're the absolute ideal evening mate to team with a silk shirt and footwear that works for you; yet throw on with a tee, biker and trainers and you've got the perfect dressed-down outfit. However, if you've absolutely no reason to ever look really smart, there's little point in having a pair of tailored trousers as one of your building blocks as they just won't fit into your lifestyle.

The thing you need to focus on is what sort of trousers are best for you. We now know that you're dressing for the lifestyle that you have, the shape that you are and the style that works for you. Also, remember that if you are VERY much a trouser person and really aren't into skirts at all, then it makes sense to have, as part of your bottoms

Wide-leg trousers, full length
or cropped, can work for
pretty much any shape and
any height.

building blocks (don't say that after a drink and actually don't say that out loud as, frankly, it does sound quite weird), a couple of different trouser options that offer alternative looks.

Wide-leg trousers

The most important thing to remember with wide-leg trousers is, thinking back to dressing for your shape, proportion. With a wider shape on the bottom, we're looking for a neater silhouette on the top and outerwear that is either fitted or long and loose to lengthen your look. The obvious issue in rainier months is, if you have them long, then there is the very uncomfortable issue of a soggy hem to deal with. My personal preference for full-length wide-leg trousers is to wear them long. In fact, I like them to be so long that, when I walk, I look like a Dalek. Which, I appreciate, doesn't sound aesthetically pleasing in the slightest – the eagle-eyed among you will have noticed that there isn't a Dalek category in the style icons – but wide-leg trousers that have fabric slightly pooling on the floor is, for me, the epitome of chic. Maybe I should have said Katharine Hepburn instead of Dalek...Trainers are my shoe poison of choice, and any sturdy flats such as loafers or brogues are just as great. Heels or wedges are a fab option if you're on the petite side.

There are the cropped versions to consider, too, which are an ideal winter option but also perfect for the warmer months. Boots that fit under the trousers are a superb choice for when it's cold and wet – either a flat boot or a heeled one works. Just make sure that there is no flesh on show. Keep the look streamlined so that the trouser fully covers the top of the boot. Yes, it looks better, but it also prevents a chilly calf.

In the spring and summer, either wide-leg length options are your friend. The only thing to remember is to keep your top fitted, although a looser top works in a light, floaty fabric. You're looking to balance your proportions again, so with a wide leg on the bottom, ideally we'd have less bulk on top.

Style-wise: Minimalist Elegance team with ballet flats; Classic Chic and Androgynous Flair team with heels, brogues or loafers; Seventies Magic and Boho in loose, floaty fabric, with either sandals or wedges; Parisian Chic and Laid-Back LA team with trainers.

Tapered-leg trousers

Also known as a carrot or a barrel leg. These are ideal for the pear-shaped among us, as they're looser over the hips but taper neatly into the ankle. Ditto for those who are on the thinner side. The most popular length for these is to hit just above the ankle bone, making them the perfect trousers for those of you who have gorgeous ankles – the shape of the trousers draws the eye down to show off one of your best assets. Can be worn either with flats or heels. In the winter, it's possible to tuck them into an ankle boot. Alternatively, it is perfectly acceptable to have a little bit of flesh showing. Optional, depending on how nesh you are when it comes to the cold!

With regard to tops, the devil that is proportion is sitting on our shoulder, reminding us to balance out the bottom with the top. So, because we have created a silhouette that is giving us shape below the waist, we're looking to keep it neater on the top. These types of trousers are ideally suited to something that you can tuck in, or half tuck, or a top that has a cinched-in waistband (a sweatshirt or jumper) to create a nipped-in silhouette around your middle. Coat-wise, though, fill your boots with oversized, thigh length: a trench or pretty much any jacket that works for you.

Style-wise: Ideal for Minimalist Elegance and Classic Chic. Also perfect for Laid-Back LA and Androgynous Flair in heavy chino cotton.

Cargo or combat trousers
These are, in fact, a similar(ish) shape to the tapered trousers, above, but definitely fit neatly under the more casual banner. They are exactly what they say on the tin: once used for practical purposes, they aren't usually tight, but are loose and comfortable and sometimes have useful pockets for putting stuff in. Nowadays they're seen as a staple part of many wardrobes and are ideal if you have a more casual bent to your lifestyle. Because they are usually loose, you're probably better off on the top with a style that doesn't drown you – we're not looking for big, baggy jumpers here. Instead, add a big knit in the form of a chunky cardigan if that's the vibe you're looking for.

Footwear-wise, while I did mention heels, that is a very specific look and, for most, a more casual addition to your feet works better. Trainers, sandals or ankle boots are probably the most suitable for completing your outfit.

Style-wise: If we're talking Laid-Back LA or Classic Chic, they can definitely give your outfit a cool, casual vibe; or they can work as part of a more Eclectic Vintage look (add heels for the Carrie from *SATC* vibes), depending on what you team them with.

Joggers
The even slouchier cousin of the combat/cargo trousers. Now, there is no denying that pre-Lockdown Years these would not have made an entry. But ever since we were confined to our sitting rooms for months on end, loungewear has taken on a whole new wardrobe meaning. Joggers that were once confined to purely activewear have become part of our daily

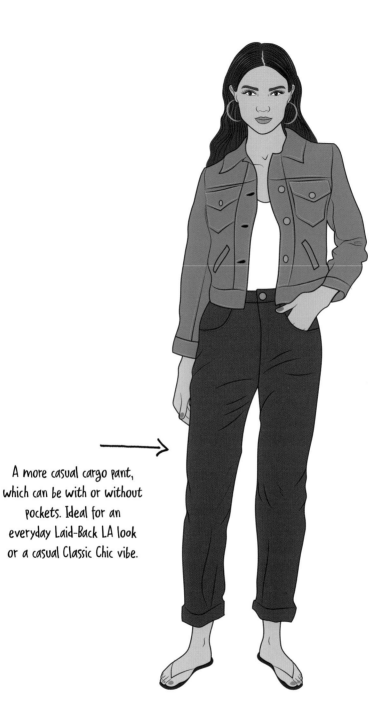

A more casual cargo pant, which can be with or without pockets. Ideal for an everyday Laid-Back LA look or a casual Classic Chic vibe.

Leather leggings.
More flattering than you think.
Dress up or dress down with
knits and boots. Also perfect
for curvier shapes. Think about
pairing with a looser tunic
that's not too long.

routine. Loungewear became king. New fabrics and tweaks to the classic jogger shape meant that suddenly they became a lot more wearable when we were allowed out and about. Obviously some burnt theirs, having lived in nothing else for months, but others saw them as the comfortable and yet elegant alternative trouser option.

No longer consigned to the purely casual, joggers in faux or real leather, cashmere, tweed, silk or a luxury jersey can hold their own. A style very much in their own right and, dare I say, possibly now my favourite (my hobby in lockdown, it appears, was collecting as many joggers in as many different styles as I could). They work all year round and can be, depending on the fabric, smart enough for a work environment, worn in the evening or dressed down during the day. Or, as they were initially intended, for an afternoon on the sofa.

Style-wise: Fabric-dependent, there is a pair for most styles. Minimalist Elegance, Classic Chic, Parisian Chic and London Cool in silks and faux leathers; Androgynous Flair in a tweed and Laid-Back LA in a jersey. Not forgetting Seventies Magic in sequins.

Leggings

Speaking of things that made a revival during lockdown, the humble legging made a majestic comeback. And while you may all be thinking of the jersey leggings of yesteryear – or, heaven forbid, an actual pair of activewear leggings – these have come a long way and are now most definitely acceptable as day and night wear. Thanks to the multitude of fabrics they are now available in. Leather and faux-leather offer a super-flattering option. Yes, I'll say that again as I can hear the GASPS from those at the back. Genuinely – it really does not matter what size you are – there will be a pair of leather/faux-leather leggings out there for you, if it's a style that works. The trick is to make sure that they're the right size, and a matt fabric is universally more complimentary than a shiny pair.

The other key to wearing them is what you put on top. This is where we can go wild in the oversized aisles. Think longline shirt, big, chunky knits and long, skimming cardigans. Unless you're 3, a teen whose dad hasn't clocked that she's going out with her mates, actually DOING exercise or a Victoria's Secret model, you will be a lot more comfortable if you pair your leggings with a top that covers your derrière. At least covering your hips – most people will want their bum covering too.

Style-wise: It very much depends on the fabric and what you team them with but, as a pantry staple, leggings can pretty much work for all styles.

Jeans

I've thought long and hard about where to put these as, frankly, I could write a whole book on them. On just jeans. And another book on moaning about how to find the perfect ones to wear. It's an inevitable fact of life – up there with death and taxes – that trying on jeans is a nightmare. It's hideously difficult. I've also thought long and hard about why this is. Why is it so much harder to buy a pair of jeans than a pair of trousers? I think it's because we have a fixed idea in our head about what they should look like, rather than thinking about what styles work for us. Once you've found the pair that works for your style and your shape, don't overthink it – just wear them.

Jeans are just another pair of trousers. So all the shapes that we've discussed above work as jeans – they're just another fabric. And denim itself comes in so many guises that it can work for all different styles and shapes. As we've said, if you're blessed with curves, then a denim with a high elastane content is going to be your best friend. The taller and straighter among us, if you're looking for a looser pair, will favour a stiffer denim with a lot less stretch.

As well as being just trousers in different textures of denim, they are also available in a whole host of colours. Not just shades of blue – they tick off ALL the neutral shades now. And there's absolutely nothing wrong with having not one other pair of trousers in your wardrobe bar jeans. If that's what you wear. One tiny note on cost: there is a theory that the more you spend on jeans, the better they are. I can categorically state, after having tried on more jeans that I've had hot dinners (essentially, I see it as exercise), it's nothing to do with the price and everything to do with the fit. A pair of supermarket jeans can be as good as a designer pair, if they fit you properly and are the style and wash that you're looking for.

They can also cover your smart bases. OK, so I perhaps wouldn't advocate going to the most corporate work meeting in a pair of jeans. BUT if smart casual is the most debonair you need to be, there will always be a pair of jeans that fits the bill (out of interest, on that note, my go-to would always be a pair of jet-black jeans, as they do essentially look like a pair of black trousers and now pretty much come in all styles).

Style-wise: Hand on heart, there is a pair of jeans for each style. And, actually, every style can wear almost every type of jeans. It's more about ensuring that the cut is right for your shape and that the rest of your outfit marries with your style.

Dungarees

Oh the dilemma about whether to include these as I'm not sure Barbara

De-Worzel the dungas
with ballet flats, trench and
a crisp white shirt.

from *The Good Life* is reading. And then I gave myself a slap, listened to my own advice and thought about dressing for the lifestyle that you have and not the one that you want. There may well be other Barbaras reading who really do wear dungarees a lot of the time. 'Overalls' (as our friends across the pond call them) are no longer purely the uniform of the gardener, the decorator or the kids' TV presenter. They are very much part of a more mainstream everyday uniform. That's not to say that you have to wear them – don't get me wrong, I still look like Mario in drag or one of Dexys Midnight Runners if I don a pair of blue denim ones – they're not a style that works for everyone. But on some, they look effortlessly chic or fabulously casual, depending on the styling. On those who know their style, who know how to pair tops and bottoms and match their footwear, the look is sublime and on the money AND they exude confidence and style.

The key – as with most things of course – is to ensure that the top works with the bottoms. And that the fit is right. Essentially, there are two sorts of fit: a looser pair and a tighter pair (we're not talking a dungaree-style catsuit here, just one that is more fitted). As a general rule of thumb, if you have a generous chest, the placement of the bib on a pair of dungarees isn't going to do you the hugest amount of favours. They are one of those items that those with less up top are better suited to. The looser style can, however, offer great coverage over a less-than-toned tummy. The tighter versions, as they leave little room for hiding anything, you may assume, are therefore the domain of the more slender among us, but actually a well-fitting pair in your size can work on a curvier figure if you're happy to flaunt the silhouette you were given.

What to wear underneath very much comes down to style but, again, you are curtailed by fabric. It's safe to say, anything with bulk or weight to it, isn't going to look the best. You need to think of tops that are fitted or are of a light, flowing fabric that will lie neatly under your dungas. Tees, floaty blouses and neat-fitting shirts are all options. Remember, you can also play with sleeves to balance out your proportions if you're wider of hip but really do love the dungaree style. Feminine blouses are ideal to de-Worzel your dungas – something more frilly, floaty and frothy is the perfect juxtaposition with a more practical-look pair of overalls. Or, keep it chic with a Breton top and a longline blazer for a more minimalist look.

Fabric-wise, yes, they're historically in denim but it doesn't have to be a blue denim. In fact, in jet-black denim, velvet, cord or linen, ecru, khaki or any other colour, they immediately take on a very different image. They're probably not the most popular wardrobe essential for many, but for some they are the pantry staple they turn to every time.

Style-wise: Parisian Chic, London Cool, Androgynous Flair and Laid-Back LA look to a more minimalist fashion; Boho, Eclectic Vintage and Seventies Magic think party on the top, business on the bottom.

Shorts

Oh how I deliberated putting these in. And then I gave myself another good slap – just because I personally don't wear them (I have baby Les Dawson faces as knees and the rest of the world doesn't need to see them), to many, they are the mainstay of a summer wardrobe. As they indeed should be.

Shorts can work in a multitude of styles. They can be smart and actually worn for work (OK, we're not talking hotpants here) and are the perfect suit option for warmer months.

Shorts look super chic as classic, modern work attire in tailored cotton or linen, teamed with a blouse and matching blazer. Alternatively, they are perfect for a casual dressed-down occasion, again in linen or cotton or the classic denim. Cut off, hemmed or rolled up at the bottom – despite me saying I don't wear them, if you do want to – there is a pair for everyone. Just find the shape that flatters you the most – the waistband can be low-rise or high, the shorts can be more fitted on the legs or looser over the thighs. There is, of course, the hotpant option – you do you if you want to – but perhaps for the majority of us, a slightly longer length will appeal.

Style-wise: As with jeans, there really is a pair of shorts out there that will work for every style. Tailored with a clean, neat line will work for Minimalist Elegance, Classic Chic, Androgynous Flair and Parisian Chic. The denim versions in whatever shape are ideal for Boho, Eclectic Vintage, Seventies Magic, London Cool and Laid-Back LA (and as denim shorts are so versatile, I know many Classic Chics who love them, too).

Skirts

You don't necessarily 'have' to choose from this category. As with trousers, it's about having the perfect bottoms to work with your shape, style and lifestyle. It could be ALL skirts, or all trousers, or a combination.

Mini

Ignoring the fact that there are many people out there who believe that after a certain age miniskirts should be retired (I'm saving my rage and vitriol on this topic for 'The elephant in the room' later on, see page 234), let's talk miniskirts.

There are many, many, MANY of you who have amazing legs. And for you, the miniskirt is the perfect option. We're not necessarily talking mini mini here (a flash of foof is never a good idea, no matter how great your legs are), but even a couple of inches above your knee can look great in the summer. A loose tee and a miniskirt with sandals can be the epitome of summer chic. But I do know that there are many who aren't fans of exposing the bare flesh of the lower limbs. The easiest way to wear them, though, is in the autumn and winter with the legs encased in opaques. All hail the forgiving nature of Lycra. A thick pair of matt (make sure they're matt – shiny opaques aren't as forgiving on legs that don't belong to a supermodel) opaques works for everyone. Colour, of course, is up to you, depending on whether you're staying within your neutral zone or making a statement with a coloured pair.

Miniskirts also come in a variety of shapes but, in the interests of talking about wardrobe staples, you're probably best sticking to a classic shape – obviously in a neutral colour – that offers more versatility. That's probably what we all think of as being a narrow miniskirt (which you can readily find in all fabrics: cotton, cord, denim, velvet, leather), but there's no reason why it couldn't be a fuller skater-style miniskirt, which would also work perfectly.

With regards to what you team your miniskirt with, again, think about proportion and your shape. Generally, a slimmer skirt is great with something slightly looser on the top, while it's possibly better to keep the top more fitted with a fuller short skirt.

Style-wise: Very dependent on how you style them and the fabric of the skirt. They definitely fit very neatly into the categories of Boho (oversized knit in the winter; floaty embroidered top in the summer); Minimalist Elegance, London Cool and Parisian Chic (semi-fitted knits, opaques and flats/boots); Classic Chic (neat blouse or knit); Eclectic Vintage and Seventies Magic (the world is your oyster – the skirt is just the base – it's the fabulous layering on top that gives these styles the edge); and Laid-Back LA (denim skirt and loose tee is the epitome of your summer style).

Miniskirts can work for all ages and all shapes with the right outfit. Opaque tights are your friend and a looser top or chunkier knit add balance to your outfit.

Midi-skirts are, for many,
a wardrobe staple. The length
is a personal choice, from below
the knee to nearer the ankle.
Again, depending on your shape
and style. Try a few options and
see what you prefer.

Midi

The only tricky things about a midi-skirt are finding the right length to work for you AND whether it's your style. I say 'only', although they're actually two pretty big things. Oh, and while I'm here, the other thing to remember is that we're talking pantry staples. Wardrobe basics – the building blocks on which the rest of your outfits are formed. Hence, the neutral element to it. So if you're thinking floral, lace or any other print, then hold those thoughts as they don't necessarily count as a staple. That's your extras (and we come to them later in the book, see page 170).

Right now, we're focusing on things that are timeless and that you can keep for years. My personal midi-skirt of DREAMS is an A-Line black leather skirt with pockets. It is my absolute go-to outfit (I do wear a top with it – usually a fitted knit) for when I want to feel my most ME. The polished version of me, not the 'things aren't really going the way I planned me' or the 'trying to juggle all the balls me', which is definitely 'me' a lot of the time, but not the one that I perhaps want people to see.

And therein lies the beauty of having these pantry staples that you know work, that give you that extra boost of confidence we often all need. Yes, a skirt can do that (with a jumper, of course. If I were to walk around in just a skirt with my bazookas swinging free, suffice to say, confident would not be the primary emotion I was feeling).

Length-wise, it really depends on your height and the shape of your legs. If you're more petite or of average height, then halfway between your knee and ankle is probably ideal. If you're more generous of calf, then you may want your midi-skirt ever so slightly longer or shorter so it doesn't hit the widest part of your lower leg. For the taller among you, try going lower. Halfway between your knee and calf will result in there being a lot of leg on show, purely because the length of your legs means you have a lot of leg to show! Longer is definitely better, not necessarily to make you look shorter but simply to get the look of a midi-skirt where a LOT of leg shouldn't be seen. I would say a couple of inches above your ankle is probably the ideal length.

Style-wise: Boho and Seventies Magic look at cord, suede, leather, velvet, any rich, luxurious fabric that you can layer over; Minimalist Elegance, Classic Chic and Androgynous Flair consider leather, wool, suede, silk or satin, A-line or pencil; Eclectic Chic go for leather, suede, tulle, A-line; for Laid-Back LA it's linen, silk or satin, bias cut or A-line.

Maxi

Usually maxi-skirts aren't neutral or plain. They've returned to fashion in recent years and look like they're going nowhere, but the majority that are wearable are print. Floral or animal print are popular BUT we're talking neutral wardrobe staples here...A plain maxi-skirt isn't prevalent in many wardrobes for aesthetic reasons: too much plain fabric in an outfit can end up drowning most people (death by maxi-skirt; you heard it here first). But there are a few exceptions to the rule. OK, actually only one. As we said previously with the midi, we are looking for skirts that can be the base of a plethora of outfits for you. And there is no denying that when we're dressing for the lifestyle we have, a plain midi is easier for most of us than a plain maxi (slightly less *Handmaid's Tale*...). But if you're looking to branch out and be a little different (thinking about your style icon), you may want to consider a tulle maxi-skirt as one of your pantry staples. It's absolutely NOT a wardrobe basic for everyone, but some are able to rock their tutu in many different ways. Well, in as many ways as you can rock a skirt. With a tee, biker jacket and chunky boots; with a silk blouse, blazer and heels; with a thin knit, trench coat and trainers.

Style-wise: Think about the juxtaposition of a pretty skirt with pretty much anything else in your wardrobe for Eclectic Vintage but definitely channel that rock-chick vibe for London Cool.

Tops

Shirts/blouses

As with the bottoms, your tops can vary according to the style you love. But most people will have either a shirt or blouse of some description as there really is an option to suit everyone.

White shirt

Starting the tops section with shirts and blouses, which are pretty much the same thing, to be honest. Some may say that a blouse is looser and more feminine than a shirt. The devil is in the detail, but it's safe to say – as an all-encompassing phrase – they're 'tops with buttons'.

A white shirt is one of those things that is possibly more useful than you thought. Scarred by school uniform or days of corporate office wear, you may well no longer reserve a place in your wardrobe for the humble white shirt. That's fine, as there are alternatives; and good for you if you stick to your guns and your style decisions – you can't wear all of the styles all of the time.

But for many, a white shirt is the backbone of myriad outfits. An oversized shirt is the perfect partner for a pair of skinny jeans or leggings, while a slimmer-fitting shirt is perfect on its own with trousers and skirts, and ideal for layering under knits and tanks. Think about what works for your shape.

To collar or not to collar? That is the question. And even then, the collar can be rounded, with large lapels or even a frill neck. There are countless shirt options out there. The only decision you need to make is: which works best with your style and shape?

Style-wise: Minimalist Elegance, Classic Chic, Androgynous Flair, Parisian Chic, London Cool and Laid-Back LA can all look at loose or fitted, untucked or half tucked.

Denim shirt
This is probably the item that most people have in their wardrobe and never throw away. Along with the denim jacket. Both really do stand the test of time and can be a lot more useful than you think. Is a denim shirt for everyone? Absolutely not. But if you love a denim jacket, you will LOVE a denim shirt. You can divide the world into those who love double denim and those who think the 'Canadian tuxedo' should only be worn by actual cowboys.

For those who love them, the denim shirt is a wardrobe chameleon that works all year round and is the finishing solution for myriad outfits. There's the obvious wear-as-a-shirt option, but you can also wear it as a layer underneath a knit or as a jacket during the warmer months. You can even take it to the extreme and use it at the beach as a cover-up. Fabric-wise, there are thick

denim versions or you can find them in soft chambray, and there is a wash for every taste: vintage and faded, dark denim, medium or even very pale, almost bleached. Fitted or oversized, the choice is yours. As with the white shirt, there are collars to suit every shape. And the joy of buttons is that they work for every bust size.

Then there are also the blouse versions of the denim shirt. Essentially a blouse in a denim fabric, this could have a pussy bow, a ruffle here or there, or it could be collarless. Once you start adding too many details, though, just be aware that its function as a building block and essential go-to piece in your wardrobe wanes. We're thinking about versatility here, so to tick the pantry staple box, you're probably better keeping it classic.

Style-wise: Boho, Eclectic Vintage, London Cool and Seventies Magic look at a vintage-style wash, either fitted or oversized; Minimalist Elegance, Classic Chic and Parisian Chic consider a more fitted, plain version; and pretty much any style works for Laid-Back LA and Androgynous Flair.

Silk blouse
I confess this is possibly the favourite top in my wardrobe. On description it sounds very, well, not very wearable and a little bit prissy, but the reality is that,

like a denim and a white shirt, there is a silk blouse for everyone. I will add the caveat that when I say 'silk', it can be the real thing, but there are also some other incredible fibres out there that give you the same drape (recycled polyester for a start) but with less tricky washing instructions and no need to iron – things that the slightly/very incompetent and lazy being inside me loves.

Oh yes and also the 'blouse' word. For years, this word was up there with crimplene and petticoat – surely no one born after 1935 would be wearing these? All hail the Stupidity of Youth (youth-ish – I was probably still 40 when the word made me snigger). A blouse is a supremely awesome addition to your wardrobe (as is a petticoat, to be fair... and give me a good couple of hours rummaging in a vintage shop and I bet I could find a wardrobe gem in crimplene). It's just a word for a top that is versatile, that is the ideal foil for any pair of trousers and that, once you find the style and shape that works for you, you will wonder how you lived without.

The joy, for me, of the silk blouse is that it has the ability to transform an outfit into something extra. As I'm typing, I'm thinking, that sounds amazing and yet one of those weird, fashiony, random claims. Soz. I know, it does. But there are some items in your wardrobe that can be so...transformative. And for me it's the silk blouse. I would go so far as to say that the silk blouse is the epitome of the wardrobe basic. It has the ability to transform a pair of jeans, a leather skirt, even leggings and a pair of combat trousers, into something Outfit Worthy (admittedly, we are shoe-dependent here; the shoe advice is on the way, see page 161). At the same time, it can be dressed down and worn every day and just be a super-easy top to fling on (the shoes are the crowning glory here, I admit).

The other joy is that, like the white and denim shirts, there is a shape for everyone and there are lots of options to choose from. So a looser, long, tunic style works if you're used to wearing skinny jeans or leggings, and a more fitted style is better if you're looking to tuck it in.

And the magic of a silk blouse, as opposed to a white or denim shirt, is that it is a dream when it comes to tucking in. One of the most popular questions people ask me as a stylist is, how do you tuck something in without it looking messy or adding bulk? It's down to the fabric. The finer and more drapey the fabric, the easier it is to tuck in without, frankly, making a mess. Less bulging fabric, smoother lines, a lot easier and a lot more flattering. It's also easier to half tuck – where you tuck some of the fabric in and leave some untucked (as mentioned in the 'Dressing for your shape' chapter, see page 74) – as weird as it sounds, it does work but it works better when there aren't bunches of fabric billowing over and under your waistband. A small tuck with a silky fabric is a lot more seamless, with smoother fabric underneath and on the portion left untucked.

Neckline: there are perhaps more options here than with the white and denim shirts. My personal favourite is the pussy-bow tie – you can imagine the levels of childish sniggering at 'pussy-bow blouse', can't you? Luckily my maturity levels have improved somewhat in the past ten years and a pussy-bow blouse is now nothing but a thing of beauty to me. Especially as you get at least two necklines in one blouse. First off, there is the option of the actual bow being tied high at the nape of the neck (my go-to style), or you can tie the bow lower at around the bust level (and it doesn't even have to be a bow: just tie the two ends over and let them hang down, which is a lot more flattering if you're larger of bust). The tie is occasionally detachable. This is obviously the best kind as you then have the option to wear it sans bow and tie the bow anywhere you like – the long scarf works wonders as a belt – or not at all (you don't HAVE to wear them together).

Style-wise: As with jeans, I absolutely believe that there is a silky blouse for every style.

T-shirts

As ridiculous as it may sound, I do truly think that buying a T-shirt is almost as difficult as buying a pair of jeans. One man's meat is most definitely another man's (or woman's) poison.

The most important thing to understand is which style works for you. And that doesn't necessarily mean that you have to be restricted to one style, but it is worth considering those that work for your shape.

Necklines, fit and arm length are the main things to consider. And then it just comes down to fabric. Now. Here is where it gets interesting. Lots of people are very fond of 100 per cent cotton but, giving you a sneak peak of the sustainability chapter (see page 222), you're better off keeping an eye out for organic or recycled cotton. I personally much prefer a fabric that has an element of a drape: common fabrics are ones such as lyocell, rayon or modal, all of which are made from a natural element – cellulose – derived from wood pulp. Often they also have a small percentage of elastane in them, which helps to keep the original shape of the tee.

Your options are:

- **V-neck** (universally flattering but ideal for those with bigger busts)

- **Scoop neck** (again, a shape that will work for most, but definitely one for those blessed of breast)

- **Crew neck** (perfect for those with a flatter chest)

- **Boat neck** (depends on how wide and how low the 'slash' neck extends but can work for every bust size)

- **Bardot** (off-the-shoulder which can work for everyone if you can find the perfect strapless bra but will probably be those with a flatter chest who prefer this style)

- **Sleeveless** (can either be a low scoop, a V-neck or a high neck. Rules are the same as for a tee with sleeves, but generally these are great if you don't mind flashing the flesh on your arms).

Style-wise: There is a T-shirt for every style. They really are the perfect base layers on which to build different outfit looks. Or just keep it simple and let the tee do the talking. It's more down to finding the right one for your shape.

Knits

Also known as jumpers. The world is your oyster and, as with jeans (and don't even get me started on coats), this is an area on which I could wax lyrical for hours. A book and then some. But in the interests of keeping people awake and focused – and FOCUS is the name of the game here – the more prep you put into thinking about your wardrobe, the more benefit you will see when you come to detoxing, sorting and buying new things if needed.

It's also important to remember that we're thinking of building blocks for your wardrobe. So jumpers that are classic and will stand the test of time – ones around which you can build other outfits. For me, along with a silk blouse and a sleeveless high-neck vest, the most important staples in my wardrobe are knits.

Fabric here is very interesting. Different fabrics work for different people and for different budgets. Some detest the feeling of wool and others may not have the budget for cashmere. The good news is that these days there is so much choice – some may say too much (but we'll save that for the sustainability chapter, see page 222), there is definitely an option for every style, shape and purse. Recycled materials, as with tees, are a great way to sustainably buy a man-made fabric. They're purse friendly but also a lot easier to wash and maintain than wool or cashmere.

V-neck

Generally the universally flattering knit to wear. Ideal for those who are blessed with breasts and an ideal layering garment for those who love to wear a tee, blouse or shirt under a jumper. We're not talking fully oversized here, we're thinking of a fitted or semi-fitted, not too long, classic jumper. Fit-wise, a V-neck really does depend on the style you're looking to emulate and your shape.

Style-wise: Perfect for any style to wear as a base layer or to build an outfit on with other components.

Crew neck

Also known as the round neck. A classic shape that can be loose or more fitted; either work, depending on your style or shape (again, not getting on to the oversized element just yet). Another ideal shape for wearing on its own or, if you do have it slightly on the looser side, perfect for layering under. Fit is important when it comes to layering – if it's too tight, it has the propensity to suggest the 'stuffed sausage about to burst' look, which perhaps isn't what we're going for.

Style-wise: As with the V-neck, depending on the fit of the crew neck, it works happily for any style as either a stand-alone knit or as part of a layering look.

Polo neck

The jumper that divides. First, on the name – polo neck, roll neck, turtle neck? So, in the UK, the polo neck and the roll neck are the same thing (the polo neck being the older name for it). In the US, a turtle neck is exactly the same as a polo neck but with a different name. BUT, in the UK, a turtle neck is a half-polo neck: imagine a polo neck turned half down at the neck. Still following? All you really have to know is that chances are you either love 'em or hate 'em. And it's very usually boobage dependent. If you are curvier and blessed with breasts, then it's probably best to avoid them. However... if you love the look, have more of an hourglass figure and are happy to invest in a great bra to give your boobs the proper scaffolding they deserve, a polo neck CAN work. Think Marilyn Monroe. As a general rule, though, they are usually favoured by those left hanging in the chest department and who, as their consolation prize, are able to rock a roll neck. Long-sleeved is the traditional style, but short sleeves can add a different dimension. As we're not talking oversized yet (be patient, my oversized jumper lovers), it's more usual to find these in a finer and not chunky knit.

Style-wise: As a classic jumper, like the V- and crew necks, so long as it works for your shape, there is a style opportunity for everyone with a classic polo neck.

Oversized

The comfort knit. Probably best known for its ability to hide a multitude of sins and, for that, we will always love it. It's most definitely why it will always have a special place as one of my wardrobe basics. But it's so much more than that... although it shouldn't actually be so oversized as to have its own postcode. There is a fine line between looking lovely and comfy and looking like you're being buried in knitwear. The key to the perfect oversized knit is to find one that does hide the evidence but at the same time doesn't drown you. It should be just oversized. The Goldilocks of oversized. And how do you know? We come again to trust your judgment and that gut instinct. Essentially, you want it to look too big. But not so you could smuggle an entire buffet breakfast bar for lunch later (OK, maybe a couple of muffins, a banana and some rolls...). Length is also important. There are the shorter versions of oversized knits that end around or just below the waistband and can be worn with a more voluminous bottom (wide-leg trousers, boyfriend jeans, a loose skirt), but it's generally a harder look to pull off. The easier oversized-knit look to perfect and one that, if it's your style, you will turn to again and again, is a mid-thigh-ending knit over skinny jeans or leggings. If you're taller, the knit can end slightly lower, and if you're petite, make sure that it doesn't hit lower than mid-thigh. Pondering a neckline doesn't have to throw another spanner in the works: so long as you suit it to your shape, it will work. So either V-neck, round neck or polo neck.

Style-wise: Boho, Minimalist Elegance, Eclectic Vintage, Parisian Chic, London Cool and Laid-Back LA can all rock an oversized knit – it's the rest of their outfit that will really finish their signature look.

Sleeveless, aka the tank top

A rank outsider in the classic jumper stakes. Oh, and I should also point out that our American friends call this a vest. What we call a vest, they call an undershirt...which, frankly, makes a lot more sense. But, semantics aside, a tank top is a personal favourite of mine – of the knitted variety (as is a vest of the cotton variety!). The neckline can either be V-neck, low scoop or crew neck. Tanks can be worn on their own or layered over, well, pretty much anything you want to layer them over, the most common being a shirt, tee or dress. A rather handy little wardrobe basic to give different looks to your outfits.

Style-wise: The versatility of a tank top means it earns its place in any style wardrobe, depending on whether you layer it or wear it as a stand-alone knit.

Bardot

Absolutely not for everyone. Your first port of call with an off-the-shoulder bardot-style knit (you can also get it in other other fabrics – a stretch jersey is a total winner, as is a '70s-style loose cheesecloth blouse) is a good strapless bra. And we all know how hard they are to find, especially if you're more well endowed than the average person. BUT if you are pear-shaped or blessed with some middle-age loving around the tummy, these are ideal for adding balance to your shoulders by widening the top of your body. You might not believe me but the clavicle on show is one of the sexiest things a woman can expose (even more so if you're able to tuck your boobs into your waistband like I am).

Style-wise: Like most knits, it depends on what you team your bardot top with and what fabric it's made from. There is a bardot for every style – it's more down to whether you're comfortable wearing it.

The Breton

Is it a T-shirt, is it a knit? Well, it's both. It can be one or the other, or both. And there is a Breton for everyone, if you should want to wear one. For the purposes of pantry staples, we are talking a classic – dark navy or black. Of course, there is now a plethora of variations on the theme, but we are sticking to the original. To be fair, I say the original... it's basically what we have come to think of as the original. I remember years ago going down the rabbit hole of the Breton when writing an article. Apparently, purists believe that to be a true Breton it should hail from Northern France and have 21 stripes (one for each of Napoleon's victories), as per the original seaman's uniform from the 19th century.

But in the interests of fashion, we have adapted the name to mean a white or cream striped top with navy (or black) stripes. It can be in heavy cotton with long or three-quarter-length sleeves, or in a cotton or wool knit (in pretty much any shape that you fancy). There are even V-neck striped tees that we can throw into the Breton category – massive apologies if I've offended anyone with my liberal sprinkling of the Breton title; please be assured it is done with love, affection and utter admiration of such an incredibly versatile piece of clothing. Depending on the shape of your Breton, it can pretty much be worn with everything in your wardrobe. For your shape – just remember the guidelines on the neckline and the fit of the top.

Style-wise: As with jeans, a Breton will work for almost every category: Parisian Chic, Minimalist Elegance, Classic Chic, Androgynous Flair, London Cool and Laid-Back LA. Admittedly it's probably not the first top of choice for a Boho or Eclectic Vintage vibe, but for Seventies Magic, a Breton and a pair of high-waisted flair jeans and clogs? Bring it on.

Neckline styles

- V-neck
- scoop neck
- crew neck

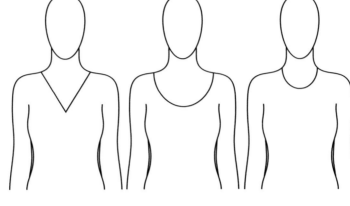

- shirt neck
- boat neck
- off-the-shoulder

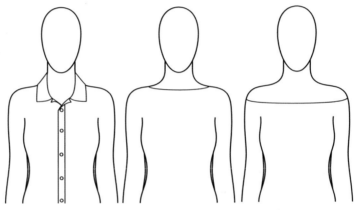

- sleeveless
- pussy bow
- polo neck

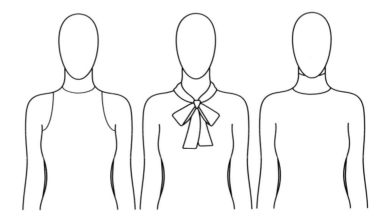

Outerwear

Jackets

Does everyone need a jacket? I think you'll find it's the perfect outerwear item for spring and autumn (and in the summer) and when you see the number of options available, your answer will be affirmative.

Blazer

How long is a piece of string and how long have you got? There is no denying that a blazer isn't going to feature as a must-have in everyone's wardrobe. At all. But if you love a blazer, boy do you love a blazer. The opportunities are never-ending to dress it up or down, and it's really worth spending time finding one that is perfect for your shape and for your style. They are undoubtedly the staple for a corporate wardrobe but can be easily segued into a more casual look. Ideal with jeans and a tee and any footwear to suit your style, be it trainers, loafers, heels or ankle boots.

I would go so far as to say that if you do fancy a staple blazer but think it's not your style, try rethinking the fabric. Velvet? Cord? Bouclé? Leather? If you stretch your imagination to include alternative shapes of blazer and different fabrics, you may just find that there is one that fits the bill and becomes the perfect wardrobe staple to finish off a plethora of outfits. Yes, a classic dark wool (or wool-mix) blazer is typically more suited to Minimalist Elegance, Classic Chic, Androgynous Flair, London Cool, Parisian Chic and Laid-Back LA. But you could mix it up with a linen blazer (also perfect for Laid-Back LA and Parisian Chic), rich, draping velvets or a soft needlecord in neutral colours for a Boho or Eclectic Vintage look. Tweed can be an ideal alternative for Eclectic Vintage and Androgynous Flair. A blazer doesn't necessarily need to be fully structured – it depends on the fabric. You could also think about different lengths – cropped, mid-length or longline work in all styles.

● **Double-breasted, either oversized or fitted.** Not often worn done up, but oversized has a boxier, looser shape, whereas a more fitted style has a shaped waist. Very different shapes, their only commonality is their double-breastedness (not an actual fashion term). To wear or not to wear really comes down to whether it works for your shape.

Style-wise: Boho, Eclectic Vintage, Androgynous Flair, London Cool, Laid-Back LA and Parisian Chic look at an oversized, loose shape, depending on fabric; Minimalist Elegance, Classic Chic, Eclectic Vintage, Androgynous Flair, Parisian Chic, London Cool and

Laid-Back LA consider a fitted shape, also depending on fabric.

● **Single-breasted, either oversized or fitted, cropped or longline.** To be honest, the same concept as its double-breasted sibling, except with less fabric at the front of the jacket and with one set of buttons rather than two. The better option for those with larger appendages up front.

Style-wise: A single-breasted blazer, depending on the fabric and the fit, works for any style.

● **Collarless, either V-neck or round neck.** Usually single-breasted, can be cropped and boxier or fitted and mid-length or longer line. Admittedly I am stretching the definition of blazer here, but it's a structured shape so I reckon it has earned its blazer stripes.

Style-wise: Depending on the fabric, pretty much any style can find one of these jackets to work as part of their staple wardrobe.

● **Bouclé.** I've given the bouclé blazer its own category, which is a punchy move as, by rights, it's a fabric so should sit neatly in one of the categories above. In fact, it can sit in any of the above categories as you can get them double-breasted, single-breasted and collarless; fitted, loose, cropped, mid-length or

longline. But, I really do think they are a blazer style in their own right, thanking you kindly there Coco Chanel.

Style-wise: Most definitely not just for the Parisian Chic (although, yes, that is the obvious choice). Minimalist Elegance and Classic Chic are also clear choices but Eclectic Vintage and London Cool can both rock the bouclé – worn as part of their typical non-traditional styles.

Leather jacket

So...as with the blazer above, I would hazard a guess at there being many people out there who believe they have no need for a leather jacket in their life. Style-wise most people automatically think of a biker jacket when they hear leather jacket, and that most definitely isn't going to be for everyone. And that's totally fine. It would be an insanely dull world if we all wore the same things. There is also the suede option (placed under this header as it's a leather fabric), which gives a softer, more feminine look to a typical leather jacket. Faux leather and faux suede are also options that are ideal for the ethically minded or budget conscious. There are also lots of different leather options but, when it comes to classics, the biker and the blazer are probably the most ubiquitous. As a rule, other leather jackets I'd be more likely to place on a pedestal in your wardrobe gems (see page 170).

The classic biker. Once only for actual bikers and James Dean, now a staple piece in most wardrobes. Many styles are available, in many fabrics. I challenge you to find your perfect piece.

● **Biker.** Perhaps the most typical of leather jackets. They've been around forever and keep bouncing back into fashion but are most definitely a wardrobe staple for certain styles. Shape-wise, there are slight variations on a theme but they are usually double-breasted, loose but not generally oversized (although they certainly do come as an option and are often slightly longer line) and a mid- or cropped length. Suede or leather, studded or pared back. If the biker fits your style, it will be the jacket you turn to for years and years.

Style-wise: Boho, Eclectic Vintage, Seventies Magic, Androgynous Flair, London Cool and Laid-Back LA look to suede or leather; and because it's become so mainstream it can even work for the Classic Chic among us, especially in a softer colour that's perhaps not black – midnight or charcoal is more likely to be of interest.

● **Blazer.** Oh the dilemma of whether to put this in the blazer or the leather category. It could have gone in either, but I've placed it here as I believe it's the perfect solution for those who think they would never wear a leather jacket but are dyed-in-the-wool members of the blazer fan club. A leather blazer, I appreciate, can sound all sorts of wrong diddly. But, actually, a buttery-soft leather or suede (or faux fabrics of either), in a fitted single-breasted style can be just the ticket to add a new dimension to your wardrobe. Or how about a collarless, cropped or mid-length fitted version? When you're in a style rut but don't necessarily want to change your style direction, a tweak of fabric here and there can add a different edge to your look without changing the entirety of the aesthetic. You could even throw caution to the wind and get one with a belt.

Style-wise: Minimalist Elegance, Classic Chic, Parisian Chic, London Cool and Laid-Back LA look at structured single-breasted or collarless cropped or mid-length fitted shapes in either suede or leather; Boho, Eclectic Vintage and Seventies Magic look for any shape in vintage leather or suede.

Denim jacket

Do we think there is anyone who doesn't have a denim jacket? OK, so yes, I can hear you at the back and, yes, there are definitely going to be people who are not lovers of a jacket of the denim variety. There ARE lots of different style options but, suffice to say, when we're talking about wardrobe classics, we're really talking about the basics that you have for years. That classic, essential denim jacket that is perhaps (I know for sure it is for many) the oldest item in your wardrobe. As they really haven't changed since…well, forever. The classic, jean-style denim jacket, aka the trucker jacket.

Like jeans, you can get them in any denim wash imaginable and, while the generic style of the classic 'jeans jacket' is almost always the same, there are different fits and there is most definitely one for every shape. Fitted, cropped, longer line, oversized or boxy. Dark denim, faded denim, bleached, white, vintage – every style can find a denim jacket to suit them IF they so desire. It may well be that it's just not your bag and you have a perfect jacket alternative that is your wardrobe staple. They do also tend to be mostly a spring/summer/autumn jacket, although I know some people who layer them under an oversized coat to maximize the denim offering all year round.

Style-wise: Boho, Eclectic Vintage, Seventies Magic, London Cool and Laid-Back LA go for loose, fitted or even oversized but in a more faded, vintage-style wash, mostly shades of blue, could be black; Minimalist Elegance, Classic Chic, Androgynous Flair, Parisian Chic and Laid-Back LA look at a more generic loose or fitted style in a clean dark, pale, black or white denim.

Coats

How many coats are too many? Asking for a friend...Coats are one of those wardrobe items that, for many, it's merely the space limitations that curtail the number they have. Were space (and budget) no option? Well, sustainability would stop us buying ALL the coats as you can't wear all the coats, but if you could, there is most definitely a coat for every occasion.

However, many coats fit into the category of wardrobe gems (coming up... see page 170) and, in this chapter, we're all about the pantry staples. Those coats that will work day in, day out, year in, year out, that aren't slaves to a statement, that don't do all the talking and that work for many different occasions and complete many different outfits. That's not to say they can't add a certain flourish to an outfit, but it's in an understated, elegant and chic way. A classic of your style that will last you for years.

And the important thing – yet again – about ensuring that an item really is a wardrobe staple for you, is to make sure that it works for your style. It always surprises me that often people don't include their coat as part of their outfit. For me, it's often the place where I begin when I think about what to wear. Maybe it's because of my job, as I'm not at a desk all day and am out and about a lot. Even so, my love (obsession?) for coats began years and years ago, when I most

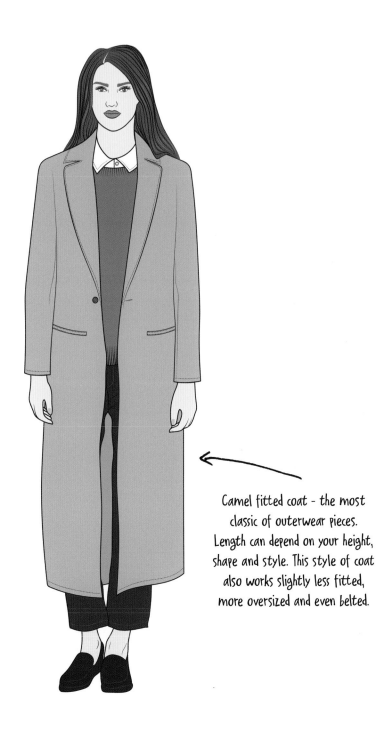

Camel fitted coat - the most classic of outerwear pieces. Length can depend on your height, shape and style. This style of coat also works slightly less fitted, more oversized and even belted.

definitely did have a desk job but was still utterly enamoured with how they could be the finishing touch to an outfit.

So, once you've decided on the neutral tone that will work best with the items in your wardrobe, it's down to style…

Tailored coat

Pretty much does what it says on the tin. A coat that is tailored. It can be calf-length, knee-length or longer; sometimes double-breasted, sometimes single. It doesn't have to be worn buttoned up to get the tailored look. The joy of these coats is that they are shaped and so do the work of being super flattering with absolutely no effort required.

The only other thing to think about is the proportion of your outfit with a tailored coat over the top. It makes sense to pair it with tailored clothes underneath to keep the simple-looking lines unified. Frills, flounces and lots of fabric should be kept to a minimum, (but style-wise if you choose a tailored coat, it's unlikely to be a problem). It doesn't necessarily have to be an incredibly structured outfit and it doesn't necessarily have to be 'smart'; a fluid silk shirt and flowing wide-leg trousers are the perfect foil, as they sit seamlessly underneath. Just as a pair of jeans, a tee and trainers can be the ideal weekend pairing with a classic tailored overcoat.

Fabric-wise, the most popular staple for your wardrobe is a wool, a wool style or a wool mix. Tweed or herringbone can also work as a basic neutral shade (even though they are actually patterns…oops).

Style-wise: Minimalist Elegance, Classic Chic, Androgynous Flair, Parisian Chic and Laid-Back LA can all channel a tailored coat, length depending on what works for their outfit.

Oversized coat

There is a theory that the more oversized pieces are really suited to people who are taller – and I would like to say it's more of a myth than a theory. I think the confusion comes when people assume that they'd be wearing the same size coat, when, as we discussed in the 'Dressing for your shape' chapter (see page 56), it's all about finding items in the size that works for your height. So when it comes to an oversized coat, while, yes, a BIG oversized coat will look fabulous on an oversized person, an oversized coat in petite proportions can look just as fabulous on a petite person. It also comes down to knowing your style and owning your look. If the rest of your outfit is perfectly attuned to the styling that works with an oversized coat, you will look simply fantastic.

The key to this style is in the title. Oversized: wide in body, often longer than you may wear in other styles and with wide arms (which, interestingly, don't have to be long and can, indeed, be slightly shorter, so long as they have the width – an almost three-quarter-length arm style really can work on an oversized coat and is certainly ideal for the more petite among us). Oversized coats lend themselves perfectly to a more grungey bohemian style, but can also have a perfect minimalist vibe that makes them classically elegant.

When it comes to fabric, again, there is a wool or wool-mix option for a classic long-lasting style. My personal favourite is double-faced wool. This is essentially a coat that is the same fabric on the outside as it is on the inside, hence, it's double faced (but not usually reversible, although never say never, as occasionally it is). To some, that just means it's a bit rubbish as it's unlined (which it is), but to me, it means the perfect coat is more wearable throughout the seasons. To counter the lack of warmth, layering, layering, layering is your friend.

Style-wise: Boho, Minimalist Elegance, Classic Chic, Eclectic Vintage, Androgynous Flair, Parisian Chic and Laid-Back LA can all very much adapt an oversized coat into their style – the look will depend on the outfit beneath and, of course, the footwear.

Peacoat or military

I should start by saying that they're not entirely the same thing, but the defining feature of both is the button detail. And often (not always, but often) there is a bit of epaulette action going on. Which makes them initially ideal for those who are looking to balance out their proportions at their shoulders, as an epaulette does an instant job of widening your frame and balances out wider hips. Having said that, they are alas trickier to wear if you're blessed with curves and if they're double-breasted, which is the main feature of a peacoat. They often also finish just below the hips, which, if that's where you're at your widest, you're not looking to draw attention to. 'Well, what the hell has she put this in here for?' I hear you cry.

Because a double-breasted peacoat can work perfectly for certain styles and for certain shapes. For those who are tall and thin and are looking to break up their height and add dimension with the fabric of an undone double-breasted coat. (The nature of a peacoat means that it's unusual for women to do them up, unless they have a very flat chest – that's definitely more of a masculine-style look. A very dapper one at that, but not one you often see women sporting.) Often they have an addition of gold buttons, which, again, are great for those who are tall and wanting to break up a mass of dark fabric.

However, a military coat can offer the perfect solution for those who like the soldier look. And it definitely adds an eclectic touch to an outfit.

Often military-style coats can also be single-breasted in style but with double buttons on each side of the opening, giving the illusion of a double-breasted coat without the extra fabric. They can be short or long, working for most shapes and styles.

Fabrics for peacoats and military coats can either be a classic wool or wool-style mix but they can also be in a heavy gabardine.

Style-wise: Minimalist Elegance, Classic Chic and Laid-Back LA look at the classic peacoat; Androgynous Flair, Eclectic Vintage, Parisian Chic and London Cool go for the military coat.

Trench

And, finally, my favourite classic coat of all time. The Trench. Interestingly, it's not necessarily the classic tailored trench that is my choice of poison. Instead, a fluid, flowing, long trench is the most ubiquitous coat in my wardrobe. Yes, there is the classic camel-coloured trench that we all immediately think of, but a black one can be just as useful.

Let's start with the trench that we all think of as being The Trench. A camel fitted-style 'mac', belted, sometimes double-breasted but you absolutely can get single-breasted too. Length-wise, there are variations on the theme and one to suit every height. They are the epitome of fashion for certain styles and can finish off a look with utter panache as well as being (often but not always) practical (as in, they're waterproof).

However, they're not always the most flattering shape to wear. They're not great at disguising lumps and bumps as the traditional fabric is often stiff and rather unforgiving, and especially brutal when double-breasted. One definitely for the straighter, slimmer figures, although they can be worn by both petite and tall, length depending.

Don't be disheartened if you're a rounder version of your former self (for a start, there's more of you to love). There is a trench that is made for you. It's a trench that works for everyone and it's, as I said, my absolute fave: the fluid, drapey version. There's obviously a downside in that they're rarely waterproof. Very much style over practical substance (although I do keep meaning to try the waterproof fabric spray but have been too scared of it not working and my coat being ruined, so I have just invested in a plethora of brollies – primarily as I seem to leave them everywhere, hence I *may* have more than one).

Length-wise, they can be long, they can also be short. It goes without saying that if you're more petite, a shorter version is probably going to be better. If you're tall, can I suggest spending time on hunting down as long a trench as you can find? It may well end up being your ultimate wardrobe staple.

For me, as with the double-faced coats, the joy of a trench is that they are practically all-year-round coats. So versatility-wise, they tick every box. There is an apparent downside of them not being the warmest of outerwear items, but layering is your friend. Which, because of the loose, drapey nature of the coat, is easy to achieve. You can layer to your heart's content as the looseness of the style allows you to.

Shape-wise, because of their fluidity, they are perfect for not accentuating things you don't want accentuated – the fabric drapes rather than clings. If you have a shapelier figure, the softness of the material allows you to belt the coat without having bunches of stiff fabric around your middle. Also, because of the versatility of the style and the nature of the fabric, they work to solve the coat dilemma of so many different outfits. Longer dresses and skirts, especially those of a voluminous nature, are ideal teamed with a fluid trench. Jeans, trouser- or skirt suits, any single trouser style I can think of – this coat just works. What you need to consider is whether or not it fits into your style.

Style-wise: Minimalist Elegance, Classic Chic, Androgynous Flair, Parisian Chic and London Cool look at the structured 'classic' trench. All styles work perfectly with the fluid trench.

The one pieces

LBD

The Little Black Dress. Except it doesn't have to be black. Or little. I call it a little black dress as the concept of an LBD is that it's the perfect dress in your wardrobe for all occasions: work, party, holiday. The dress that you reach for when you're going somewhere but have no idea what to wear. It could be an interview, it could be a dinner or lunch. The dress that makes you feel like the best version of yourself. The dress that you know no one is going to question. As, believe me, it doesn't matter how confident you are, there are always times when everyone has doubts and it's easy to have your self-assurance knocked by a stray glance or what you think is a funny look – regardless of how many bags of confidence you have brought with you. Those occasions when you need an extra OOMPH of courage require the most trusted and reliable LBD. It could be navy, charcoal or you could even go all Chris de Burgh and pick a red one. Or… it could be a print. I know. She bangs on about neutral basics and then she goes throwing in a red or a print number. But sometimes, when you're just wearing one thing, and it's a stand-alone piece, it works.

Style-wise: Every style has their version.

LBJ

Fear not if a dress isn't your thing. And here's the good news even if you are a dress fan. One of these can go into your pantry ALONG with the dress…it's a little black…JUMPSUIT!

Which isn't actually a thing at all but well it should be so let's make it one. A little black jumpsuit. As useful as any little black dress and the above rules also apply. It doesn't have to be black. It also doesn't have to be little (unless a playsuit, aka a shorty jumpsuit, is your thing in which case, knock yourself out, but I prefer a little/lot of knee coverage).

A jumpsuit is not only a completely viable option if you're not into your frocks, but it can also be another fabulous tool in your basics arsenal. So many options to suit all shapes and sizes and, so long as you choose one in the right fabric and by this I mean something with a little more fluidity in it (universally more flattering and versatile) as opposed to the stiffer, boilersuit-style options, they are the ultimate piece to dress up and down.

Style-wise: Knock yourself out with the jumpsuit for whichever style you are.

Footwear

And finally, possibly my favourite part of the book. The SECRET WEAPONS. I genuinely believe that footwear can be the ultimate key to adapting your style. Would I say that shoes are the most important pieces in any wardrobe? Well, I would certainly put up a good argument for the case, although you obviously need an outfit as well, as you can't 'just' wear something on your feet. But I could certainly convince you that they are AS important as the clothes you wear. They offer a versatility to your style and wardrobe that very few other items can. They can completely change the look of an outfit, hence the term secret weapons.

I know, earlier, I posed the question: how many coats are too many? When it comes to shoes, my inner Imelda Marcos comes screaming to the fore and the answer is: there are never too many. Luckily my inner Imelda isn't let out too often as, of course, there are too many. But there is definitely a case (and this would stand up in any fashion court) for having more styles of shoe than you would other things in your pantry staples.

Not only are shoes your secret weapons, they're magic too. They can transform a pumpkin pair of jeans into the most incredible stagecoach fit for a party. Cinderella is proof that a pair of shoes can change your life! They can make a dress that you bought to wear to a wedding work so much harder in your wardrobe by making it suitable to wear to the supermarket as well (simply add trainers). We talk about sustainability later (see page 222), but a set of pantry staples footwear adds a level of versatility to your wardrobe that means you'll be buying less but wearing it more.

I'm often asked what items you should invest in. It's such a difficult thing to answer as it's down to budget and style, and everyone's are different. But investing time in thinking about which style of shoes can add that diversity to your wardrobe and then ensuring that you find the right ones – that should be your priority. It's not about owning lots and lots of shoes, it's about owning the right ones for your style and your lifestyle. When it comes to dressing for your shape, there are small tips and tricks that you can adopt to make your footwear more flattering, but there's no doubting that it's easier to find a good selection of footwear to suit everyone than it is to find clothes.

Which is why I LOVE shoes. I have boots that, on first purchasing them, I *may* have loved more than a child (not really but for a nano-nanosecond...). Confession time now: I have been known to sleep with my new footwear purchase next to me on the floor so it would be the first thing I saw when I woke up in the morning to start my day feeling JOYOUS. Alas, a small chewing puppy put paid to that years ago (yes, tears were shed when she chewed the back of my vintage crackle-leather Stan Smiths that were unrescuable and no longer made).

But I digress, and I will try and stay focused in this chapter, as the danger of allowing me to extol the virtues of footwear is that we could end up with *War and Peace In Heels*.

I'm just going to fly quickly through the various footwear options – I will obviously have missed some out, but these are the main ones to consider as pantry staples. No list is ever truly exhaustive when it comes to fashion.

Shoes

Flats

Starting with flats as, let's face it, these are the most practical. While there are some people who don heels every day, I think it's fair to say that the majority of us spend most of our time in flat, or flattish, shoes. And there are flat shoes for everyone and for every style.

● **Trainers.** Yes, trainers. Once saved only for exercise and the daily uniform of an athlete (clearly why I didn't wear them for years), they are now the Shoe of the Masses. The trainer has gained cult status in recent years and although there are still workplaces that won't allow them, frankly, they're wrong. When I am Prime Minister, I will make it law that everyone is allowed to wear trainers (and that all dresses and skirts should have pockets). The thinking is that trainers can be too casual and too, basically, crap. And I get it. If you say trainers, you give licence to people to rock up in an old pair of beat-up runners that they've done the marathon in (or just jogged round the park out of breath with the dog, speaking for myself). But boots are a standard part of a smart dress code. And, using that reasoning, no one turns up in wellies, do they? So I would like to think that the majority of people would turn up in 'fit-for-purpose' trainers, yet of course there will always be the few that spoil it for the many.

I'm sure the time will come when there is a wide understanding of the difference between types of trainers but, until then, we can just continue to spread the trainer love. Because they ARE the most versatile shoe that you can have in your wardrobe, to make so much that was once unwearable as day wear, totally fair game. A floral maxi- or midi-dress that once you would only have been able to wear to Ascot, a wedding or a 'proper' party? Throw it on with trainers to make it day wear. The same applies to suits that once would only have been appropriate for work, a funeral or court. Put on a pair of trainers and hello dressed-down casual. There are other tweaks that you can also apply to the outfits: a denim jacket with the dress, a slogan tee in lieu of a blouse or shirt with the suit. But it's really the juxtaposition with trainers that makes the outfit work and deformalizes your once only formal clothes.

Different styles, of course, work for different people. Flatforms are ideal if you're more petite, and a chunky trainer can also add height. Plus there are lots of wide-fit options for those with a sturdier foot.

For the purposes of thinking about pantry staples, while, yes, there are jazz-hands trainers (not their official title but trainers with a bit of bling to them...), it's probably better to think about ones that are more versatile. Having said that...do you know what? I love shoes SO MUCH that I actually think a shoe that does make a bit more of a statement can be a neutral. So long as it fits in with your style. Things such as a subtle metallic (or any of your precious metals) or a pair of leopard-print trainers or hightops. A personal statement that stamps your style on an outfit.

Or there are my personal favourites: a classic white trainer. You can never, ever, ever go wrong. You don't have to spend a fortune and there is definitely a style to suit everyone.

Style-wise: Minimalist Elegance, Classic Chic, Androgynous Flair, Parisian Chic, Laid-Back LA and London Cool consider a classic white trainer of any style. Boho, Eclectic Vintage and Seventies Magic could go for a classic white trainer, but this is probably where you should let your trainer imagination loose...

● **Sandals.** Right, this is where I have to be careful as the temptation is for me to start writing and to never finish. Sandals. I love them (I will get to a style of shoe I'm not that enamoured with, I promise. Maybe. Hopefully...although realistically...probably not). And they are an utter necessity in the summer. As sun is to day and moon is to night, so sandals are to summer as boots are to winter. In fact, I know a lot of people who go straight from boots into sandals and back into boots again. Interestingly, here is where it does get tricky when you're thinking about sandals. Because there are simply so many options to choose from that it's very easy to start gathering oodles of them (put them DOWN Imelda…). The trick is to find the pair of sandals that works best for your style and your lifestyle. Again, we're lucky in that, when it comes to shape, there is a lot less to consider than with clothes (although, yes, sizing can still be an issue at either end of the scale, although there are more options from smaller businesses online than there ever were before). Of course, you don't necessarily have to have just one pair, but if you spend time thinking about your style, your lifestyle and what would work best with the majority of your outfits, you'll be buying fewer and wearing them more.

> **Chunky.** As there is generally more support in a chunkier sandal, they are ideal if you have a life that is rather active and involves a lot of moving around. That's not to say they're purely practical. While lots have an androgynous edge to them, there are more minimalist styles around. Or look for a jewel detail to add a more feminine vibe. They can have two straps, one strap, they can have buckles, they can have ankle straps, they can have toe posts (I do have a separate section to discuss them…read on…), they can have a back strap. The options are endless.

> **Greek-style.** Usually a flat-soled leather strappy sandal that can be as strappy or as minimalist as you can find. Generally in tan or black and often a more delicate sandal than its chunkier counterparts.

> **Toe-post.** I am going to throw in the classic flipflop here although it's classic only in its familiar, beachy nature. I wouldn't consider it a style classic, although there is no denying its place in our wardrobes on holiday. But there is, of course, the updated version of the flipflop. The leather version – a sturdier sister to the rubber beach fave. You can get jewelled versions, you can get metallic versions, you can get chunky versions, you can get ones with a little wedge. The only thing you have to answer is…to toe post or not to toe post?

Style-wise: There is a sandal for every style. And within the styles of sandals, there is a style for every style. It's down to what you find most comfortable and which you prefer.

● **Loafers.** And the first of the 'proper shoes', as my husband would call them. The thing is, though, in this day and age, for some people there is no need to wear a proper shoe. As bonkers as that sounds, it's true. Some people genuinely have no real reason to own a 'shoe'. But others are bona fide shoeaholics. Or just prefer a shoe to a trainer, a sandal or a boot.

And it could well be that loafers are your poison of choice. They can be chunky, they can be a penny loafer, they can be on the lighter side with a horsebit buckle across the top. They can even be a mule-style loafer for warmer months. They can be worn for work or for play. They work with trousers, jeans and even skirts for a preppy look.

Style-wise: Depending on the style of loafer, there is definitely one for everyone. Eclectic Vintage can obviously throw anything on; heeled loafers may work for Seventies Magic; and classic loafer styles really can add different vibes to different styles, depending on what they are dressed with.

● **Brogues.** Very similar style of shoe to the loafer in that it has a more androgynous feel to it, so can be worn in a smart, suitish kind of way, but, at the same time, it could be used as a juxtaposition to a more feminine, floaty dress or skirt to create a more eclectic and personal style. Alternatively, you may like the Mary Poppins, Mrs Trunchbull (sorry, she's perhaps not the best style icon for me to quote!), English traditional look: it can actually have a fabulous eclectic edge to it. The modern alternative to the brogue is a flatform brogue. These are the ideal option for those who want the casual look of a trainer but perhaps aren't allowed to wear them for work.

Style-wise: Classic Chic, Eclectic Vintage, London Cool and Androgynous Flair will all rock a brogue, depending on the style.

● **Ballet flats.** Like the previous two styles, these are definitely not for everyone, but if you love a ballet flat, you love a ballet flat. I can just look at a pair and I come over all Audrey Hepburn. There are variations on the theme as well. They're not necessarily an entirely delicate entity. You can get ones with a block heel, which are superb if you're not a fan of a totally flat shoe. There are also flatform versions, which offer height and a bit of weight – ideal, especially, if you are on the petite side. There are pointed versions, rounded versions and ones with ankle straps – the latter being excellent for the taller, lean-ankle brigade.

Style-wise: Minimalist Elegance, Classic Chic, Parisian Chic and Laid-Back LA.

● **Clogs and Mules.** These perhaps aren't the most typical shoes that you may think of as, well, they're only half a shoe. They're backless. But as they have a toe covering, by my reckoning, that makes them more of a shoe than a sandal. Can you tell I've spent rather too long thinking about this? And, yes, I am a RIOT at dinner parties! But back to the scintillating matter of clogs and mules. Up there with one of my favourite items of footwear. Admittedly, one pair of my mules is a flat loafer version (snuck that in there), but there is something about the hybrid nature of a shoe/sandal that I love the aesthetic of. As well as there being chunky, wooden-soled clog versions, there are also more delicate options: pointed flat mules in satin, suede or velvet, which can add a very feminine feel to a pair of jeans or are the perfect evening option should you not want to wear heels.

Style-wise: Because there are so many different options within the category, there is a mule to suit everyone, although a clog may be more suited to Boho, Eclectic Vintage, Seventies Magic and I'd also go Laid-Back LA.

Heels

Yet again, I could write for hours on the virtues and the simply gorgeousness of heels. But…when it comes to pantry staples, how many of us actually rely on heels to complete our everyday look? Which is the crux of what we're looking for here: those pieces that day in, day out can be the solution to wardrobe dilemmas, the reliable staple that you can always fall back on. So while I say not many of us rely on heels for everyday wear, there most definitely are some who do (perhaps the more petite among us), and many of us probably look to heels to transform our day clothes into…drum roll…our out clothes.

Yes, I can prove that heels are also secret weapons in your wardrobe. They're also your secret weapon to making great inroads in the sustainability stakes (more later in the book!). One of the main objectives of this book is to ensure we all wear more of what we actually own, as opposed to constantly buying new things for every occasion. A pair of heels (which can really stand the test of time) are the perfect tool in making sure you're optimising the clothes you love.

Heels also have the ability to add versatility to a humble pair of black trousers, a ditsy day dress or a pair of faithful jeans, giving them all a new life out in the evening. The list isn't exhaustive. I can go on and on and on; jumpsuits, leather skirts, even leather joggers, all can be remodelled into an evening, a smart lunch, even a wedding wardrobe with the addition of a pair of heels.

From court shoes, to heeled clogs, to strappy sandals, from mid-heels to stiletto heels, to high or low wedges: if you are a heel lover, there is a staple pair of heels for you out there. And we haven't even started to talk about heeled boots…

Style-wise: You can find a heel for every single style. The heel world is your oyster.

Boots

I should probably confess that, up there with coats, I have what I would term a weakness for boots (in hindsight, I do seem to have said this about pretty much every category so far…). My husband, in a non-charitable moment, may call it an addiction, but he's wrong as I definitely don't think I need help for it. I love boots. While I'm not that person who goes straight from boots to sandals (I may or may not also have a trainer fetish), I absolutely could be.

Like all other shoes, I think a pair of boots adds an instant personality to an outfit in a way that nothing else can. Not to mention that they are also PRACTICAL! What's not to love about that? OK, so they *can* be practical… And that makes them perfect as a pantry staple, something you can always fall back on. It needn't necessarily be a practical pair; it could also be that one pair of incredible boots that makes everything seem OK with the world when you wear them. Yes, I am writing that and thinking…hmmm some people may think that's far-fetched… but the reality is that when you have an important event at which you want to feel your very, very best, it sometimes takes a pair of awesome boots (or it could be shoes…) to give you that extra boost of confidence. It's finding the footwear that makes you feel like that – and it could well be a pair of boots.

Boots don't have to be practical, they don't have to be chunky or heavy. They can be dainty, they can be short, long, low-heeled, mid-heeled or high-heeled. There are some styles that make excellent wardrobe classics, and there are others that fit squarely into the category of wardrobe gems.

● **Ankle.** Possibly the most popular boot out there as there are simply so many different options to choose from. The key to finding one that you will get the most wear out of is, again, thinking about which clothes work for your lifestyle and matching a pair of boots to the style and set of basics that you've chosen. So it may be that you prefer a low Chelsea boot to wear with skinnies or with dresses; you may favour a kitten-heeled pointy boot, which would work with different types of trousers, skirts and dresses; or a classic side-zip block-heel almond-toed boot that offers versatility to team with a plethora of outfits. There are also the higher-heeled options: a block heel, a cone heel, a stiletto, of mid- or vertiginous heel height. Suede or leather, ideally in a neutral colour (although I think you could sneak in a 'neutral' leopard-print option…she says, thinking of a pair in her wardrobe that are her favourite go-to boots).

Style-wise: Choose your poison for your style.

● **Knee high.** The lesser-seen older sister of the ankle boot. A boot that comes in and out of 'fashion' in its many guises, but for some is always here to stay. A classic boot that can be flat or heeled, round-, almond-, square- or pointy-toed. The heel, as with its ankle boot equivalent, can be flat or high – cone shaped, stiletto, block or wedge. It can be knee high, or even over the knee – which is therefore not knee high but we'll just leave them in. And while we're here, let's chuck in a mid-calf pair as, to be fair, it does depend on how long your legs are as to where your knee-high boots hit. Whether it's a flat riding-boot style or a 1970s block-heel platform, you'll know if you're a fully paid-up member of the knee-high-boot fan club as these are the ones you'll reach for to finish off so many of your outfits. Over skinny jeans and leggings, under wide-leg jeans and trousers, and with all shapes of skirts and dresses.

Style-wise: Again, there are so many options to choose from that there absolutely is one that works for the style you're looking to emulate.

● **Cowboy.** Well howdy partner is what I bet you're thinking. OK, possibly not. You're more likely to be thinking: cowboy boots, a STAPLE? Surely they're squarely in the Eclectic Vintage category. They possibly could be. But the thing about cowboy boots, rather like the rest of their western outfit counterparts – the denim shirt and denim jacket – is they've sort of become a real staple in fashion folklore. They've made so many comebacks over the years, they've finally earned their right to stay. The one proviso I think it is fair to make with cowboy boots is that there is a risk of tipping over into costume territory if you wear them over blue denim jeans, and that may be not your intentional style move. The whiff of actual cowboy can easily be in the air with a combo of blue jeans tucked into cowboy boots, so, again, it's possibly better to think of a juxtaposition of styles. If costume territory does take your fancy, then *Little House on the Prairie* is a good a place to start with long ditsy floral or needlecord dresses and a pair of trusty cowboy boots. The more vintage-looking the better. Not a pair of boots for everyone but, for some, they are old faithfuls and they are here to stay.

Style-wise: Eclectic Vintage, London Cool, Seventies Magic, Boho.

● **Chunky practical.** I will admit the title of these bad boys doesn't sound the most appealing, but if you lead any sort of an outdoor life, chances are that in the winter, these are what you are wearing day in and day out. Just because they're practical doesn't mean that they have to be dull, boring or unattractive (although do remember that beauty is in the eye of the beholder). This is an area in particular where I find it joyous that fashion has become so inclusive. I remember the days when hiking boots were most definitely only sold in Millets camping shops and there was no option for a stylish, practical boot. Yet now, you can find a pair of designer hiking boots for four figures (I'm not sure you could do any proper hiking in them – not sure anyone has yet made it up Everest in a pair of chunky Guccis), and you can of course find a squidillion variations on the theme on the high street. There are now endless lace-up versions, Chelsea-boot versions, knee-high versions, fur-lined versions (imagine both practical AND warm – it's like boot Christmas).

The inclusion isn't just the acceptance of the style of boots as everyday fashion, it's also the diversity of the looks they can be worn with. Like trainers, they have become an acceptable style to wear with dresses, joggers, skirts and pretty much any style of trouser you choose to team them with. And that makes them a pretty darn useful wardrobe staple that you can go and walk the dog in, as well as wearing out to lunch. Because of our open-arm welcoming of new fashions and the long-awaited general acceptance of individual style, these relatively 'new' items to arrive in the fashion sphere are most definitely here to stay. So go forth and adopt them as one of your pantry staples, making sure you love the style and it works with your outfits.

Style-wise: Boho, Classic Chic (yes, even a Classic Chic can rock a pair of hiking boots for a dressed-down look), Eclectic Vintage, Androgynous Flair, London Cool and Laid-Back LA.

Hero ingredients

At last we've reached the end of the tome that is pantry staples, but before we move on to accessories, there is a special mention needed for your hero ingredients. Which are basically your wardrobe gems. These are what give you your internal superwoman cape.

While pantry staples give you the ability to rustle up a superb outfit that you feel fab in, no matter what the occasion, a hero ingredient is the icing on the cake. Like that special favourite ingredient you love to include in your meals. The one thing that always makes people ask, 'What's that flavour? It's amazing but I can't tell what it is.' It perhaps shouldn't work, but it does in the way you cook with it. And it's usually something people wouldn't normally add. Like anchovies, Marmite, a random spice or herb (I have a friend who throws tarragon into everything and even people who don't like aniseed love her cooking!), smoked honey, truffle oil, chorizo, liquorice – OK, I need to stop now as I'm just making myself hungry. It's not an accessory, it's an integral part of the outfit that elevates it to something that's unique to you but that simply makes the outfit.

And, more importantly, it's something that, when you wear it, makes you feel at your most fabulous and most confident. For some, it's one or two pieces: many people love having a more neutral wardrobe with lots of super-versatile things in it and the odd hero ingredient to spice it up. For others, it's the majority of their wardrobe.

The key to a true hero ingredient is that it's something, frankly, a bit bonkers. A bit jazz hands, and it most certainly doesn't work with everything. BUT the outfits that it does work with, it utterly transforms.

If you don't have a hero ingredient, to get your creative juices flowing, here are some ideas of what might constitute a wardrobe gem. Or it may help you to look at something in your wardrobe in a different light.

- **Trousers.** Rather than neutral, a fabulous print.

- **Skirt.** Simply so many options. Frills, any sort of print that you can possibly think of, sequins and even feathers.

- **Blouse and shirt.** Ruffles, frills, print,

print and more print. It could also be a sleeve detail or different shape. Or maybe an oversized collar. Something that makes your blouse or shirt that little bit more unique.

● **T-shirt.** Slightly more difficult to make a tee unique, but the most popular option is a logo or graphic design. On a personal note, I would like to add that they absolutely last the test of time and you can possibly never have too many. Especially if you have a daughter who is also partial to them/yours…Alternatively, a twist on a Breton: a striped tee in a more unorthodox colour combo.

● **Jumper.** Texture is a big definer here. Think mohair, an alpaca mix or a loose chunky knit. As bizarre as it sounds, a print jumper is also most definitely a thing: Fair Isle, argyle or an intarsia logo knit. There are also striped knits in a variety of colours.

● **Jacket.** Now here is where the fun begins. There are many people who keep the majority of their wardrobe neutral and go wild in the aisles with their outerwear. Jackets in lace, tartan or check; with sequins or extensive embroidery; brightly coloured; with incredible button, collar or sleeve detail; with full-on faux fur or any print that takes your fancy – floral, check, leopard or any other animal.

● **Coat.** As with jackets, it's really only your imagination and style constraints that are stopping you here (there are also the issues of budget and closet space). A coat that does the talking and that you love can be transformative to your confidence and make you feel fabulous. A maxi or cropped faux-fur coat in any colour or print, a leather trench, an embroidered frock coat, a suede 1970s number, check in any size and colourway – there really is no end to the level of coat awesomeness you could reach.

● **LBD.** Get rid of the L and the B and just focus on Dress here. If dresses are your jam, find a few that make your heart sing and make you look like a queen (not the Queen; although she is cool, you might want a frock with a little more pizzazz). And more importantly make you FEEL like a queen. A dress that embodies your personality or is the image of the person you know you want to be can work wonders for your confidence. It can be mini, midi or maxi. It can be straight or voluminous. The detailing can be in the colour, the print, the texture, the frills, the ruffles, the sleeves, the belt – there is really no end to the opportunities, and we certainly don't have time to dissect each and every one. Even though I'd love to. I know I said that I have a major obsession with coats and boots, and possibly something else I've conveniently neglected to remember or mention, but I may have a Minor obsession with dresses. Yes that is a capital M as it's sort of a major minor…as in basically just major. BUT that is because, as I said when I was talking about the beauty of an LBD, there is something about the ease of a dress, the comfort of a dress, the countless opportunities to dress a dress (!) up and down that make it such a great wardrobe gem. The key, as always, is to find one that suits your style and shape AND, as a hero ingredient, it must have that special *je ne sais quoi*.

● **LBJ.** As much as I always say an LBJ is pretty much the trouser version of an LBD, the reality is that it's harder to add jazz hands to a jumpsuit without morphing into…well, something you possibly won't want to morph into. Kids' TV presenter from the 1980s may be your vibe but it's definitely harder to find a jumpsuit that isn't a fabulous classic. They don't really make them, probably because they don't really work on the majority of people. That's NOT to say that if you find a print jumpsuit that you love and you look and feel great in, you shouldn't wear it. It's just that you might struggle to track one down. The secret to making a jumpsuit look great is in the accessories. Hold that thought for the next chapter (see page 174). Alternatively, a wardrobe staple LBJ could be crying out for a hero ingredient of the footwear variety…

● **Shoes.** I know I said it's coats and jackets that are the leaders in the hero ingredients, but shoes are chomping at their heels. Think every colour under the sun, think embellishment, different fabrics, different laces, embroidery or hand painting.

● **Heels.** The same goes for heels as for shoes: the rules are identical, as in there are no rules.

● **Boots.** Well guess what I'm going to say. Yup, no rules, think of the fun you've had with shoes and heels and then think about how much BIGGER boots are, and that gives you an idea of how much more EXTRA they can be. Like with jackets and coats, the rest of your outfit can be completely plain. These pantry staples can really work hard and you don't need a huge number of them. All the personality of your outfit, all the versatility in your wardrobe can be down to your footwear.

Nutritional information

Choose one from each main category;
from the subcategories you may choose a couple.

Bottoms
Trousers – Wide leg, full length or cropped ☐ Tapered, sometimes known as barrel or carrot ☐ Cargo or combat ☐ Joggers ☐ Leggings ☐ Jeans ☐ Dungarees ☐
Shorts – ☐
Skirts – Mini ☐ Midi ☐ Maxi ☐

Tops
Shirts/Blouses – White shirt ☐ Denim shirt ☐ Silk blouse ☐
T-shirts – V-neck ☐ Scoop neck ☐ Crew neck ☐ Boat neck ☐ Bardot ☐ Sleeveless ☐
Knits – V-neck ☐ Crew neck ☐ Polo neck ☐ Oversized ☐ Sleeveless ☐
Breton – ☐

Outerwear
Jackets – Blazer ☐ Leather ☐ Denim ☐
Coats – Tailored ☐ Oversized ☐ Peacoat or military ☐ Trench ☐

LBD
Little Black Dress (of any colour) ☐

LBJ
Little Black Jumpsuit (of any colour) ☐

Footwear
Shoes – Flats ☐ Trainers ☐ Sandals ☐ Loafers ☐ Brogues ☐ Ballet flats ☐ Clogs and mules ☐
Heels – ☐
Boots – ☐ Ankle ☐ Knee high ☐ Cowboy ☐ Chunky practical ☐

Hero ingredients
Wardrobe gems are the cherries on top of your pantry staples and the rest of your wardrobe. Statement pieces that bring your basics to life, be it a pair of print trousers, a full-on faux-fur coat, a pair of leopard-print shoes or boots, a sequin blazer, a print silk shirt.

Accessories

To many, I will be preaching to the converted. But there are also lots of others out there, I am fully aware, who just can't quite get to grips with accessories. Don't get me wrong, I know that many of you love them on someone else, but can't get their head around how to accessorize themselves.

'I feel ridiculous.'
'They just don't work on me.'
'I don't know where to start.'
'I can't see the point.'

And some may not even realize that often what makes an outfit are the accessories. You don't realize it because they just appear to be a generic part of the look.

The best way I have of describing the importance of accessories, to hopefully give you a better idea of their function, is to think of a burger. How do you elevate the humble burger into a gourmet extravaganza? You accessorize.

Yes, I am obsessed with burgers (for the record) and I've never shared this analogy with anyone (who's a meat eater, although I do throw in some vegan analogies as well) without them ending up hungry, so I apologize right now.

The basics of your burger are the patty and the bun (yes, my kids do watch too much *SpongeBob* and so the meat or veggie middle will forever be a patty). Be that veggie, vegan, beef or chicken (and be your bun bread or the gluten-free version). Once you've NAILED the basics, it's time to think how to pimp that burger.

This is the same as finding your perfect wardrobe basics (or pantry staples), whether that's the perfect jeans and tee, your ideal trousers and a silk shirt, or the black/navy/khaki perfect dress. As an outfit it works on its own. And there will be times when that absolutely suffices.

As does, occasionally, just a plain little burger. As my mother-in-law always says when she visits a very famous burger place where you may happen to park under some golden arches...' There are times when all you want are two little plain burgers. You forget how great they are.' (Don't ask me why one isn't enough, it's always two; her excuse is that she doesn't eat chips and she's sticking with it.) But other times you fancy a cheeseburger. Or maybe it's a cheeseburger with bacon, tomato and lettuce. Change it up at the weekend for gruyère, BBQ sauce and onion rings.

Accessories offer you the same level of versatility in your outfits that a fridge full of condiments and other such goodies offer a burger. They also add completely different flavours to your outfits, just as changing up the add-ons in a burger can elevate a basic cheeseburger to a slap-up feast. Or go quirky – beetroot with pineapple and/or egg anyone? (Apparently a Kiwi tradition, but I am yet to be convinced enough to try it.)

And, in a nutshell, you have the joy of the accessory. You can create unlimited new versions of outfits just by changing what you add to your building blocks. You can make them completely personal – what works for one person, won't necessarily work for another.

Your accessories are the secret weapons that add versatility to your wardrobe, bring longevity to your clothes and breathe new life into your pantry staples that you may well have got that little bit bored of. As I always say with clothes, there is no need to throw the

baby out with the bathwater. If you have items in your wardrobe that still fit and still have life in them, you WILL be able to reinvent them (and I tell you how to spot these later in the 'Wardrobe detox' chapter, see page 196).

The one thing we possibly need to discuss before we crack on to what accessories we could be thinking about is 'how much?' – not as in ££ but as in how far down the 'do we want to look like a decorated Christmas Tree?' route we should venture. Well, therein lies the joy of already having worked out what style look you're aiming to emulate. Who you think of when you look at an item of clothing and think 'would *insert style icon* wear that?'.

Some may quote Coco Chanel, who said, 'Before you leave the house, look in the mirror and take at least one thing off.' I love Chanel's approach to fashion, but I can't quite get to grips with this for the normal person. For a start, I don't know about you, but it would make me three hours late for anything and everything. 'Take what off? Why? What's wrong with it? What do I take off?' And from a practical point of view, it could well mean 'but then I'll be cold'.

I MUCH prefer Iris Apfel's quote: 'Coco Chanel said take one thing off. I always said put another one on.'

Now this won't work for everyone. And it needn't work for you all of the time. Think of accessories as being armour.

You can add as little or as much as you need. They're a great way of expressing personality (as ridiculous as that sounds writing it down; it is a hideous fashiony thing to say but it is true). Even more than that, they're a superb confidence builder.

They can also act as the most fabulous distraction. Spot on your forehead? Bright red lipstick to distract the eye. Don't want to draw attention to the breasts that you've been blessed with? Large earrings to lead the eye away from them. Same with necklaces: some who are larger of bust love a long necklace and that can be great if you're more petite and want to create a lengthening look. But it can also draw the eye to where you don't want people to focus, whereas a higher, larger necklace that falls on your breastbone will be the first thing that people see.

As to knowing what works for you, well again, it's back to what we practised with colour. If there's something you're not used to wearing, the first time you see yourself in the mirror it will look strange. But it's because you're not used to it. It's like when you first get a new haircut and think 'who even is that?' when you look in the mirror. You need to get used to something new – and you also need to get used to other people remarking that it's different. The more you get used to it, the more you will like it, the more confident you will feel and the more confident you will look.

Of course, there are always exceptions to that rule. There are times when you try things, think you're not sure, leave them on for a day and conclude that they are absolutely not for you and you feel like a wally. THAT IS OK! The world did not fall off its axis and there will be an alternative that works for you.

I will say, though, that the more preparation you do, the more you think about the style that will work for you and the lifestyle that you have, the fewer mistakes you will make.

But for starters, let's think about what accessories you should be thinking about and how they can work. I'm going to start with inside ones, as in ones that you wear all the time, inside and out; and then outside ones (unless you carry your handbag or wear a large scarf inside all the time, in which case, feel free to ignore me being didactic on where they should be worn).

Jewellery

This may sound like an obvious one but jewellery is one of those things that people often don't even see. Especially if someone wears it all the time – you can take it for granted as you would, say, eyebrows (and let me tell you, anyone over the age of 45 knows NOT to take eyebrows for granted).

You only realize how important eyebrows are to your face when you look in the mirror and see yourself looking back with a smattering of amputated spiders' legs where there once were eyebrows. (It virtually happens overnight. I fear they actually migrate to under your chin – essentially the icing on the ageing cake.) Likewise with jewellery. You see someone without their jewellery and you recognize how integral it is to their 'look'. And you can change up your look depending on the size, style and volume of jewellery that you wear.

I also think jewellery is the easiest way to create a signature look. This may or may not be something that you are interested in, but I do think there is something quite – hmmm, how to say this without sounding like a fashion wally? – sophisticated (hides behind hands cringing but it's the best I can come up with) about having a 'signature look'. And actually, it's not cringe. The writing down of it may be, but in reality

this is how style is created. Personal style. Something that people associate with you – in a good way. If baggy, stained joggers are currently the signature look you're rocking and the image people associate with you, the simplest way to change that is to come up with a stylish, easy-to-wear alternative and jewellery could well be your answer (and maybe a clean pair of joggers that fit).

At the same time as offering an aesthetic addition to your look, jewellery also puts your own personal stamp on the style you're creating. Whether that be a necklace you always wear, a bracelet or earrings, or a combo of all three. For me, the main pieces that I never take off are a large silver cuff – when I bought it, I did contemplate two, but on each wrist there was more than a hint of Wonder Woman about it and, despite the sentiment being there, the reality was I just looked like I was missing the rest of the costume. So one cuff it is. Plus two necklaces: a large silver bean that I had worn for 24 years until I lost it and my husband found a vintage one the same for Christmas last year (he's a keeper) and a small gold bean of the same style. These you will find me wearing every single day. I sleep in the necklaces (no, mysteriously they don't get tangled up. I am asked this ALL the time and it appears that when God was giving out gifts, mine was the ability to wear two necklaces at the same time and not have them tangle. Others got the ability to run a sub-10-second 100m. I got the necklace thing. Not bitter at all...), but the cuff goes on religiously every morning.

That's not to say you need to keep your selection of jewellery all the same all of the time. Less when it's needed but more when required – mood, outfit and occasion depending.

Earrings can be a game changer. Either subtle and discreet with some diamond (diamanté does the job too) studs; thin hoops offer a slightly more statement solution; and full-on oversized ornate numbers can do the style talking for you. All can be interchanged with a plain outfit to create very different looks.

My personal favourites are the arm candy. As I said previously in the shape section (see page 67), for me, this is my armour for disguising long arms and sleeves that may be a tad on the short side. I never take my perfect-for-this-very-reason, large Wonder Woman cuff off (and obviously I like to think of myself always as Wonder Woman, or at least

that's what I say to my kids and, no, they don't think it's funny either), but I do change up the bracelets on my other arm. A collection of stacked bracelets, a chunky watch or a statement cuff can work wonders in making arms look less orangutan-esque, filling in the empty wrist left by a jumper sleeve that isn't quite long enough.

Necklaces come a very close second, though. Yes I love my two that I wear all the time, which sit just on and below my collarbone, but I usually wear a choker as well. Another shape-saving trick I use: being tall and having a very long neck, when I wore my hair up, I always felt like I was morphing into giraffe mode (not an actual thing – I just felt like my neck was abnormally long). By layering necklaces to hide flesh, similar to the arm-candy ruse, it makes me feel less exposed.

Doesn't have to be delicate and high though. Large, statement necklaces can be superb for transforming the plainest of outfits into something event worthy. Different styles and different colours offer total versatility: a collection of necklaces is something that will always serve you well. Plus, what goes around comes round. We'll see this in the wardrobe edit (see page 196), but it's always worth hanging on to them once you've bought them.

Belts

Another area where you can keep it completely classic or go utterly wild in the aisles. If keeping it classic, I think a must-have belt in everyone's wardrobe is (depending on the colour palette you mostly wear) a plain leather belt to work with jeans or trousers. This, to me, is like butter in a sandwich. And if you don't like butter, then mayo, marg or anything else moist. I always remember my Nana's friend saying, after being given a sandwich without butter by my mum, who was trying to cut down on Nana's cholesterol – way back in the day – 'Blimey, Jill, nowt moist in here?' Is a sandwich without butter actually a sandwich? It just doesn't work.

There's obviously no need to wear one all the time if you're wearing a jumper or loose shirt over the top of your jeans/trousers (unless, of course, for practical reasons, which is what a belt is primarily there for – no one needs to see half an arse when someone gets up and their trousers don't). But if the waistband is on show, then I always think a belt is the perfect finishing touch to an outfit. As with the butter in the sandwich, some people prefer it without, but to the majority, without it, there's just something a bit off. You can keep it as plain or as jazz hands as you like. Again, think about your style icon. What would they wear? What would work for the look you're trying to achieve?

Are you going to team it with a white shirt and jeans? A simple black fitted knit and kick-flare trousers? Or a logo tee and loose jeans? Boyfriend jeans, silk blouse and a sequin jacket? Your outfit will dictate the kind of belt you can play with. Plain, pared back and simply elegant? Or a stud or two on the belt with a slightly more bling buckle to release your inner rock chick?

Alternatively, it can transform a set of pantry staples. A plain white tee and jeans can look very sophisticated with a plain belt, but a studded belt automatically gives it an edgier vibe. Just one example of how interchanging the same accessory in a different style can transform the look of your building blocks.

The other gift that belts bring to your wardrobe is to completely change the shape of an outfit. Namely dresses, but they do also work over coats (at this point, I will just say thin coats...if you start belting anything with a bit of bulk to it, unless you're a Victoria's Secret model, even the most slender of normal people will most likely have a hint of the Michelin Man about them).

But a belt with a dress? Ideal for adding both a waist and sartorial elegance. A belt can completely transform the look of a dress. From a loose smocked look to a nipped-in-at-the-waist look, be the dress long or short. Even if a dress already goes in at the waist, a belt can be – going back to the butter analogy – just the finisher the outfit needs. If you're tall, it can be great for breaking up the line of a print or block colour, so seeming to reduce your height; if you're on the petite side, go for a belt in a similar tone to the colour or pattern of the dress to continue the seamless, lengthening look.

The other thing to add is NEVER throw a belt away. As with jewellery, these bad boys come around again. In my wardrobe, the oldest things I own are necklaces and belts.

Glasses

Just to touch on these, as if you don't wear them there isn't a lot you can do to add them in as an accessory (OK, you could go all non-prescription, just-glass look – an option. A slightly random one, but an option). And most people only have one pair, so it's tricky to change up your look with a selection. The idea is to try and nail the look that you want to achieve most of the time.

Your choice of frame comes down to whether you're happy making more of a statement with a larger, more prominent frame with a thicker rim, or prefer a subtler, less obvious vibe, with a smaller, lighter-rimmed frame, perhaps metal. It also depends on your face size, BUT I would say that having spent a lot of time waxing lyrical with my optician, who designs his own range of glasses, if you like the statement look and are petite of face, it is still possible to achieve it. Again, it comes down to that word we are all going to love and embrace by the end of this book: CONFIDENCE.

Glasses, for those of us who have to wear them, are such a huge part of our look. I genuinely think we should see them as an opportunity to have fun. Think of them as an extension of your style, the chance to showcase your personality and your look, be that traditional or modern, minimalist or maximalist, elegant or electic.

In this day and age, truly anything does go. The rules, as I always say, have been ripped up and it's possible to create your own look, defying the old idioms that we used to be slaves to and just owning what we wear.

Make-Up

No, I haven't lost my mind here: make-up can be the perfect accessory and is such a simple way to completely change your look.

The easiest way to imagine this is with good old lipstick. A red lip (or any other bold shade that takes your fancy – a definite variation on the theme that works for you is totally fine). Is it the easiest thing to wear though? Well… I would have said no for years. I was not a bold lipstick person. I was all about the eyes. Club-level smoky eyes for a daytime look but with a verging-on-nude lip. This was very much my signature look.

It's ridiculously easy to create and own a 'signature look' that works as part of your style with minimal make-up. (To be honest in my headier, younger years it was more about not having removed the make-up the night before which made for the perfect smoky eye… a look that stemmed from pure laziness. I promise that I do now apply fresh make-up every morning. I have learnt my lesson!). And talking of signature styles, the same can be said for donning lipstick. I have friends who rock the red-lippie look and I have always been hugely envious. It's such a glamorous look and can transform a plain black outfit (as anyone who remembers the video of Robert Palmer's 'Addicted to

Love' will testify. Anyone brought up in the 1980s has surely had a moment when they thought, 'that's so how I want to look when I get older'. For at least three seconds anyway!).

But then came lockdown, and it was the perfect time to start experimenting with lipsticks. Obviously not when wearing a mask…but the Zoom calls, Microsoft Teams, being online and visible from the waist up really changed how many of us did our make-up. Could you really be bothered with an entire face full of slap just for an hour's meeting when you weren't going anywhere afterwards (and you were probably sporting your jama bottoms and slippers anyway). Suddenly, it was the perfect time to embrace The Lip. The quickest route to an instant level of 'dressed up' was to chuck on some mascara, eyebrows (the need to now apply – an absolute necessity as previously mentioned) and a bolder lip.

As with everything, this does take some getting used to. Funnily enough, when I put on a red lip and looked in the mirror, it wasn't a babe from the Robert Palmer video looking back at me, it was a much older, wrinklier version with exceptionally grey roots and split ends. BUT...but, but, but. With all these things, it's the initial shock at seeing something so different that so often puts us off making a change. It's the expectation we have in our heads that often doesn't match up to reality that makes us stay in our comfort zone and not branch out and grow.

And we're back to that old gem: confidence. You need to try something on for size and then live in it a bit for comfort. This pretty much works for everything and, in that, we can include lipstick. Especially a bright lip that you're not used to. A bold lipstick can be a game changer when it comes to outfits. I would get yourself used to it first before you let yourself loose on the rest of the world. Walk around the house in it, experiment with different make-up (especially on your eyes and with different shades of blush) and try it out with different outfits. And keep looking at yourself in the mirror to get used to it. There are many shades of red (in fact, many shades of bold lipsticks – you may be more of a coral or a wine girl), so it can take time to find one that works for you. I have found trial and error the simplest way to find a good lippie. And then I pray I don't lose the one that's my current favourite (only me?).

A plain tee and jeans (as with a belt) can be given a whole new lease of life with a bold red lippie applied – think of it as adding lobster to your plain burger for a bit of surf and turf.

Referring back to your armour and having a red lipstick as your secret weapon – have you ever looked at someone with red lipstick and not automatically assumed they were super confident? The more you feel it, the more you will BE IT!

Scarves

Our neat segue from the indoor clothing to the outside outfit finishers, scarves cross the boundary between the two: some you can wear inside, others are very much for completing a look when you leave the house.

Indoor scarves (as they're not really known but that title sort of works for now) are ones that you wear inside (see?). Obviously we're not talking chunky woolly numbers here but finer knit or silk versions. The classic silk scarf seems like the obvious choice but in the past few years it's fallen out of favour. Yes I know that I'm always banging on about anything goes these days, and I stand by that. I'm not saying that there isn't an occasion when a silk scarf tied round the neck is a good look, it's just a trickier style to pull off without giving off an air-hostess vibe. Actually we're not allowed to call them that any more, are we…flight attendants? Either way, it's a very specific look that, when we think of style icons, isn't one that necessarily springs to mind. But if you have a collection of silk scarves that you love and have been accumulating for years, OF COURSE you can wear them tied round your neck if that's the look you love. But there are some other great options too.

If you do want to wear a scarf round your neck, rather than tying it in a knot, how about rolling it (I am a huge fan of rolling silk scarves!) and wearing it like a choker? Very 1970s elegant.

Providing it's long enough, it's ideal worn rolled up as a belt too. Granted, it's not going to be the most practical if you rely solely on your belt to keep everyone from having a grandstand view of your pants, but, for aesthetic purposes, a scarf fashioned into a belt can add both print and colour to an outfit.

Shorter scarves can similarly be rolled up and tied round your wrist. Who says arm candy needs to be of the metal variety? A bracelet-style scarf can, indeed, like its larger sister the belt scarf, be the perfect addition to elevate a plain outfit into something a bit more interesting. From experience, before you lose your shizzle, do rope someone else in to help you knot it round your wrist. Been there, done that, used all the swear words.

Rolled up and worn as a headband in the summer for a chic 1970s vibe, a scarf can be both a great accessory to a look and also functional, especially on those warmer days when you don't want to be festooned with jewellery or lashings of lippie. On the beach with a cossie (and sunnies – see page 188), a scarf worn as a headband also works as a fabulous distraction. Not that I give two rooting tooting hoots what anyone thinks about me in a swimsuit. There is no denying that I am a lover of life and not necessarily of exercise, and so drawing the eye UP to a gorgeous headband and a huge pair of sunnies is never an unwelcome means of distraction.

Or wear it as a headscarf...OK, think more Grace Kelly than the Queen... no knotting under the chin please! But worn to cover the hair and tied at the back. Ideal for summer looks and for adding instant interest to an outfit, as well as offering up a practical answer to not having washed your hair while also protecting it from the sun. For me, the not-having-washed-your-hair solution is the clincher there (spot the lazy person...).

And from the beach to chillier climes. Moving neatly on to outdoor accessories. As in, those that you wear when you go outdoors.

I wanted first to cover the accessories that complete an outfit, which you will always be wearing. It's all well and good to spend lots of time thinking about a thick scarf, a hat and a handbag, but when you're indoors, you don't – necessarily

(not arguing with anyone who might; hats off to you, or not as the case may be) – wear those things and, if you rely on them as your only accessories, when you take them off, it can be the equivalent of feeling slightly naked. Believe me, when you get on board the accessories express, NOT having any on will feel very strange indeed! So we're covered (literally) for the indoors, and now it's time to consider those that can finish off our outfit when we leave the house.

Scarves yes. But this time the thicker version and the level of chunkiness is completely up to you. Ramp them up for full-on chilly walks, while finer knit versions are great for bringing colour and/or print to an outfit without adding bulk. However, the question I am asked all the time – the thorniest of thorns in the garden of accessory roses – is how to tie them. Look no further. The main thing you really need to remember is to HOLD BY THE CORNER! That's it. This works for large rectangle and square scarves of any fabric.

For a longer, thinner scarf – think Doctor Who – tie once around neck with both ends hanging down and then knot again if not too chunky; same with a super-thick, longer, narrower scarf. Or you can throw the ends over your shoulders...I'm sure Ali MacGraw used to wear long woolly scarves and sashay around New York in the 1970s in the snow with her scarf tails flowing behind her. Although I have had a look and can't find confirmation so that may well have been a dream. But a good dream – we can channel that look.

And, finally, the silk scarf has an outdoor use as well. Not on you per se

Scarf-tying masterclass

1. Hold your scarf up by corner (A) above your head, with the rest of the scarf hanging down in front of your body. Hold corner (B) next to your waist.
2. Move corner (A) behind your neck and down by your waist. Keep it parallel with the side hanging down by waist.
3. Keeping corner (A) still by your waist, loop the side with corner (B) in front of your neck and around the back of your head.
4. Loop the scarf back down in front of you so the two corners (A & B) are both in front of your body.
5. Either leave the ends loose, or tie in a knot and ruffle the bulk of the scarf fabric to create the look you want. You may prefer a looser look that gathers on your chest, or a neater, tighter scarf up around your neck. Just play and practise with it.

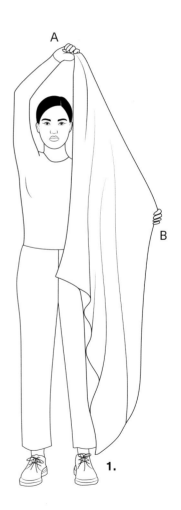

but on an accessory (coming up soon – see page 190): your bag. Accessory ON Accessory. Both large or small silk scarves, depending on the size of your bag handles, can be used as decoration around said handles. Very Hermès indeed, except it matters not a jot if neither bag nor scarf are of that brand (mine most definitely aren't). Wrapped around the handles or tied loosely, both are great options, especially if your outfit and your bag are of the neutral variety. Also works a dream in the summer around a basket handle and is then handily there should you need it to double up as a headscarf. It's all in the versatility.

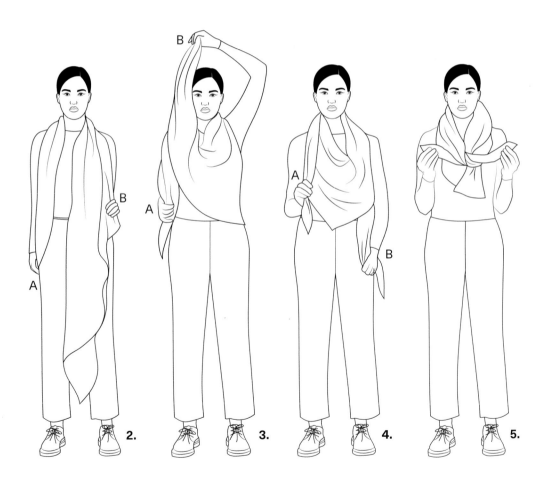

Sunglasses

Oh how I love a pair of sunglasses. And mine are most definitely not only for the summertime. Oh no, I am a massive all-year-round sunnies advocate. In my justification of wearing sunglasses during the winter months (I am aware that I can look like a tit but, I like to think, a stylish tit...), I have very pale eyes that water in any vaguely bright light – so sunnies are a must. That is my excuse and I shall be sticking to it.

Due to my obsession with sunglasses, it may come as no surprise that I have many. Admittedly, part of this is down to the fact that I lose them on a very regular basis. Lose as in 'screaming at the rest of my family when I'm in a rush and can't find them when they're actually in the car/on my head/in my handbag' lose. So not actually lost. Hence, I have a few pairs.

In my defence, I will also state that I think they are THE most useful outdoor accessory there is. Very few people don't actually look better in sunnies. Bold statement, I appreciate, as lots of people have utterly gorgeous eyes, but there is something about the mystery behind the lenses, the elegance, the sophistication, that adds that *je ne sais quoi*.

And with myriad specs in your accessories repertoire, you can ensure you have one to suit every occasion.

Going for the 1970s vibe? Simply cement the look with a pair of glasses that you could have kept since the great decade itself. Oversized, statement versions are the ultimate finishing touch, so much so that the rest of your outfit can really be an understated nod to the theme (we're not looking for fancy dress here – I hear you at the back!). Alternatively, for a pared-back Parisian Chic look, keep your outfit simple and top with a pair of dark but bold frames to suit the style of your face.

There absolutely is a pair of sunnies for every style, every face shape and every occasion.

Hats

You have two choices when it comes to hats: the practical and the aesthetically sartorial...although, of course, the two are not mutually exclusive.

A fabulous woolly hat for cold days is obviously a must and, yes, they can be purely practical, but over the years (and, yes, another item that stands the test of fashion time: a cosy beanie will never not be useful or not worn) I have collected quite a colourful stash. Some neutral ones for those pared-back days when I want to be tonal, but I also have some fabulous full-on colour numbers to make those cold winter days just that little bit more cheery. I admit, I am also very partial to a fingerless glove (obviously a pair, as I am fortunate enough to have two hands). I haven't listed gloves as an accessory, even though they clearly are, mainly because we have a lot to get through and they do tend to be more practical than an outfit changer.

But a hat, oh how I love a head covering. Just like a scarf headband, it's also super useful for those days when washing your hair feels like a step too far (we've all had them and if you haven't, frankly, I'm not sure this book is for you as you have your life SORTED).

We can now move on to the hats that complete a look. That are as integral to the finished outfit as a necklace or a belt. Think beret, think fedora, think large, floppy, summer straw number – yes these bad boys work all year round and can really lift an outfit.

Again, as with anything, it does take a degree of confidence to pull off a hat, but until you actually leave the house in one you're never going to know if it works for you or not. My advice would be, as it always is: if you love it, WEAR IT! I would also ask you: how many times have you seen someone in a hat and thought they look super cool? They may well have been having the same hesitations as you, but you'd never know. As no one will know if you wear your hat with a smile (and other clothes, obviously – I am no advocate of JUST a hat and a smile, regardless of what Joe Cocker says. Leave your hat on, yes, but also the rest of the outfit...).

Bags

Finishing with my favourite accessory of all time. I may have said previously that one of the others is my ultimate fave, but I was telling white lies as there is nothing that I love more than a bag. Well, obviously my kids and husband. Obviously. Sometimes at the very least...because there is nothing that fills my heart with joy like a new bag. Or even using a bag that I love and have had for years.

A bag is so much more than an accessory to me (and to many – I am not alone in what could well appear to be utterly barmy rhetoric), it's like finding a best friend. OK, to be fair, typing that does make me sound like a raging lunatic but...well, there is just something about a bag that makes it feel like part of the family and not just part of the wardrobe.

I see a bag maybe as an extension of me, which essentially is what personal style is – and, yes, that does include accessories and bags. Maybe it's because as well as being an aesthetic addition to an outfit, a bag, for most women, contains our lives. It contains our past (with the exception of the neat freaks among us, who don't have an old receipt or an old lippie secreted somewhere in the depths of our handbag) and our entire present. From keys, to a phone, to make-up, to poo bags (for the dog, obvs), to a purse, it's the vessel that contains everything that we need to function. Which is perhaps why I feel so strongly about it and so incredibly attached to mine.

And that's why you can really put a lot of thought into your bag. Cost per wear, it is also a great investment. You use it pretty much every day; regardless of the weather or your outfit, you ALWAYS need to carry your handbag with you, and they last for years. Most are classics. There are trends in bags but, as a rule, they are pretty timeless. And they ALWAYS fit, no matter what shape you are!

Because of their longevity, it's also OK to build up a little collection (she says, justifying her own not-so-little stash). Of course, there is the option of a classic neutral that goes with every outfit, but there are also print and colour options to raise your outfit game when needed. Once you've decided on the colours that you know work for you in your wardrobe, a matching or contrasting bag can really cement a look. Alternatively there is always – one of my all-time favourites – the leopard bag. I confess to having more than a couple of these. As with clothing, a leopard print works as the most perfect neutral. Other animal prints are available, depending on your taste, and, as laid out in the print chapter (see page 112), will work with anything you put them with.

Style-wise: The world is your oyster, depending on the style avenue you've chosen to go down. AND you don't necessarily have to stick to one option. If you do, however, the plainer and the more pared back (think minimum hardware and a very neutral tone and style), the more versatile the bag will be and the more outfits it will complement.

'I have too many handbags' said no woman ever. If you love them, you will always use them (and if you don't, your daughters, mother, sisters or friends, will).

Nutritional information

Accessories are the ultimate outfit maker.

Jewellery
Statement earrings, bracelets, cuffs, and layered or ornate bracelets.

Belts
From classic plain leather to a full-on Liberace-style buckle number, a belt can transform a plain pair of jeans. Consider elasticated-waist belts and vintage leather belts.

Glasses
Subtle or statement, there is a style to work with your style.

Make-up
The quickest weapon in your arsenal to go to battle in. One lipstick can change a whole look.

Scarves
For indoors or outdoors. Silk scarves are multi-purpose as a neck scarf but also as a headband or bag/wrist accessory. Functional oversized wool ones work wonders to complete your look in the autumn and winter.

Sunglasses
You can change your whole look with a pair of sunnies. Elton John can be your spirit animal. Never be knowingly under-accessorized on the sunglasses front.

Hats
From summer straw numbers to practical winter woollies.

Bags
Cost per wear, the best investment to perfectly finish an outfit.

Accessories stand the test of time. You will never regret keeping accessories that makes your heart sing, as the smallest additions to an outfit can make the biggest impact. They are the ultimate weapons in your fashion arsenal.

3
Method

Wardrobe detox

In this chapter we will start the practical method of your fashion journey. The first place to start isn't in a shop, it's in your wardrobe.

By this point in the book, we've got to grips with our situation and our lifestyle; questioned the root cause of how we feel about ourselves at the moment and what we need from our style; and we've narrowed down how it is that we would love to look as we have found our inner style icon (or icons...we are allowed more than one). And we've worked out how to dress for our shape.

You know how you want to look, you know what you need to have in your wardrobe to be able to wake up every day and put on an outfit you love and feel great in. That you feel confident in. That is you.

Keeping all that in mind and knowing how rewarding the end goal actually is, it's time to move on to the next stage. The practical part. The Method. How do we find and put together the ingredients of our stylish new identity? You may think that the first step would be hot-footing it down to the shops to buy a whole host of lovely new things to wear,

but back up your truck there. We have some work to do at home first.

Because you already have clothes. And while you may think that they're a significant contributor to the malaise you currently find yourself in, please don't tar every item in your wardrobe with the same brush.

It's time for the wardrobe detox.

It's a common phenomenon that too many of us wear 20 per cent of our wardrobe 80 per cent of the time. What did the other 80 per cent of your wardrobe ever do to you? Why isn't it getting any loving? Are you sure there aren't any gems in there that you can wear? And if not, WHY are you holding on to it all?

The thinking behind a wardrobe detox is that there isn't a person among us who doesn't have a whole load of tat in their closets that they haven't worn for years. Actually, I take that back. I'm sure there are many among us who have wardrobes fit for an Instagram #wardrobegoals tag, who regularly declutter, who worship at the temple of Marie Kondo and who never have anything in their wardrobe that doesn't fit, work, need ironing/dry cleaning or mending, or that they hate. If you are one of those people, go forth and relish in your tidy, organized life as this chapter will simply be teaching you how to suck eggs (and know that the rest of us hate you ever such a teensy-tiny bit – of course, not really, we're just green with envy...).

If, perhaps, you are more like me and not one of those super-tidy people who have a spreadsheet of their wardrobe contents (and, believe me, I have come across people who do...), you categorically WILL have things in there that still work for you. I don't care if they're 20 years old or they're still sitting in the corner in the carrier bag with their tags on (we've all been there...), now is the time to have a serious conversation with your whole wardrobe. NOT just the pieces that you've been wearing and those other offending items that you think you don't like. Your WHOLE wardrobe.

Because, as obvious as it sounds, if you want to be able to get dressed in the morning with no fuss, no bother; if you want to love the outfit that you've put on and feel utterly superb in it; if you want to easily be able to select a get-up for every occasion without having to resort to a panic smash-and-grab on the way home from work (we all know how successful those can be...said no one ever), then you need to know that everything in your wardrobe has a purpose.

Before we start on how you get there, I'm going to introduce you to the Rule of Three. OK, so as I explain later, these aren't rules per se...they're guidelines. Which, if you follow them, will change the way you dress. For the better. And the best thing is, it's so easy. You just need to remember **Think Three.** Three is the magic number...

PLUS (and spoiler alert here) they are also the key things to remember when you do make it to the shops or online... I absolutely promise you, you will never make a shopping howler again if you always bear in mind (what I actually mean is tattoo on your brain) the **Rule of Three.**

So, I can now hear from the back, 'get on with it'. So here is the Rule of Three in very simple terms. We'll explore in more detail what it actually means when we go through how to detox, but essentially, this is all you need to know.

Rule of three: Think three

Three occasions. Three outfits.

1. You must be able to think of three occasions when said piece in your wardrobe will work.

2. You must be able to wear said piece with three outfits that you already own.

How hard can that be? OK, so it's slightly trickier when it comes to buying new clothes, but right now we're just talking about clothes that you already own. And since you bought them, there's got to be a (maybe slim) chance that you loved them once. Even if you no longer plan on wearing them in the outfits that you originally bought them for, there is a good chance that they will still work in some guise going forward.

What you need:
- A wardrobe in need of a detox
- Space
- A full-length mirror and/or a willing photographer
- Two items of clothing you like – ideally a neutral top and a neutral bottom
- Style icon(s) in mind
- Access to Instagram/Pinterest/or other forms of outfit inspiration
- Pen and paper – for making a list of your 'wardrobe holes'

1 **Set aside time**
We're going to start with the practicalities. Set aside some time. To do this properly, even if you don't have too many clothes, it's probably still going to take longer than you think. And if you have loads of clothes, kiss goodbye to a fair few hours/days. Think of it as investment in you (vom-inducing self-help speech again – this time making no apologies for it). It's a one-time labour-intensive exercise that is really, really worth doing. In the long run, it is going to save you time getting dressed every day and, more importantly, money. Not to mention, doing your bit for the planet as well. There is absolutely ZERO point in going shopping for new clothes if you don't actually know what you already have. How on earth are you going to be able to properly judge whether you can make three outfits (remembering our Rule of Three) if you don't actually know what's in your wardrobe in the first place?

2 **Lay it all out**
So, to start with…you've set aside time…you now lay everything out. EVERYTHING. This is, of course, assuming that you do have space, but, in an ideal world, I would like you to empty every single thing out of your wardrobe.

IF you don't have the space, you can work through the contents of your wardrobe while they're still in situ, but

I promise you it's a lot more satisfying to see an empty wardrobe that you're then able to fill with clothes that you already know you'll wear. AND you won't have spent a penny. Plus, the temptation to leave those niggly few items at the back is always there. You say you won't…trust me, you will.

As I previously covered, there are many among us who have things lurking at the back of our wardrobe that haven't seen the light of day since Santa was a child. Well this, my friends, is the time to get reacquainted with them. To meet those work suits that you retired pre-maternity leave (and your eldest may or may not be 16 now), to get out those jeans from the 1990s that are so low cut you can actually flash foliage, and to come face to face again with those jumpers that are full of holes that you MEAN to take to be repaired but never quite get round to it. Not forgetting those dry-clean-only gems that, frankly, who can ever be arsed to dry clean when it costs a quarter of what the darned dress cost in the first place?

3 **Categorize**
Now, you could simply throw everything on the bed in a fit of defiance BUT I do find it easier to apply a semblance of organization to the process. The answer to this is, I find, piles. Not piles of colour but piles of items: jeans in one group, trousers in

another; divide up into T-shirts, jumpers, dresses, skirts, and so forth. Shoes go into similar piles: trainers in one, flats in another, boots to the right (or left).

4 Preparation

And the KEY to making this a successful process: a full-length mirror. Without one of these, getting a true feeling of what an item or outfit looks like is really hard. The only other option is to rope in a willing compatriot. Ideally one who doesn't have a caustic tongue and who relishes proffering their opinion where none is required – and get them to take a photo of you in each piece.

When I say each piece, I don't mean put on a T-shirt and parade around in your undies. The best place to start is to find TWO items of clothing that you love – one that goes on top and one that goes on the bottom. In an ideal world, both of these things would be plain and neutral. They're really there not to create an outfit with, but as a backdrop to the item you're trying on, and to give you an idea of how they will look when teamed with other perfect things. It's very tricky to ascertain whether a pair of trousers is worth keeping when you're flashing your best assets and have a lot more flesh on show than you ordinarily would. A little modesty goes a long way to focusing on the item in question.

5 Testing

When you have the item on, it's time to consider its longevity and use. And, while the Rule of Three is key to working out whether or not the item is worth keeping, there's one test it has to pass first. The most important test of all – and if the answer is no, then it's future is MOST definitely in doubt.

Does it fit?

If it's too small, then bid farewell, sayonara, ciao, adios, au revoir. Straight into the no pile. Please don't feel bad about having kept things that you had planned on slimming into. I'm willing to bet that there are more than a lot of us out there. More than a lot. Loads.

Of course, they're often things that we utterly love or that were really expensive. Which makes it even trickier to say goodbye. In that case, there ARE options...you can put that sentimental but too-small item in the maybe pile.

If it's too big BUT it passes the Rule of Three were it to fit you, again, place it in the maybe pile.

So, if we've established that the item fits, you move on to the Rule of Three.

Can you think of three occasions when you will be able to wear said item?

Can you make three outfits with said item from things that you already have in your wardrobe?

And that you would actually wear. Just throwing that in like it's something rather insignificant, but it's actually the key to a really successful wardrobe detox and is the main differentiator between having clothes that fit you and outfits that you LOVE.

6 Inspiration on the way

As we discussed in chapter 1 (see page 20), one of the main inhibitors to feeling truly confident in what we wear is feeling that you don't look GREAT. It's feeling out of our depth in outfits, it's feeling that they don't represent the person we want to be, it's looking in the mirror and not loving the person we see looking back.

And that is often because we don't have the right clothes for our lifestyle. To feel truly comfortable in ourselves, as trite as it sounds, we need to actually feel comfortable in what we wear. That doesn't necessarily mean swanning around in a onesie and Uggs all day – surely the ultimate in actual comfort (bar going to the loo...there's nothing comfy about going to the loo when you're wearing a onesie but, that aside, what's not to love about an oversized babygro?). It means comfort, as in you feel happy that your outfit is appropriate for whatever it is that you may be doing.

If your wardrobe is testament to a life that you once had, it's not going to work if you lead a very different lifestyle now...

UNLESS you rethink the way you used to wear your clothes.

This is why it's so, so important to lay everything out in piles, to constantly keep in mind those images of the people you would love to emulate...your inner *insert style icon of choice*; to keep asking, what would *style icon* wear? And to try things on. Unless you try things on, this will not work. It doesn't matter how talented a stylist you are, there are times when you genuinely think an outfit will work, it looks incredible on a flatlay, on a mood board, in your head and on the hangers. But actually on a person? Couldn't be more awful. Think troll in fancy dress. Sometimes it just doesn't work.

There are lots of other places you can go for stylish inspiration: Instagram is a case in point, another great place is Pinterest. Simply look up the item that you're thinking of styling along with a word like 'outfit' or 'style' or 'ideas' and a whole host of glorious images will be at your fingertips to get your creative juices flowing. One top tip is to not get sidetracked by the actual 'person' who's wearing them – trust me, they're usually young, thin and very pretty, which you may well be too, but if you're a couple of adjectives short of that description, like most of us, there's no point getting disheartened. It's about adopting the essence of the outfit, for example, teaming a trench coat with cropped jeans and a pair of loafers (as opposed to perhaps the boot-cut or wide-leg jeans and trainers you may have always worn).

7 Experiment

There are just as many times, actually there are MORE times, when you try items on together that you wouldn't normally have put together in an outfit and it's fashion kismet. All the styling planets align and you come across an outfit that can change the way you dress.

It's an opening of the floodgates to so many more outfits – and so, so often, that can come from things that you already own. It just takes a little bit of openness and an investment of time to understand that you CAN completely change your style while still wearing clothes that you own, simply by wearing them in a slightly different way.

One way I love to experiment with outfits while trying everything on, is to think: juxtaposition. I'm sure that there are a great many of us who have clothes from a previous life that are the polar opposite to those we wear in the lives we currently lead. Wardrobes full of them, I'm willing to wager, and we don't wear them any more as we have no need for a corporate suit or a silk blouse.

Well, may I tell you, yes you do. Don't think of them as a suit, think of them as separates (another great reason for splitting items into piles, as so often you see them in a different light when they're not hung with what you're used to seeing them with).

A pair of former suit trousers – be they wide leg, tapered or culottes – could be superb with a tee – either a pared-back simple tee, if you're looking for more of a Scandi vibe, or a full-on band number to throw on with a biker jacket if you're channelling your inner Chrissie Hynde. An oversized knit and a trench coat is the answer to transforming a pair of work trousers into an androgynous outfit that Katharine Hepburn would rock.

The blazer from the suit can easily be stripped from its workwear roots. As I mentioned before, it's all about the juxtaposition, teaming it with outfits that you would never normally have thought of wearing. A formal blazer over a long, flowy, floral maxi-dress. Sounds bizarre but it entirely works (so long as the proportions are right). How about with jeans and trainers? Think about giving in to your inner rock chick: a slogan tee and statement belt breathe new life into an old blazer.

Think about dressing things up as well. A blazer, a silk blouse (or any top that takes your fancy) with a pair of jeans and heels – suddenly you have an 'out out' outfit right there. All from things that you already had but perhaps never wore together.

ITEM OF CLOTHING	DRESS UP	DRESS DOWN
SILK BLOUSE		
Top options	Blazer	Biker
Bottom options	Leather trousers Tapered trousers Jeans	Jeans Joggers
Shoe options	Heels Sparkly flats	Trainers
BLAZER		
Top options	Midi-dress Silk blouse Tee	Tee
Bottom options	Full midi/maxi-skirt Jeans	Jeans
Shoe options	HEELS! Heeled boots	Loafers Trainers
SUIT TROUSERS		
Top options	Silk blouse Cami top Sequin jacket	Tee Knitted top/jumper Trench coat Biker jacket
Shoe options	Heels	Trainers Loafers

8 Does it represent you?

I genuinely find the outfits that are the most successful are the ones that you really thought wouldn't work. The genius in experimenting from your wardrobe is that once upon a time, you did love all these things – enough to buy them at least. So, in a way, they are a representation of you. If you put them into an outfit, you've checked the proportions, you love it and you feel like it represents who you are, it will work.

9 Finding the holes

NOW, what you MIGHT find (and what you will hopefully find) if you've very much kept your fashion icons at the forefront of your mind while trying everything on, is that you're ALMOST able to put together three outfits from each item that you've put back in your wardrobe. But there is very often a key piece missing. And you may well find that it's something you're totally missing from your wardrobe. You are absolutely allowed to have holes in your wardrobe – the need for a few key pieces that will tie all your existing outfits together.

Could it be that it's the perfect thin-knit jumper that would work with your skirts, jeans and trousers? Or a plain V-neck black or white T-shirt? Do you need a new trench that you've perhaps never had and would work for your new wardrobe? Or a casual jacket – maybe a camouflage shacket (shirt-jacket) or

a leather biker? I can guarantee there will be a running theme of a couple of must-have items that you'll constantly be thinking 'this would work with an X'.

So, as you go along trying on different outfits, make a note of your wardrobe holes – this will be your future shopping list. This is super useful for two reasons: it channels the mind when you do hit the shops or online, and it stops you making mistakes you will regret. But once you've read the chapter on shopping (see page 212), you won't be making any of those…

10 Shoes!

While we're talking about game changers, another thing to think about when you're trying on outfits is shoes. As obvious as it sounds, it's something that people don't always consider.

Let's go back to the suit. You could even wear the jacket WITH the trousers BUT change up the shoes: swap your workwear pumps or flats for something you would never normally wear to work…chunky sandals, trainers, flatform brogues or loafers…and, suddenly, you've dressed down what was once a much more formal get-up.

The same can be done with dresses. A tea dress that perhaps you used to wear a gazillion and one years ago that now feels like it's not working for you? A floral dress you invested in to wear to a wedding that's been sitting in your wardrobe giving you the evil eye as you've not showered it with any affection since you wore it ten years ago to that wedding in Italy? Get it out. Reinvent it with different footwear. If it was something you always wore to formal events, dress it down with footwear that is much more casual and that you feel comfortable in. If you're looking to bring a tired dress back to life, a nod to a more modern and on-trend pair of shoes, trainers or sandals can work wonders in giving it a second bite of the fashion cherry. And that dress can then go back into the wardrobe.

11 Keeping it for best?

Which leads me neatly on to another point I want you to think about when working out whether or not something is going to make the grade in your new wardrobe: have you been keeping it for best?

Come on now...it's time to face the music, and don't be shy about looking the truth in the face as we have ALL been there. Are you not wearing something in your wardrobe because you're saving it? WHAT FOR? The whole point of coming face to face with your fashion demons is so that you can LOVE what you wear every day. It's NOT about spending a whole load of money on a whole load of clothes. It's about conscious dressing, and a huge part of that is wearing what you already have. How many times were you planning on wearing that

ridiculously expensive dress? Dare I say that ultimately it will probably end up being a handful? Which, when you think about it, is criminal. Cost per wear, you have let that item down massively. It deserves to be worn, it deserves to be loved, it deserves to make you look fabulous.

If you think it's too formal, think back to the juxtaposition. Pair it with something to dress it down: ankle boots, cowboy boots, trainers, chunky dad sandals. Jacket-wise, wear a biker or a trench coat and accessorize with a huge scarf and a woolly hat.

We want to get to the point where we are no longer wearing 80 per cent of our wardrobe only 20 per cent of the time – we should be wearing it 80 per cent of the time! That sounds fair, that sounds right, that sounds sustainable.

12 The piles

And, speaking of sustainable, we have two piles of clothes after our trying-on sessions that are no longer in the wardrobe, and we have to decide what to do with them. A no pile and a maybe pile. The no pile is easy. You have choices here. You can either sell them or you can give them to charity (lots more ideas on both of these in the sustainability chapter, see page 222). The maybe pile is slightly more complex. You can either decide that, no, you don't want them, and sling them in the no pile. Or, if you're perhaps not as ruthless as me, you can take another look at them.

If they're there because they're too big or they need fixing in some way or other (moths love my house regardless of what I do!), are you going to alter or repair them? Be honest…are you? Because if you were going to, wouldn't you have done it by now? Of course, you could be as big a procrastinator as I am. But if you do finally get around to it, a repaired jumper, an altered pair of trousers, a nipped-in waistband on a dress or a mended zip on a skirt means a brand-new item to wear in your wardrobe that you haven't had to go out and buy. It's like falling in love ALL over again but practically for free. What's not to love about that? (*Stops writing and immediately heads to the alterations lady*.)

There are, then, the dry-clean-only items. Oh, how we all hate you. Well. Here's the thing. I don't have any of these anymore. I know. *Polishes halo*. Because I throw everything in the washing machine. Rebel? Fool? Well, no actually. I will add a caveat here that I do have more consideration for wool trousers and structured coats and blazers (I also have a pair of very snug and now short wool trousers that may be the key reason for this…that was a lesson in understanding fabrics). BUT the huge majority of things that recommend dry clean only are able to be handwashed. When I say handwashed, I mean in a

washing machine on a cold handwash, using proper handwash detergent (KEY!). Can I recommend you handwash everything that says dry clean only? No. Not at all. As that could lead to a set of lawsuits after everyone washes their cashmere jumpers and they come out of the machine fit only for a Tiny Tears.

Can I tell you what I personally wash and have had success with? Yes. Cashmere jumpers, wool jumpers, silk dresses, silk skirts and silk blouses. The main thing that I've learned (after a couple of washing-related disasters – you have to break some eggs to make a cake) is that the fabric is the main indicator of how successful your washing roulette will be. Unembellished silk works for me, as does cashmere and knitted wool items. Polyester I have also had success with. Viscose I tend to take a view on as it CAN go one of two ways. An Internet search can also be a huge help in knowing whether to bet on your machine or the dry cleaner. My general advice is, though, if it's something you absolutely love and you would be utterly devastated if it got ruined, take it to the dry cleaner (although, having said that, I am fully aware of some disaster stories from trips to the professionals).

The other, far easier option, of course, although not necessarily popular, is to just not wash things as much. The current thinking is that western society is far too happy to fling things to be washed after one or two wears when really it's not necessary. I'm a fully paid-up member of the sniff society (sounds grim but it works). Things really don't need washing as often as we think they do.

If there are still things in your maybe pile that you simply can't bear to get rid of as they hold sentimental value, were heinously expensive (do consider selling them though) or you just can't think of how you'd wear them now but REALLY want to keep them, then pack them up and put them in a bag in the attic. If it's only one or two pieces, you *may* put them back in your wardrobe as hopefully it means you will revisit them more often than you used to. Otherwise, I would recommend getting that bag of maybes out of the attic every year and re-evaluating them. Be more ruthless next time round, that's all I'll say. And actually, because you'll have had a year of a superb wardrobe, you'll be a pro and it will be easy. The other option, of course, is to share the love of the item you can't bear to get rid of and donate it to a friend or lucky family member. But be prepared for outfit envy when you see them rocking it!

Hopefully, now, you should have been able to salvage some things from your wardrobe that you had previously never envisaged wearing again and have a small shopping list of things that you need to complete your perfect wardrobe.

Confession time...

I am going to hold up my hands and admit that there is more than one item in my wardrobe, languishing at the back, which 'one day I will fit into'. And while we're 'fessing up, I will admit that one dress that immediately springs to mind (and I can't get rid of it as I washed it and shrunk it and somehow think it will miraculously expand just by hanging in my closet), I keep thinking I *might* be able to stretch by ironing it. SERIOUSLY? (Yes, seriously, says a small voice in my head.) Have I ironed it? Have I chuff as like. Why? Because if I do iron it, I secretly know it's not actually going to stretch that much but that will leave me with the VERY REAL knowledge that unless I lose four ribs from each side, it's never going to fit me again and I will have to say goodbye to it.

So it sits there, chastising me every time I look at it, as it's the one thing – another confession looming now – that I did handwash when I should have taken it to the dry cleaner. ERROR. In my defence, it was vintage and didn't have a cleaning label on it, but deep down I knew that it was a wool mix and, well, it was a painful lesson learned on my sustainable journey to try to dry clean things less. As I said, you have to break some eggs to make a cake, but I'm not going to lie, I do weep a bit every time I think about that vintage, irreplaceable egg that I broke.

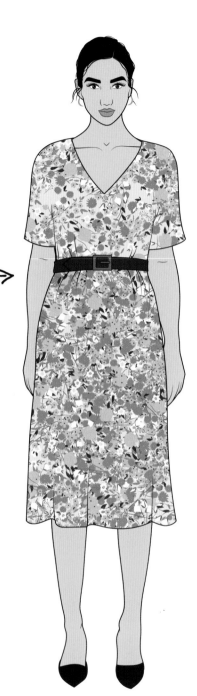

Dress with or without a belt. Perfect on its own with heels for work or a smarter occasion.

Wear into autumn and winter by layering with a knit and a trench.

Change seasonal footwear to boots.

Dress down for spring and summer with a denim jacket and trainers.

Nutritional information

I would love to say there is an easy, quick fix for this one but there isn't. HOWEVER, please know that the first time is always the hardest and the most daunting. It's possibly the biggest mountain to climb on your journey to having a wardrobe full of clothes you love but it will most definitely be worth it. Keep the faith, stay strong and make sure you remember the following:

Wardrobe Detox
> Set aside time.
> Get everything out of your wardrobe.
> Make sure you have a full-length mirror or a trusted friend with a camera.
> Find two neutral items of clothing to team tops and bottoms with.
> Make sure you have your inner style icon first and foremost in your mind.
> Get trying on.
> Does it fit? Too small, on the no pile. Too big, on the maybe pile.
> Understand the Rule of Three.
> Does it work for your lifestyle?
> Does it fit into the wardrobe of your inner style icon?

> Keep experimenting and trying lots of different pieces on together to make different outfits.
> Always remember the juxtaposition: dressing things down and dressing things up.
> Bear in mind you are allowed to have holes in your wardrobe – you can create a shopping list of things that will tie existing outfits together.
> Think about the shoes. Change the shoes and the whole outfit changes.
> Do not keep anything for best.
> Get rid of the no pile.
> Reassess the maybe pile.
> Get your bum down to the alteration place immediately.
> Do some dry-cleaning soul-searching.
> Put everything back in your wardrobe and arm yourself with the start of your shopping list.

Your perfect wardrobe doesn't have to be a pipe dream. It will take time, some soul-searching and some growing, but it can be a reality.

The art of shopping

In this chapter we enter the fray. We will look at helpful ways to strategize your shopping expeditions and turn them into a form of art. We will supplement our Rule of Three with Three Shopping Tests so you always think clearly and avoid costly mistakes.

And now…it's time for the MAIN EVENT. Are we ready? Yes is the answer by the way – you may not think it is, but it is. Please trust me, we've got all the way to this point without too much kicking and screaming I hope. Surely it was easier than you thought?

We know the style icons that we are emulating, we understand our body shape and we know what's going to work and what isn't. We're comfortable in understanding the colours we're looking for and the prints we're going to introduce. We know what our wardrobe basics are and we have a list of our wardrobe holes so we know what we should be adding in. And, most importantly, we know what we already have in our wardrobe so we're not buying more of the same.

You are ready to rock and roll and GO SHOPPING! This is the fun bit, the absolute best bit. Even if you don't think so right now, please tell me you're a little bit excited at the prospect?

But, hold your horses, as I have a few things to run by you first of all (teensy understatement, but, at the end of the day, it is a few – the explanations are just wordy…). Now, theoretically I should call these rules. Except they're not rules. I hate rules. Probably because I am ridiculously compliant, which makes me hate them even more as I am always the one who ends up following the darned rules (Catholic upbringing – the Guilt is real, yes, with a capital G, and is invariably almost worse than not following the rule in the first place). Rules were not made to be broken in my book, they were made to be followed and made to put me in a foul mood.

SO. These are categorically not rules. This is advice. These are advisory guidelines. I like to think of them (in my more modest moments) as nuggets of wisdom that will transform the way you shop.

Let's talk about SHOPPING! 'How hard can that be?' I hear some of you cry. 'VERY', yell most others. To be honest, even if you find shopping a doddle, I will again bet my (still hefty) mortgage that there isn't a person among us who hasn't made a howler every now and again.

It's so easy to do. A drink of wine at lunchtime, a flattering mirror, a balmy little boutique when on holiday (note to self: things purchased from a Greek shop in 35°C with a cracking tan do not work on the school run, in the office or generally at all in a country where the average temp is 18°C on a good day, with drizzle), a persuasive sales assistant, a moment of pure madness when you are convinced that you're *actually* Carrie Bradshaw from *Sex and the City* and, yes, that tulle skirt will work for every conceivable occasion you can think of and, no, you won't resemble an extra from *The Nutcracker* at all (you may well not – you most likely will). We've all been there.

Plus, let's be honest – deep breath here – don't we just all own too many clothes? (If I could put an emoji in a book, it would be the one screaming, holding its face, which is me on too regular a basis). Hopefully, though, if you've been working through the chapters, by this point you will have come to terms with the demons in your wardrobe and will have realized that a large number of the humdingers in it are down to errors made while shopping. Please, please don't think that you are alone in this. All over the country (and, in my wildest dreams, the world) there are women nodding, thinking about the howlers that never made the outfit grade. As I said earlier in the book, one of the goals that I think it's admirable to achieve is – very simply – to buy less and wear it more.

Sounds easy? In theory it is. But the reality is that it's too easy to get sucked into an impulse purchase (see above reasons and, while we are here, just in case you think you might not ever have done it, we can also add shopping at the wrong time of month and buying something under pressure for an occasion. Nothing like the fear of going to a wedding in your pants to make you lose your marbles and come home with something that fills you with buyer's remorse forever. And, no, it's never the cheap dress…).

However, by remembering these guidelines (see what I did there – it's not following rules, it's remembering guidelines – so much less dictatorial), I can guarantee that you won't make a shopping mistake again. OK, so maybe not guarantee...but how about, I am very, very confident. Confident that you will be working towards curating a wardrobe of clothes that you love, that make you happy, that make you feel confident, upbeat and 'on it'. (I don't really know what 'on it' means, but I do feel it's something that we should all feel at one point or another). And that is easy to get dressed from!

First of all, we need to remember the Rule of Three that we used in our wardrobe detox (see page 198). Here's a refresher.

Remember, we've all made massive shopping errors. We've all looked in the (ridiculously unflattering) shop mirror and seen a potato staring back and we've all been nearly stuck in that dress in the changing room. You WILL have to kiss a lot of frogs before you find your Prince of an outfit. Shopping DOES take time and practice, but it most definitely will one day be fun.

I promise!

Rule of three: Think three

Three occasions. Three outfits.

1. You must be able to think of three occasions when said piece will work.

2. You must be able to wear said piece with three outfits that you already own.

Next, we have **Three Shopping Tests** to prompt us when we're in the deepest throes of shopping. This is to get you asking yourself the right questions all the time and challenging yourself before making a purchasing decision.

Are you going to wear it?
Three Shopping Tests

1. The Changing Room Test

This is possibly the easiest and most obvious piece of advice to follow but I'm not sure how many of us do it. Maybe subconsciously, but I want this to be something that is tattooed onto your brain as I promise you it's the easiest thing to remember and it genuinely works. If you prefer what you were wearing when you walked into the changing room to the item that you tried on **Do Not Buy It**. How many times have you tried something on and thought,'yup, that works', got dressed back into your own clothes, looked in the mirror and thought, 'that REALLY works'?

We rarely go shopping in our absolute best outfits, so chances are it's a day-to-day outfit that we like. Well, I want you to start only buying things that you LOVE. Things that you can't wait to get home and wear. And if you prefer what you were wearing when you walked into the changing room, the question you should be asking is, do I love this enough?

2. The Bag in the Corner Test

We've all been there. You bought something new, you loved it. You were planning on wearing it all the time and with everything that you own. You've 'three is the magic numbered' yourself ad infinitum and you wanted to skip out of the changing room wearing it (for the record, don't ever be tempted to do this, as trying to get a magnetic security tag off a top while you have it on is not the most glamorous thing you'll ever do in your life. Trust me. Been there, done that, draped myself with stomach hanging out, perilously close to whacking a boob into the cashier's face, while they tried, uncenemoniously, to de-tag me and I prayed that no one was videoing me. No one needs a video of this. It's a memory that wakes you up in a cold sweat for longer than you'd like it to, believe me). Yet...yet, yet, yet...it sits in the bag in the corner of your bedroom for weeks. Maybe you got it out, tried it on with all those wonderful outfits you'd thought of in the changing room and that weren't 'quite' as wonderful as you thought they might be (and how many times have we all done that...oh, that skirt will SO go with that new tee and that blazer. *Puts outfit on and looks like a potato*. You are in good company). That's OK. Try it on with other things. Go back to when you did your wardrobe detox and remember how you tried on combinations that you didn't think would work. Try that again. You may be surprised as to what you like together and what works as an outfit...you may also realize that you've bought a complete dud and throw it back into the bag and into the corner of the room in disgust, as if it's the naughty corner for clothes that disappoint you. Again, that's OK. But DO NOT LEAVE IT THERE. Return it. **Return, return, return.** This also goes for those items in bags that do work. If you haven't worn it within the return period, which is usually around a month, the chances are you just don't love it enough. Or it's not versatile enough for your wardrobe. So back it goes.

3. The Lifestyle Test

Shop for the lifestyle you have, not for the lifestyle you want. There are some exceptions to this, which we'll look at later on (ahem, black tie, ahem, see page 219), but this is still a crucial piece of advice. Once you've detoxed your wardrobe, you should hopefully have seen what mistakes you have made over the years. You will also definitely have a MUCH better idea of what it is you do actually wear and what sits at the back of the wardrobe gathering dust. Chances are, as we've discussed, you just don't have the opportunity to wear these pieces on a regular basis. Not because you don't love them, but because they just don't work for your lifestyle. This lifestyle test is partly covered by our Rule of Three, which, if you remember, says **you need to be able to think of three occasions when you could wear this item of clothing.** However, this test takes it one step further – it is about asking yourself honestly HOW OFTEN do those occasions really happen in your life? If the answer is hardly at all, then the item of clothing you're trying on might not be passing your lifestyle test.

Shopping: The exceptions

Shopping is tricky, there's no two ways about it. But, honestly, once you've got your own style pinned down, and you're using the Rule of Three and Three Shopping Tests, you may well feel like you have this shopping lark nailed.

And then, just when you think you're safe to be let loose online or in-store with a credit card, something comes along that has the ability to derail the hardiest shoppers among us.

The. Sales.

There is something about sales shopping that can strike fear into even the most professional of shoppers. It's the adrenaline of bagging a bargain, the terror of missing out, the panic at wondering whether to play Sales Chicken with an item...how low will it go? It's the utter distress at thinking you may miss out on that one item that could change your wardrobe forever.

Exaggeration much? Well, obviously. But there is something about the thrill of shopping the sales that sets it apart from the normal perusal of the high street for a bargain or for the perfect pair of jeans and turns into the equivalent of a gladiatorial sport. The bar is high. The pursuit for the ultimate bargain is real. The Game is On.

What's also high is our level of utter stupidity. It's as if we leave our brains at home in the quest to bag the bargain of the year. Believe me, I know. Trust me, as someone who is the proud owner of some very dubious items that you could be forgiven for thinking I'd had a lobotomy while purchasing, instead of using my, usually exceptionally sensible and finely honed, shopping brain (another moment of pure modesty...).

So, may I advise (as these aren't rules) that in order not to make some (usually expensive) howling errors, we not only follow the sacred shopping guidelines, as above, the Rule of Three and the Three Shopping Tests, but we also add in Three Bargain Checks when it comes to sales shopping.

These are perhaps glaringly obvious BUT, as my brain turns to putty at the mere hint of a 50 per cent off (and don't even start me on 70 per cent – that's enough for me to revert to the mentality of a toddler with a fistful of dollars), it's worth remembering them.

Sales shopping: Three bargain checks

1 **Does it Fit?**
If I had a £ for every time I thought 'Oh I'll slim into that', I would be writing this on my own private island, supping Cristal. I'm not. And you won't. It's one thing to buy something that can be altered, but it's a whole different (smelly) kettle of fish to make a purchase that no amount of altering will fix. Plus, you won't really be able to tell how it looks if it doesn't fit you properly. It could also be that regardless of how much weight you lose, it's just the wrong shape for you. Do. Not. Buy. It.

2 **The High Street Test**
This is simple. But ridiculously effective, as we all know there is nothing like the lure of a bargain. If it's cheap, especially if it's reduced, you can kiss goodbye to common sense and the need to BUY, BUY, BUY somehow takes over. A good reduction is a thrill like no other. But slow yourself down: imagine that the sale price is FULL price in your favourite high street store. Would you buy it? Or would you think, no way José. If the latter, then put it back. You're just buying it because of the label or because it's reduced.

3 **Is it on your Wish List?**
Before engaging in any sales shopping, a brilliant tactic is to have planned in advance. At the beginning of and during the season make a wish list of things that you love but can't quite justify purchasing. Those items that are basically out of your budget, but you love. And you WOULD wear. The other thing I would advise doing is, when you've made your list, write down what you would pay for the items. Write it down as you go along during the season – don't cheat and add to it at the end, as that's when the panic sets in and, trust me, that sales adrenalin is a shifty bugger. Even if it's on your wish list, make sure it passes your other bargain checks before parting with your cash.

Exceptions...

Now, these aren't exceptions to the rules, as clearly these are not rules. Advisory guidelines that will streamline the way you shop and take out all the anxiety from the shopping process. However, as with all great things in life, there are times when you have to throw caution to the wind and just live life on the edge. To give you an idea of how dull my life is, for me, that is buying an unsuitable pair of shoes. Rock and roll, right there.

The truth is, there are times when we might want to make a purchase even though it doesn't quite pass our Rule of Three, Three Shopping Tests, or Three Bargain Checks. I call these, the Three Excuses...

Three Excuses

1 **Black Tie**
Speaking of unsuitable shoes... there are those occasions for which we need an outfit that we're really going to struggle with ensuring is versatile. Some may say any dressy occasion, but I hold little truck with that concept. As we've discussed in 'Wardrobe detox' (see page 196), I'm a fully paid-up member of the Nothing is for Best club. There are outfits you can choose that really will work for a wedding, for the races, for any special occasion but that you'll also be able to wear on a daily basis. I promise. However, there is one event for which it IS possible to find something to wear that's versatile, but most of the time it does come under my exception banner, and that's black tie. There are options that preclude buying a dress you'll wear once and once only (as we touched upon in 'Pantry staples', see page 160), but I will acknowledge this one does have its difficulties.

2 Summer Holiday Clothes

Unless you're me when I was 19 and used to wear my swimsuit to a club with a pair of tiny denim shorts, the chances are slim of you being able to shoehorn a bikini into any dress code other than on holiday. Obvs. But then there is also the thorny subject of those super-summery, wafty beach dresses. Perfect for swanning round a pool or on the beach in post-30°C. To the supermarket in June in the rain? Not so much. Of course there ARE those ridiculous days we get in the UK when all we want to do (all we CAN do, thanks to our non-existent – as it would be utterly redundant for 360 days of the year – air-con) is lie round in our pants – then these dresses come into their own. But it's tricky to get your head around the Rule of Three with items that are so exceptionally weather dependent. Same applies to ski gear, which I can't be bothered to write about as I am inherently lazy (way too many things to carry, too much to pack, too much walking, too much exercise and basically just too cold. Give me a beach and a teeny-weeny bikini any day).

3 Fancy Dress

Three options. First, you make do with what you have in your wardrobe, failing that, in your partner's or kids'. Second, you hire it. Third, find something cheap in the sales or in a charity shop. I once went to a 1970s party and managed to snag a green velvet flared sleeveless jumpsuit from Zara in the sale for £7.99. As you can imagine, it wasn't something that people were clamouring to purchase (I think it was 90 per cent off – for good reason, believe me). There isn't a cat in hell's chance that I will be wearing it again APART from to another fancy dress party. My main advice is DO NOT buy a whole new full-priced outfit, spending ££££ on something that you will never wear again. Side note to anyone reading this who knows me: please only invite me to a fancy dress party if it's 1970s themed.

Nutritional information

The art of shopping

Rule of Three
> Three outfits
> Three occasions

Are you going to wear it?
Three Shopping Tests
1. The Changing Room Test
2. The Bag in the Corner Test
3. The Lifestyle Test

Sales Shopping
Three Bargain Checks
1. Does it Fit?
2. The High Street Test
3. Is it on your Wish List?

Three Excuses
1. Black Tie
2. Summer Holiday Clothes
3. Fancy Dress

A healthy diet

So if it wasn't hard enough getting to grips with this whole personal style, shape, lifestyle, wardrobe detox, shopping malarkey, there is just one last teensy-tiny thing to consider. OK, it's not so teensy-tiny at all – it's actually really important and will ultimately be a massive game changer for us all. Sustainability and ethical practices.

This is, in the long term, how we maintain a healthy fashion diet that keeps the planet alive and ensures that the people who make our clothes are looked after and safe. In the short term, there are easy steps that we can make in the right direction.

There is no doubting that we have an awfully long way to go on our sustainability journey - there are many, many changes that can be made. And if we all start making small changes immediately, a lot of small changes will slowly and surely end up being a big change.

Where to shop

It's also not an us and them scenario, as in Consumer vs Retailer. Both sides have found themselves in positions where they carry some of the blame. For the last couple of years, I have been very vocal in my opinion that retailers manufacture and sell too much stock, which is invariably left over. Which is why there are too many sales. How many sales?

End-of-season sale, pre-season sale, mid-season sale, pre-mid-season sale, mid-mid-season sale...it seems that there are more sales than there are not sales. What happened to the good old January sales and summer sales? Now there are new drops (new arrivals of styles) every other week (every week in some stores) and they're not just one or two items. There are oodles of them. Yes, some things sell out, but LOADS don't, and hence the plethora of sales when they have to get rid of all the crap they thought people might want but clearly didn't. It seems that retail buying has come down to 'if we throw enough shit at the wall, some of it will stick'.

And, yes, we as the consumers aren't blameless. We have bought into a culture of newness, of immediacy, of constant change. It's the classic conundrum of supply and demand, and right now we can't dictate the supply but we can start to change the demand.

Essentially, we need to shop less. But the GREAT news is that – one of the massive upsides about finding yourself through fashion; identifying your style; ensuring that you dress for the lifestyle that you have and not the lifestyle that you want; understanding your shape and dressing for it NOW, not the shape you once were and not the shape you hope one day you will be; and taking all the rest of the tips and tricks I've shared so far on this journey – you are more than halfway there. You are there. You WILL make those changes, you'll be dressing better and shopping less, just by wearing more of what you own.

As well as saving money, you've ticked the saving the planet box too; admittedly, it does take more than one tick to facilitate the change that's needed. BUT, if we all shopped less, retailers would be forced to produce less. Fact.

We have become a nation of fast-fashion fanatics, and whether we have driven retailers to produce more stock or whether we buy more because there is so much new stock available all the time – well, it's chicken and egg, but the main thing is: it has to stop.

The media has definitely made significant steps to promote our awareness of being more sustainable in our shopping decisions but, having sat on many panels over the years and had this discussion, I've always felt slightly uncomfortable by the level at which we're told changes can be made. A few snippets of advice I have heard: 'don't shop on the high street, we need to avoid buying fast fashion', 'only buy sustainable fabrics', 'save and invest in a higher-end garment rather than buying three cheaper high street dresses', 'shop vintage'…and many others in the same vein. All excellent and noble advice. IF you have the funds, the knowledge or the capacity to be able to do that. The assumption is that it's down to inclination. Whereas, actually, it's down to budget and spare time.

Having worked in fashion and media for ten years now and having had access to a very large and very varied audience, what frustrates me about that sort of advice is that it's only relevant to a very small percentage of people. It doesn't take into consideration budget. And yes (as I have also had this conversation), they will say, but there are many more cost-effective opportunities out there if you just look. And again – missing the point. You're still basically telling someone that because they are either cash- or time-poor, if they can't shop ethically or sustainably, then they shouldn't shop at all. I absolutely appreciate that there are goals we should be aiming for and, yes, that is to buy less and buy better, but in the short term, it shouldn't negate entire demographics from being able to buy a new dress from a supermarket or from a shop on the high street. It IS about being more circumspect about what we buy, about buying less and about how we wear it – and if you've come along the journey of this book, as I said, you've definitely made a step in the right direction.

Wearing more of what you own rather than buying extra, regardless of what it is, is the move we all need to be making (and you'll be doing that NOW!).

I also hold the high street very dear to my heart (for a start, how many people do we employ in retail? Not to mention the community aspect) and would hate to see people simply stop shopping there. Luckily retailers are very aware that people ARE becoming much more astute in their shopping habits and are also keen to show that they have listened and are making significant strides forward in their efforts to be as kind as possible to the planet and to the people who manufacture their products.

One step that retailers have made is to share information about the sustainability of their products and how ethical they are in their production processes. So for us to make more informed choices, even before we set foot in a shop or order online, checking the website for details of their ethical practices is something we all can do. There is significantly more information than there ever used to be, and the retailer's website should be more up to date than a general Internet search, which may throw up info on sustainability and ethical awareness for specific manufacturers but is likely to be out of date. If in doubt, and you would like further info before purchasing from somewhere, an email to the PR department (details are nearly always readily available on retailers' websites) should give you enough info to decide whether you're happy with where their clothes come from.

Fabric

Another great improvement that retailers have made to facilitate our shopping for more sustainable fabrics is to produce more clothes than ever in materials that are better for the environment.

In an ideal world we would all be shopping for recycled, organic and sustainably made clothes but, as already discussed, they can be prohibitive in price and simply might not be in the style you're looking for. However, I think the more we are armed with information on fabric and the more we are aware of what we're buying and make appropriate choices where we're able, the bigger the difference this will have over time.

Look out for recycled fabrics, which are becoming more readily available. Recycled cotton is made from pre- and post-consumer cotton sources and uses less water and energy to produce. Recycled polyester is manufactured from recycled bottles.

Organic cotton is grown without harmful pesticides and is obviously a better choice than cotton if you can find it. We are also seeing an increase in other sustainable natural fabrics, such as organic hemp, linen and bamboo.

Then there are the man-made cellulosic fibres, which can actually be more eco-friendly than they sound. The most sustainable of them is widely believed to be lyocell (often referred to by the brand name Tencel), which is made from dissolved pulp mainly produced from wood. Viscose, rayon and modal are similar fabrics from the same source but, due to a more intensive manufacturing process, lyocell (Tencel) gets the bigger tick in the sustainable box. Sustainable viscose is a fabric that we're seeing more of and is manufactured using the same process as lyocell.

You would think that the worst fabrics are the synthetics made from petrochemical products or petroleum-based chemicals: come and do the walk of shame polyester, nylon and acrylic. And, yes, it's true that due to the way in which they're manufactured, which produces extensive pollution and waste, not to mention the lack of biodegradability, when it comes to giving out points for eco-friendliness, they chart with a woeful nil points.

However, when you start digging, there are so many fabrics that we probably assume are much better for the environment than they actually are. Cotton, for example, is one of the worst due to the environmentally demanding way in which it's produced: a sixth of all pesticides used globally are in the growing of cotton. Animal-derived natural fabrics, such as wool, leather and even silk, will always divide people because of the ethical animal discussion but, as an aside from that, there are many other issues surrounding farming and the environmental issues in the production process.

Truth be told, there are very few fabrics that get huge ticks when it comes to sustainability.

And I don't have any of the answers. BUT we can either just ignore it, as it's too tricky and painful to think about, OR we can, as I suggested earlier, make small, manageable changes that will add up to big changes if we all start doing our part.

The more information we have, the better decisions we can make. But please don't start throwing away all the polyester that you own. The most sustainable thing you can do is buy less and actually wear the clothes that you have, more. Think about different outfit options for those clothes you already have.

Other changes to make

Sustainability can be reached in a lot of different ways. We can buy less and be more mindful about what we buy, we can wear what we already have – altering and repairing clothes instead of just passing them on; we can think about looking after our clothes better so that they last longer (note to self, order moth balls...); and we can think about washing our clothes less.

Yes, I just snuck that one in at the end, but apparently the majority of us simply wash our clothes too often. Which is an environmental shit show (not the official title) AND shortens the lifespan of our clothes. Now, if someone can do a memo to all teens that wearing a T-shirt for 30 seconds does not constitute it needing a wash, most mums would be extremely grateful (the other mums are trying to peel their teens out of clothes they've had on for a week!). Ditto dry cleaning. The chemicals obviously aren't winning any environmental awards, as well as not contributing to the shelf life of your clothes, although there are new types of green dry cleaning so it may be worth asking your local if they offer that service. But so many dry-clean labels (NOT all, I should point out) are put in to protect the retailer, and so many items can in fact be handwashed. And yes, you can do the old hand-handwash thing, and yes, that is the sustainable thing to do, but realistically sometimes it is more convenient to use a washing machine. Most, these days, have a delicate, silk or wool wash that washes at a cold temp; this is how I wash all my silk, wool and pretty much anything else that says it should be dry cleaned. In between washes, a fabric-refreshing spray such as Febreze can be your friend, or an even cheaper way to freshen clothes is to mix a capful of fabric conditioner in a spray bottle of water, spray and then hang to air. Alternatively, a good airing outside on a dry day can work wonders. Steaming clothes can also bring them back to life between wears.

We could also do well to consider possibly my favourite machine in the house – the tumble dryer. I discovered my love for it when I had three very small children and the hanging out of a gazillion tiny socks, babygros, vests, bibs and so on nearly drove me to distraction. Until I found my best friend – the tumble dryer. Who cared that it surgically bonded the stains to the fabric when I just had to throw 56 items of baby clothing into it in one go as opposed to painstakingly hanging them out? BUT. Those days are long gone and with age has come wisdom and education, and as useful as it is, the tumble dryer is just not the most environmentally friendly machine in the house. It is also not great for your clothes. This epiphany may have been reached on discovering a rogue cashmere jumper that had made it's way into the dryer and was then only fit for a Barbie doll. Suffice to say, we can all do our extra bit by air drying our clothes.

Imagine someone telling you that doing less laundry will make you more sustainable. Well, Public Service Announcement: Do. Less. Laundry. Invest in a steamer, natural cleaning sprays or a whole host of other fabulous gadgets and wizardry that are now available. Doing this means less laundry for you and good news for the environment.

You're welcome!

Moving our clothes on

We can also be more considered in how we get rid of things we don't want. One thing that it is now (and I don't say this lightly) unacceptable is to throw fabrics in the bin.

Everything can be recycled, NOTHING needs to go directly into landfill. Recycling these days is almost an industry in its own right, and when it comes to passing our clothes on, we have many choices of what to do with them:

● **Charity shops.** The obvious choice. You can also give clothes to food banks, and there are community sites that will offer your clothes to others to collect.

● **Recycling bins.** For those clothes that perhaps need mending or are worn out, underwear and other things that charity shops often won't take.

● **Charity pick-up services.** There are now many companies that will come and pick up your unwanted clothes from your home. The Internet is your friend to find one that will either sell clothes and donate the money to charity, pass them on to the more unfortunate elsewhere in the UK and the world, or will give them to women's refuges – there are many different options.

● **Give to friends.** Have a swap party or organize a local swap meet.

● **Sell online.** Auction sites and specific clothes sales sites are becoming more popular than ever.

Then, of course, there is the flipside of the coin: how we can shop sustainably. Some of that is down to changing our shopping habits. I would never say to anyone, don't shop on the high street or from supermarkets, as I think it's unfair and unreasonable. But there are also other options that you may want to consider in the future:

● **Shopping vintage.** This does take time and research, but once you have located your favourite shops – warning – it may well become your favourite pastime. My go-to pieces are jackets, boots, dresses, skirts and belts. (Best. Belts. Ever.) OK, basically anything and everything.

● **Shopping pre-loved.** Which is basically second-hand. Someone said to me that she really disliked the concept of second-hand, but as soon as she heard it being called preloved she was all over it (it's sometimes all down to the semantics!). It can be traditional charity shops (I am a dedicated rummager), but it can also be dedicated pre-loved boutiques (that sell for profit), both online and actual shops. There are now lots of curated specialist shops out there that are great treasure troves. Other larger online selling and auction sites are also worth considering. It does take time to trawl through, but once you've got the knack – warning, again – it can be addictive.

● **Renting clothing.** A new phenomenon that is definitely on the rise. And it's easy to see why. Instead of buying that one special dress for a special occasion, there is now the opportunity to rent one.

Hopefully there are some ideas here that you will be able to take on board. And hopefully our children will also learn from our example. I can take a second to polish my halo, as my teenage daughter is a vintage fiend. You can keep your spa days; our favourite day out is a good old rummage through the old clothing stores in Covent Garden. Not only do you then start collecting some timeless and unique pieces that no one else has

(the perfect way to start cementing your own personal style), but it's also invariably cheaper than a lot of the high street and you know that you're shopping sustainably. (Bear in mind that your teenager will probably think what you pick is naff, and chomp down on the temptation to yell 'I USED TO WEAR THAT' when she picks up something from the 1980s that you remember, as she will never forgive you.)

If we all start making changes NOW, future generations will learn from us and we can change the narrative. We need these changes to become a natural part of the way we shop, dress, look after and pass on our clothes. Every small change that we make will add up to the very big change that is needed.

Nutritional information

How to be healthily mindful while shopping.

Shop less
The easiest way to do that is to:
> Identify your style.
> Know what works for your shape.
> Always follow the Rule of Three when shopping.
> You must be able to wear your new purchase with three outfits you already own.
> You must be able to think of three occasions when you would wear your new purchase.

> Research your retailer's sustainability credentials before shopping.
> Understand which fabrics are preferable and choose them when you are able.
> Repair clothes instead of getting rid of them.
> Wash clothes less.
> Handwash instead of dry cleaning.
> Be sustainable in how you recycle your clothes.
> Shop vintage.
> Shop pre-loved.
> Organize a clothes swap.
> Consider renting clothes.

Small changes will add up to big change. But we all need to start somewhere. One small change is not as hard as you think.

The elephant in the room

Age. Is there an age at which you should or should not wear 'fill in the gap'?

I could make this the shortest chapter ever, as essentially the answer is: the only thing that you shouldn't wear at any age, is the weight of other people's opinions.

End of conversation.

But you may have gathered by now that I am not a woman of few words (why use one when you can use 450 and lots of brackets as well?), and as this subject makes me apoplectic with rage, I am going to just note down a few thoughts. Because, while I am happy enough to put my head above the parapet and get punched by anyone with vehement views on this topic, I am fully aware that there are many of you out there who are still in the early stages of rebooting your confidence.

And to be told that you can or can't wear something purely because of the year in which you were born can be an utter kick in the teeth. Hopefully, at this stage of the book, you will be well on your way or be giving some serious thought as to how you can make positive changes in your life as a result of dressing and feeling like the real you. To be told 'you're too old' to wear certain things before you've even started can be such a damaging dent in the confidence you're starting to rebuild.

But people can be persuasive with their (I'm not going to say moronic as that would be rude – I'd like to, but I won't) views. So rather than me just telling you to ignore it, I want to put some weight behind my theory that you can wear whatever you want at any age. Hopefully this will give you some courage in your conviction to ignore them – when you have a fabulously cohesive argument as to why it's just a big, massive pile of stinking manure.

First, at what age do these 'rules' kick in? 35, 40, 50, 60? At whichever age said ridiculous rule is applied, the answer remains the same: why? To be fair, that's the answer you can pretty much give any time anyone mutters something about age and a fashion rule. Why? Why are there these 'rules'? And who made them in the first place?

Are these a hangover from years ago (please don't for one second think that I condone them in any era, I'm just playing devil's advocate for a second) when women (oh and yes, it's always women who have these rules, by the way. Obvs. And please know that I am rolling my eyes à la teenage girl style) aged earlier than they do now? I admit that when I was younger, someone in their mid-50s and older did mostly resemble the sorts of people we now see in retirement homes (again, this was NOT the case for everyone of those ages AT ALL). But older women did seem to be 'elderly' at a much, MUCH younger age than they are now.

Is it also because we're indoctrinated by what our mothers and grandmothers may have told us? That once you reach a certain age, essentially, you're put out to pasture. To a field of sensible slacks, twinsets, tweed skirts and a comfortable-looking shoe. Oh, and while you're there, you're also only allowed to chew the responsible cud, setting a balanced, sober, pragmatic and, let's face it, dull

example to the younger generations. And again, it's certainly not all mothers or grandmothers who had those thoughts, but I definitely remember my mum sucking her teeth over someone who had long hair 'past a certain age' and her proffering an opinion that she should have it cut.

Times. Have. Changed. Everything has changed for women. And that everything includes having to hang up her personality at 40, 50, 60 and dress like a nun on day release (I have two aunts who are nuns, they won't mind me saying, there is a certain dress code they have to adhere to!).

I'm still baffled by where this magic line in the ageing sand has been drawn. I'm also bemused and actually slightly disappointed that whenever I host discussions on this topic, I am always met with a barrage of very strong opinions that weigh heavily on the side of there still being 'rules'. By women. About other women.

And what are these hideous crimes of fashion that women over a 'certain age' may commit? Take notes people. The list is extensive, but these are the most popular outfits that cause the most offence and outrage (yes, I too have an image of people clutching their pearls and reaching for the smelling salts…).

Are you ready for these? Here we go. Things that should NOT be worn by women over, I'll be honest, it's often 40, occasionally 50. I think it goes without saying that they definitely think it's 60 and above.

– Miniskirts
– Ripped jeans
– Leather jackets
– Leather leggings
– Trainers
– Items that reveal cleavage
– Cold-shoulder tops
– Leopard print
– Items that reveal the legs
– Cropped tops
– Long hair – didn't forget the long hair, Mum.

Please don't think this is an exhaustive list – oh no, they will add anything that they deem inappropriate to be worn by a woman because…well…one of the assumptions that has been bandied about is that we should be looking to be dignified. I don't know about anyone else but I didn't get the dignified memo. I can be described as a lot of things but dignified isn't one of them. And do you know what? I don't care. I may be 48 but in my head I'm still 28. Occasionally 24, sometimes 35, and actually I don't feel any different than I did at 40, 44 or 47. I can't imagine the dignity gene kicks in at 50 or that it's going to make an appearance at about 70 either. And, frankly, I feel perfectly dignified at 48, thank you very much.

For a start, I genuinely don't think it should be about the specific items that you wear. It's about how you put those items together in an outfit. It's nothing to do with age; it's everything to do with taste and style.

Now I know I have just spent the last 65,000 words encouraging you to develop your own style and your own look and to have the courage of your convictions when putting outfits together and to have the confidence to wear what you love. So I hate to say however, but…however…we all know that there are occasions when certain outfits – regardless of how much chutzpah you have or how enamoured you are with said look – perhaps aren't the most appropriate. It's not that it's about curtailing your creative. It's about dressing for the lifestyle that you have, where you're going and what you're doing. Which will include dressing appropriately for certain occasions.

For example, a lace micro miniskirt and a cropped top for a corporate work meeting? Punchy move but probably not the best career-wise. AT ANY AGE! Ripped jeans and a band tee with flipflops for a black tie event? An off-the-shoulder leopard number for a funeral? Would depend on the family's wishes, but as a general rule (and we know how much I loathe rules, so let's just call this a 'bit of advice'), there are circumstances where a certain type of dress is expected,

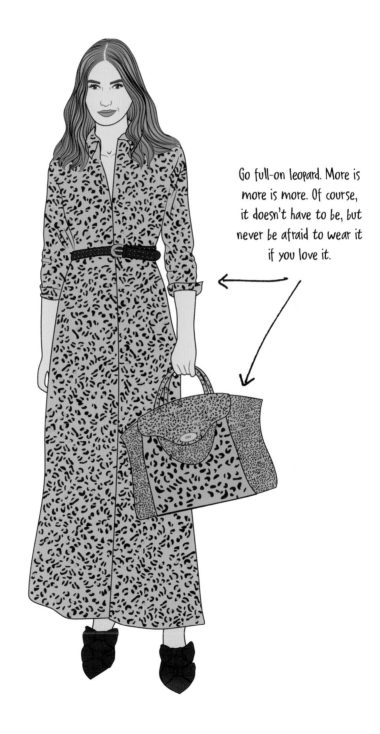

Go full-on leopard. More is more is more. Of course, it doesn't have to be, but never be afraid to wear it if you love it.

purely out of respect and courtesy. Some outfits just don't work because they're not appropriate for the occasion. It has nothing to do with age or dignity; it's just pure common sense and good manners. Regardless of how much you love it or how confident it makes you feel. And regardless of how old you are.

And, I'm not going to lie, there are times in all walks of life and in all sorts of situations when I do see outfits and I think, personally, I am not the biggest fan of that look. BUT. But, but, but. It has nothing to do with age. I can think it's a shit outfit whether you're 21, 41 or 61. As I said: nothing to do with age and, more importantly, nothing to do with me FULL STOP!

It's purely subjective. One (wo)man's shit outfit, will be another (wo)man's outfit of dreams. It's also actually not 'shit'. It's completely personal taste. And it's none of my business and it shouldn't be any of yours.

Dare I say, I always think that if someone doesn't like my outfit, I am in fact doing something right. But that's the style that I'm aiming for: Minimalist Elegance with a twist of Eclectic Vintage and a dash of Boho thrown in for good measure. And it's the latter that almost certainly is the dividing factor. I have hit my style goals if someone really isn't sure about my look! However, that's absolutely not for everyone WHICH is why people should just keep their negative opinions to themselves. As my mum used to say, if you have nothing nice to say, don't say anything at all. Don't assume that everyone is going to be grateful for your 'constructive' criticism.

The only other reason I can think that people have such an aversion to certain clothes is that as we get older, we age. Historically older women weren't as perky and toned as their younger counterparts. Newsflash: times have changed. And actually many women are more fit in later life than in their youth, and compared to younger generations.

Which is the perfect juncture to point out (again) that age should have absolutely nothing to do with what you wear. So your skin may not be as flawless as it once was, but SO WHAT? Scars, stretchmarks, and an overhang and a wobble here and there, a bit of extra love on those handles and a bit more bingo to that wing – to me, they're testimony of a life well lived.

We have enough to worry about in life and many of us lose our way on our journey as we get older. We have enough to contend with juggling all the balls and spinning all the plates – be that looking after families, parents, siblings, friends and either maintaining, building or starting a new career – without someone telling us, 'oh, and by the way, here's a list of your wardrobe contents you need to burn and shouldn't be seen out of the house in'.

Grey hair, check. Long hair, check. Age? Who cares!

Ripped jeans can work at any age. The number in the waistband is the size, not the age you stop wearing something.

The elephant in the room

This needs to change and we can be the ones who facilitate that. Like with sustainability, if enough of us talk about it, if enough of us refuse to accept these out-of-date, utterly ridonculous and preposterous theories and call out those who make them, we can start to change the narrative. And the best way to have that conversation is by practising what you preach. Change that narrative by changing you. Prove the point that women can wear anything at any age by being simply fabulous and by looking absolutely amazing.

The more confident we become as women as we get older, the more convincing we can be to everyone and anyone who ever brings up the outdated concept of mutton vs lamb (this is the first and last time I shall mention that phrase, as you can't see me typing but I have smoke coming out of both my ears and nose – it makes me that cross). The argument holds no water. I feel like I should probably type WE ARE WOMEN HEAR US ROAR now...but no.

It doesn't need for us to yell anything. The proof is in each of us: standing here, confident, beautiful and feeling like YOU. Whether that has been finding the you you once were, or discovering the version of you you had always hoped to be. Whether you are just starting your journey but feel excited about changes that you now know you can make, or whether you finally have a wardrobe of clothes that truly reflects you as a person and how you want to portray yourself to the world. So long as we're moving forward.

Past generations of older women didn't necessarily have it easy. And it's not going to be easy for us. But with baby steps, making small changes that will eventually become big ones, we will have paved the way for our daughters, nieces and grandchildren. Hopefully, looking and feeling great at any age and wearing what we want will be an expected right and the absolute norm, not just a privilege.

I hope beyond hope that this book has given you the confidence to start finding the new you by discovering your inner style and learning how to look and feel as fabulous as you deserve.

Nutritional information

If you refer back to this final shopping list with the knowledge to fill in the gaps from reading the book, I promise you that in no time this will all become second nature to you.

Remember, confidence can only come from you. Some people are born with it, most of us have to work at it, but we can ALL gain it.

Baby steps are the way forward.

Review the situation
It's so important to understand where you are NOW. It may well not be where you want to be but by acknowledging where you find yourself, you have a platform to move on from.

Identify your style
Understand that you need to dress for the lifestyle that you have and not the lifestyle that you want. And then work out who it is you want to be – find your style icon. This will help to focus and channel your thoughts, enabling you to make fewer purchasing errors.

Dress for your shape
Before we start actually getting dresses, we really do need to recognize the shape that we are. And stop punishing ourselves if it's not the shape that we want to be.

Start now by dressing for the shape you are, not the shape you once were and not the shape you hope to be one day. If one day comes, then you can change what you wear, but that's not happening tomorrow. Understanding how to make the most of your current body shape increases your confidence like you can't begin to imagine.

Colour
Not a lecture on what you should or shouldn't be wearing – this is the next step on your confidence ladder. Get to grips with what neutrals you want to be wearing, learn to recognize what colours work for you, your style and your wardrobe, and start making good print decisions. The joy of finding colours and prints that make your heart sing? I'll leave that for you to find out!

Pantry staples

The building blocks of your wardrobe. The foundations from which all other outfits can be built. Get these right and you will have something fabulous to wear every day. Don't forget those hero ingredients that are the cherry on the top of your pantry staples. From leopard boots, sequin jackets, your favourite band tee to a full-length faux-fur coat, start recognizing the things in your wardrobe that make all the difference to your outfit and your confidence.

Accessories

The not so secret weapons in your outfit arsenal. Figure out which ones work best for your look and your lifestyle, and you will always have the power to change up an outfit to make it occasion appropriate. From belts to jewellery, to hats and – that old favourite – make-up, there is something there that will work for everyone, just narrow down what yours is.

Wardrobe detox

Armed with all the relevant preparation, now is the time to get serious in your closet. Yes, it's a daunting task to begin with, but so long as you put enough time aside, it IS the most rewarding exercise and the first practical, proper step to finding the new you. Once you've mastered the task, it's one that you can repeat as and when necessary.

The art of shopping: Rule of Three

1. Can you think of three occasions when you would wear your new purchase?
2. Can you think of three different outfits that you already own with which you can wear your new purchase?

Are you actually going to wear it? Is it really a bargain or does it fall into one of your three excuses?

A healthy diet

The trick of being sustainable. To be honest, if you're following all of the above advice, you are well on your way to becoming a lot more sustainable than you have been in the past. But also think about:
> Fabrics. Organic and recycled are the easiest key points to remember.
> Where we buy from: Vintage, charity shops, rental sites.

The elephant in the room

There is NO SUCH THING AS BEING TOO OLD TO WEAR ANYTHING. It's not about anything being age appropriate, it's about being style appropriate.

It's about having the confidence in yourself that you deserve to have and that you CAN have. Just remember the baby steps.

Let's get personal – your questions answered

Q: I'm 52 but in my head I'm still 32 and not ready to accept 'middle-aged' clothes, but at the same time I don't want to feel like the dreaded mutton. How do I dress my age while still having fun with fashion and following the trends?

A: So here's the thing: as mentioned in 'The elephant in the room' (see page 234), there is literally no such thing as dressing for your age. When was the last time you saw an age tag on a piece of clothing – when you were 12? It's something that a more judgmental aspect of society has ingrained into us: the fact that at a certain age, we should morph into an 'ideal'. I'm assuming it's along the lines of twinset and pearls, slacks, headscarves and sensible shoes.

The first step is to realize that looking good has nothing to do with age: it's to do with finding your perfect style and knowing how to dress for your shape. THAT'S IT! It's having a wardrobe of building blocks that you wear year after year and to which you layer trends.

And yes, you can still definitely follow trends. One thing I would say, though, is that it's possibly better to pick one or maybe two from a season, as opposed to wearing new season trends from head to toe. Another thing that I would add is that it has absolutely nothing to do with age: this would be my advice were you 31, 51 or 71. From a sustainability perspective, it's better to invest in clothes that offer versatility and longevity in your wardrobe rather than ones that will only be one-season, on-trend wonders. Remember the Rule of Three: three different occasions when you can wear your new item of clothing and three outfits that you can make with it from things you already own.

Once you've got your style and shape sussed, you will find that buying clothes is fun again. AND you will find that there will be the odd on-trend piece that fits in and becomes a long-loved gem.

I also think it's important to remember that no shops are off-limits. One question I am asked all the time is, 'Can I shop *there*?' (mostly said about high street shops where the music is club level, you're unable to interpret any of the words and even if you can they don't really make sense, and there's a slight concern that on entering, an alarm will go off screeching 'OLD BAG ALERT!'). First off, I can't do anything about the music, although if you go with a friend, I would recommend learning to sign as you won't be able to hear each other talk. And you may well find that a lovely, friendly shop assistant tells you that her mum loves your dress when you go to purchase something. BUT apart from that, the world will not fall off its axis, I promise you. No one will actually bat an eyelid and you may well find a complete bargain that fits all your shopping criteria.

The perhaps cannier option, prior to visiting the shop, is to check it out online. Or even order online. If you're not used to the layout of a physical store, it can be daunting and tricky to find the wood for the trees. But online, you can search and filter by what you're interested in; you can try things on in the comfort of your own home and experiment wearing them with things you already own (because as much as you think an outfit 'might' work in your head, how many times have you got home and realized you look like a potato?), which does lead to fewer purchasing mistakes in the long term.

However, I would grab a friend, go for lunch and then get out where you've perhaps been too scared to venture for years. DO IT!!

Q: I've recently, due to long-term illness, been confined to a wheelchair and would love some advice on how to adapt my wardrobe.

A: The most important thing to remember is that all the advice in this book is still completely relevant. Before we even start to think about the practicalities of clothes, the most effective way to ensure that you have a wardrobe of items that you love and that make you look fantastic is knowing your style, knowing how you want to look.

When it comes to dressing for your shape, here's where the rules are slightly different. It's not that we're throwing the proportion rules out of the window; you absolutely still need to be aware of the shape that you are and you also need to think about finding and accentuating those parts of your body that you love and showing them off to their best advantage. All the rules for highlighting what you love are the same – whether that be your décolletage, wonderful breasts, gorgeous ankles, amazing neck, fabulous feet, the list goes on.

The main thing for those who spend the majority of their time in a wheelchair is to still be able to look utterly fabulous while being comfortable.

Fabric is key. First in its make-up: man-made fibres aren't your friends. You're looking for breathable, natural materials (nothing worse than sitting in a pool of your own sweat). Consider fabrics that aren't too bulky. Crisp cotton is all very good but you're after fabrics that are fluid and easy to wear, not ones that are stiff and sit a good couple of inches away from your body when you're sitting down. If you're after structure, especially in the shoulders, embrace the 1980s and get those shoulder pads out. I know, I know, but they can work miracles in giving you a great shape – I promise there won't be a hint of *Dynasty*. Try looking at lyocell, viscose, silk, bamboo, linen mixes and organic cotton jersey.

Volume of fabric is another thing to consider. This is a fine balance as you don't want things that are very fitted (I'm more than aware that they are highly uncomfortable to spend a long time in), but at the same time, you're not wanting so much fabric that it looks like you're smuggling a parachute.

Dresses that are more structured (not tight) on your top half (still follow the neckline advice, depending on your shape, see page 56) will be more flattering and more comfortable. Volume on the bottom and length are personal choices.

Loose trousers that are elasticated or drawstring are ideal. Much as that sounds like we're purely talking about joggers, after lockdown, The Jogger has been elevated to the most wonderful wardrobe staple and is no longer merely an outfit one should either be exercising or binge-watching Netflix in. They are even office worthy, depending on what you choose to team them with and what footwear you opt for. Comfort and style in the perfect pair of trews. Wide leg, tapered, cuffed or not cuffed, with or without cargo pockets on the leg (I know lots of people find the extra pockets handy!), to side stripe or not to side stripe, in a myriad of fabrics – there is a pair of 'joggers' out there for you.

Jackets, again, very much depend on your natural fit, but the important thing to consider is shape and fabric. Length-wise, a shorter style is preferable as you want it to sit neatly in the chair and you don't want to have to worry about it being bulky when you move. Softer fabrics with some stretch are ideal: from jersey to soft, stretch denim, to lived-in cargo jackets and soft leather bikers. Most people prefer single-breasted as, again, that negates the bulk and it may also be worthwhile checking out unlined jackets for the same reason.

Coats are probably the hardest things to buy; it is possible, although it will take some hunting. As with all things, it's thinking about the thickness and volume of fabric – just not too much! Length-wise, either go for long or short; a medium-length coat will just be uncomfortable to sit on as it will keep moving under your bum. And for warmth, layering is your friend. Scarves, more scarves and wrist warmers are all great ideas that you can put on and take off with ease.

Q: My daughter is getting married next year but I don't want to look like the typical 'mother of the bride'...what can I wear?

A: Personally, I think the phrase 'mother of the bride' strikes the fear of God into so many women that I'm tempted to have it banned (second thing I'll do after becoming Prime Minister and ensuring that there are pockets in all dresses). Of course, it's not the concept that I would ban (surely nothing more joyous than seeing your daughter as a bride!), but the association of mother of the bride with, basically, the Queen Mum. Or now, the Queen herself. Yes, they are both incredibly elegant and statuesque in their fashion, but if that's not your usual style, to try and shoehorn yourself into a pistachio dress and jacket with matching hat and shoes on the big day is simply all sorts of madness and a sure-fire recipe for disaster.

Forget the matchy-matchy coat and jacket ensemble. Unless it's something you can happily wear again to a party, the supermarket, to dinner, or on holiday? I thought not. Forget the traditional mother-of-the-bride colours. Where does the insistence that the bride's mother should wear a hue from the 1980s bridesmaid's colour wheel come from? Head-to-toe lilac, peach, lemon, periwinkle blue…err, no thanks.

Please don't get me wrong: if that outfit is your jam then utterly embrace it. My mum did for my wedding (and, yes, it was pistachio green), and she said she had never felt lovelier (and I would agree). But if that's not the look you're going for, fear not, there are alternatives.

I think the veering towards the macaron colour palette (coincidence only, but they are all generally French macaron colours!) comes from wanting to stand out among the guests and maybe tie in with the bridesmaids themselves. For many, those days are long gone, and the focus for mums of brides is to simply look and feel as fabulous as they can. Which opens up a whole new tranche of opportunities when it comes to finding something to wear.

The key is not to go too off-piste. As with pretty much every question, it comes down to knowing your style. Which style icon category (see page 55) would you most like to emulate in your perfect outfit? And take it from there. It doesn't have to be a dress at all. It could be a two-piece (top and bottoms, not matching coat, although there is NOTHING wrong with that – think perhaps more Jackie O than Queen Mum), a jumpsuit or a trouser suit.

And I genuinely think something that does help channel your style and focus the mind in these situations is to ask yourself the question, would I be happy to wear this outfit again? Not necessarily with hat if you're going down that route but certainly the clothes. The Rule of Three really does work because the more likely you are to want to wear the outfit for other occasions, and the fact it works with other pieces you already own, means that you will feel comfortable and confident in it.

Maybe you are willing to spend a little more than you usually would on an outfit. Going forward, it is key that you remember the valuable lesson of never keeping anything for best. Think cost per wear. So, yes, it is a more expensive dress but that is all the more reason to then wear it. A LOT! There is absolutely zero point in keeping the most expensive items you own simply for best as you don't want to ruin them.

Buy a fabulous outfit that you feel great in and then wear it, wear it and wear it again.

Q: Is it possible to mix metals in jewellery and how do you know when too many accessories is too much?

A: So this – pretty much like everything in fashion, to be honest – is a totally personal thing. There really are no rules. Some people always stick to either yellow or rose gold or silver. And that works for their style. Because, yet again, it comes down to style. As it does with knowing when too many accessories is too much.

For those who are more pared back in their look and prefer a cleaner, more structured way of dressing, it may well be that they prefer to stick to one metal colour and either layer several pieces of more delicate jewellery or wear a selection of simple, chunkier styles. Alternatively, you could be of the style ethos that more is more and a mix of metal colours and a variety of chains is the look you're going for.

Then, of course, you could create your own bespoke look. One of my personal favourites is a more classic, minimalist clothing look but adding interest with a selection of different styles of jewellery: in different metal colours, some finer chains, some chunkier.

Jewellery as an accessory needn't be metal based. You can have pearl, fabric, beaded, enamel, wood, shell, the list goes on and on and the colours can range from bright and bold to neutrals and more discreet shades – it just comes down to your personal style and taste.

As I ask earlier in the book: how to know when it's enough or too much (see page 177)? That comes down to confidence and trusting your gut. It's an instinct that everyone naturally has but it might not come naturally to everyone. However, you can relearn that instinct. The more confident you become in your fashion choices, the more instinctive you will be. Or the less you will care about what other people think, so long as you look in the mirror and love what you see.

Q: How can I move stylishly through the menopause and all that it brings, especially when my body carries weight differently? How can I project my image out into the world when I'm just not feeling myself?

A: I really think the most important thing to remember when it comes to weight gain is that you can probably count on one hand the number of women who, as they get older, it DOESN'T happen to. It could be after having a baby, it could be after lockdown, it could be after an injury or it could be down to the good old glorious menopause.

At so many times in our lives, women have occasion to not feel themselves. And the most important step in making a change is acceptance and the knowledge that it's OK! It genuinely does happen to the best of us.

There are, though, most definitely things that we can do, but it does involve us being proactive. Which, I know, when you're feeling at your lowest ebb, is such a huge mental mountain to climb. However, in the morning, you have to get dressed. And it's just as easy to put on a pair of jeans and a top that you love as it is to chuck on the old jeans and the out-of-shape rubbish tee that you should have cut up for polishing rags months ago.

The difference that knowing you look good in an outfit has on your mood and your confidence is incomparable.

So, as hard a step as it might be to take, starting at the beginning and focusing on YOU, in the short-to-medium term (not even long term!), will be worth it. And if you're here, you've already made that first step, which is possibly the hardest, and acknowledged that there is a problem and that you're willing to fix it. Start at chapter 1 (see page 20), find your style and from there, the only way is up.

The other thing it's important to flag is that you will probably need to go through a process of acceptance. If you can't change it, you need to accept it and look for the positives without focusing on what used to be. That body of yours is amazing. It has taken you into your 40s, it has served you well and you should be proud of it. It may wobble more than it used to, your shape may not be the one that you had when you were younger, but unless you have some serious dietary and exercise plans afoot, it's the body that will be taking you into the next phase of your life. Celebrate that body and dress it as it deserves: with style, flair and panache that are ALL your choosing! You have the power to change, it just takes some focus and time, but you can get there.

Life is too short not to feel fabulous. You deserve to look in the mirror and love who you see looking back at you. Best of luck, you can do it!

Kat xx

Index

Acknowledgments

Not entirely sure how to write this without it sounding like an Oscars speech, so advance apologies for the fact that it…sounds just like an Oscars speech (except that I'm typing in my pyjamas – a missed outfit opportunity there, I think we'll find).

So. I would like to thank, first and foremost, my family. My long-suffering, patient and ever-supportive husband David – you are my rock. And my three children who, frankly, have no option but to stick around; so thank you, kids, for putting up with me and the three months where I didn't make you breakfast as I had got up at 5.30am to write and was in the thick of it when you came down hungry, all those months ago. Ditto, to all my lovely friends, who didn't bear quite as much of the brunt of my trying to concentrate as it was lockdown, but a huge thank you for always being there at the end of the phone. You all know who you are.

And then on to my work-life wives, without whom, none of this would have been possible. My incredible managers Verity and Alexandra and my supremely patient literary agent Laura, plus the wider team at Gleam Talent. I started this process, knowing what I wanted to say and how I wanted to say it but not having a clue of how to get it actually out there.

Thank you, amazing ladies, for holding my hand the entire way and being the most incredible support network.

Now to, obviously, mention and credit the nothing-but-inspiring team at Octopus Publishing, who had faith in me right from the very beginning. From the first meeting when they ran the mocked-up cover by me, I knew that they were the group of ridiculously talented individuals who would bring my story to life. Thank you Alison, Yasia, Lizzie, Sarah, Ella, Caroline, Charlotte and Serena.

Not forgetting the lady without whom this book would just be words – the artistic genius Janelle, who made my fashion visions a reality. You have encapsulated perfectly the images I wanted to portray, thank you, thank you, thank you! A huge thank you, as well, to the artist Hanna Buck, whose art I have hanging on my walls and who very kindly allowed us to use representations of her work for the section openers of the book. The perfect example of where print is nothing but pleasing to my eye!

I must mention my amazing Mum, who sadly is no longer with us but who supported me like no other. She made me who I am today – shoe-, lippie- and handbag-obsessed – and I know she's looking down, bursting with pride. I love you Mum.

And finally to you. All you who over the past 11 years have been a part of my journey. Who have asked for my advice, who have listened, who have fed back, who have been willing to put themselves in my hands – hopefully I have made a difference and have helped change your life in one small way.

And now you, who have bought the book and are also willing to make that change. I promise I'm holding your hand and I will help guide you through.

Thank you.
Kat xx